Comparing Schools of Analytic Therapy

Comparing Schools of Analytic Therapy

Edited by Peter Buirski, Ph.D.

JASON ARONSON INC.
Northvale, New Jersey
London

This book was set in 11 pt. Baskerville by Lind Graphics of Upper Saddle River, New Jersey, and printed and bound by Haddon Craftsmen of Scranton, Pennsylvania.

Library of Congress Cataloging-in-Publication Data

Comparing schools of analytic therapy
/ edited by Peter Buirski.
    p.   cm.
  Includes bibliographical references and index.
  ISBN 1-56821-107-4
  1. Portnoy, Alexander (Fictitious character)   2. Psychoanalytic
interpretation—Case studies.   I. Buirski, Peter.
  [DNLM: 1. Medicine in Literature.   2. Psychoanalytic
Interpretation.   3. Psychoanalytic Theory.   WM 49 C737   1994]
RC509.8.C65   1994
616.89′17—dc20
DNLM/DLC
for Library of Congress   93-30598

Manufactured in the United States of America. Jason Aronson Inc. offers books and cassettes. For information and catalog write to Jason Aronson Inc., 230 Livingston Street, Northvale, New Jersey 07647.

To my parents, Pearl and Physil Buirski

Contents

Contributors

Elliot Adler, Ph.D. Dr. Adler is a graduate of the Psychoanalytic Institute of the Postgraduate Center for Mental Health, where he has served as Assistant Director of Adult Psychoanalytic Training, as well as serving as a faculty member, senior supervisor, and training analyst. He is currently Director of the Westchester Center for Psychoanalysis and teaches, supervises, and serves as a training analyst there. He is also in private practice in New York City and Westchester.

Stephen Appelbaum, Ph.D. After 21 years on the staff of the Menninger Foundation, Dr. Appelbaum is now in the private practice of psychoanalysis and clinical psychology in Prairie Village, Kansas. He is a professor at the University of Missouri–Kansas City School of Medicine and faculty member of the National Institute for the Psychotherapies. He is the author of three books, with two more in press, and 100 articles and book reviews.

Bruno Bettelheim, Ph.D. Dr. Bettelheim received his doctorate from the University of Vienna. After being a prisoner in the concentration camps, he came to America in 1939. He was a Professor of Education and Professor Emeritus of psychology and psychiatry at the University of Chicago. Among his numerous books are *Freud and Man's Soul,* and *The Uses of Enchantment.* Dr. Bettelheim died in 1990.

Peter Buirski, Ph.D. After 23 years in New York City, as Professor of Psychology at John Jay College of Criminal Justice and Director of Adult Psychoanalytic Training at the Postgraduate Center for Mental Health, Dr. Buirski moved to Denver. He is currently Dean of the Graduate School of Professional Psychology at the University of Denver and is a member of the Denver Psychoanalytic Society and the Colorado Center for Psychoanalytic Studies. He is also in private practice in Denver.

Shelley Doctors, Ph.D. Dr. Doctors is a clinical psychologist and psychoanalyst who completed her psychoanalytic training at the Institute for the Psychoanalytic Study of Subjectivity. An Assistant Professor of Pediatrics (Adolescent Medicine) at Albert Einstein College of Medicine for many years, she is also a charter member of the International Society for Adolescent Psychiatry and serves as a United States delegate to that body. She is on the faculty of the National Institute for the Psychotherapies in New York City, where she maintains a private practice in psychotherapy and psychoanalysis for adolescents, adults, and couples.

Judith Hanlon, Ph.D. Dr. Hanlon received her Ph.D. in Clinical Psychology from Teachers College, Columbia University, and completed her psychoanalytic training at the New York University Postdoctoral Program in Psychoanalysis and Psychotherapy. She is on the staff of the Columbia University Counseling and Psychological Services Center and she is a faculty member and supervisor in the Adult Psychoanalytic Training Program at the Postgraduate Center for Mental Health. She is currently in private practice in New York City as a psychotherapist and psychoanalyst.

Irwin Hirsch, Ph.D. Dr. Hirsch was the former Director of the Manhattan Institute for Psychoanalysis, where he is active as a faculty member, supervisor, and training analyst. He is Professor of Psychology and Supervisor in the Postdoctoral Program in Psychotherapy and Psychoanalysis at Adelphi University. He is on the editorial board of *Psychoanalytic Dialogues,* and is the author of numerous papers. Dr. Hirsch is in private practice in New York City and Long Island.

Helene Kafka, Ph.D. Dr. Kafka is on the faculty and a supervisor at the William Alanson White Institute of Psychoanalysis, National Institute for the Psychotherapies, and the Psychological Center of City University of New York. She has written extensively on the vicissitudes of aloneness and loneliness in normal development and on the masochistic and narcissistic character disorders. Her current focus is on treatment and countertransference issues in psychotherapy with survivors of childhood trauma. Her most recent paper, which unites these themes, is "To Cure or to Heal?: A Clinical and Theoretical Study of Healing Processes within Psychoanalysis."

Andrew P. Morrison, M.D. Dr. Morrison is Assistant Clinical Professor of Psychiatry at Harvard Medical School, and is on the faculty of the Boston Psychoanalytic Institute and the Massachusetts Institute for Psychoanalysis. He practices in Cambridge, Massachusetts, and writes on shame. His book, *Shame, the Underside of Narcissism,* was published in 1989 by the Analytic Press.

Joseph Newirth, Ph.D. Dr. Newirth received his Ph.D. in clinical psychology from the University of Massachusetts and completed psychoanalytic training at the William Alanson White Institute. He is currently the Director of Clinical Training and an Associate Professor in Clinical Psychology at the Derner Institute of Advanced Psychological Studies at Adelphi University. He is also on the faculty, a supervising and training analyst, in the Postdoctoral Program in Psychoanalysis and Psychotherapy at Adelphi University and at the New York University Postdoctoral Program in Psychoanalysis and Psychotherapy. He is in clinical practice in New York City and Long Island.

Gerard Pape, Ph.D. Dr. Pape received his Ph.D. in Clinical Psychology from the University of Michigan in 1982. After practicing psychology in Ann Arbor and Jackson, Michigan for many years, he moved to Paris in 1991, where he is currently pursuing training in Lacanian psychoanalysis under the auspices of the Ecole de la Cause Freudienne.

Note to the Reader

The chapters in this book cite numerous passages from Philip Roth's novel *Portnoy's Complaint*. To assist the reader in referring back to the novel, page numbers for quotations are given from two editions: the original Random House hardcover edition, published in 1969, and a recent paperback reprint published in 1991 by Touchstone, an imprint of Simon & Schuster. The wording of quotations is taken from the Random House edition.

For each citation, the page number preceding the slash refers to the Random House edition, and the page number following the slash refers to the Touchstone edition.

Preceding the text of the novel is an entry in the form of an encyclopedia definition. This page is referred to in citations as page 1.

Acknowledgments

In an edited volume, most of the thanks go to the contributing authors. All of the chapters, except for the contribution by Bruno Bettelheim, were written expressly for this book. The uniformly high quality of the chapters is a measure of the seriousness and thoughtfulness with which the authors approached this task. I appreciate their conscientiousness, patience, and friendship. We are all indebted to Philip Roth, who has populated our world with such unforgettable characters as Alexander Portnoy. I am grateful to my students, first at John Jay College of Criminal Justice and later in the Graduate School of Professional Psychology at the University of Denver, whose enjoyment of the task and creativity in its execution convinced me that such a volume might be appreciated by a larger audience. I want to extend my appreciation to Judith Kaufman, C.S.W. and Neil Skolnick, Ph.D., the directors of the National Institute for the Psychotherapies Regional Training Program at Kansas City, for sponsoring a symposium focused on this volume while it was still in process. Gerald Lynch, Ph.D., president of John Jay College of Criminal

Justice, City University of New York, has always been supportive of my professional growth and development, for which I am grateful. As always, I appreciate the good counsel of Graham Barkham. My administrative assistant, Adelaide Cohen, and secretary, Cecilia Hancock, have been invaluable, not just in their assistance with this volume, but with freeing my time so that I could focus on my editorial responsibilities. And most especially, it has been a pleasure to share this activity with my wife and colleague, Cathy Krown Buirski, M.S.W., whose analytic expertise, sound judgment, and emotional support have enriched this volume and my professional and personal life.

1

Nine Analysts in Search of a Character

Peter Buirski, Ph.D.

When a character is born, he acquires at once such an independence, even of his own author, that he can be imagined by everybody even in many other situations where the author never dreamed of placing him; and so he acquires for himself a meaning which the author never thought of giving him.

—Luigi Pirandello
Six Characters in Search of an Author

While it is not true that there are as many psychoanalytic theories of personality and treatment as there are psychoanalysts, it often seems that way. Not only is our field stimulated by numerous differing schools of thought, but there is ample disagreement among those who advocate the same theory. It is not just that we sometimes wind up comparing apples and oranges, but it turns out that apples come in wondrous variety. How are we, the analytic community, to make sense of our differences? And how are prospective patients to sort out the rotten apples from the ones that are good for you? Is a golden delicious better for you than a red delicious?

These are serious questions with few definitive answers. Is my way the right way? Or is it the better way? Or is it merely just another way? Perhaps we are all just examining, through our own magnifying glass, different sides of the same proverbial elephant? Our literature is filled with case study material in which the analyst, regardless of theoretical persuasion, reports that the patient was helped. It is rare to come across a report in which the analyst details a failure.

There have been a few courageous analysts who have voluntarily submitted their work to the scrutiny of their colleagues, but it is doubtful that they have felt uplifted by the experience. We all seem to feel that we would have done the work better, and this is especially true if we are examining the work of an analyst of a different theoretical persuasion. How can we all be right?

The quotation in this chapter's epigraph from the Pirandello play *Six Characters in Search of an Author* is intended as partial commentary on this theme. In the play, the tension is between a positivist view of reality versus a relativist view of subjective experience. In many ways, the play dramatized some of the philosophical issues that, in a different form, have been debated over the past few years by proponents of one-person and two-person psychologies, and between advocates for the stances of analytic objectivity versus intersubjectivity.

The nine analysts in this book each view the character of Alexander Portnoy differently. Some see him as neurotic, others as narcissistic; some focus on his impotence, others on his libido; some see him as a victim, others as a rapist. Each analyst imagines engaging the character in a unique and distinct interpersonal relationship. The intersubjective context is framed then by the subjective reality of the various analysts as they engage the character in a relationship of their own mutual construction.

Having posed these questions, I fear that the reader expects the "answers" to be forthcoming. But at this time, it is not answers that I am offering. What I offer is more data. It is a measure of these exciting times in the relatively young history of psychoanalysis that we have so many different varieties of apples and oranges to choose from.

Psychoanalysis, the theory of the mind and the technique of treatment, was the singular discovery of Freud. While psychoanalysis was still in its infancy, rumblings of dissent were heard within Freud's inner circle. The monolithic structure of Freud's theory was challenged by the defections of Adler and Jung. The creation of new monoliths, like the Adlerian school of individual psychology and the Jungian school of analytic psychology, became the paradigm for resolving substantive disputes of theory and technique, as well as conflicts over personal ambition. As regular and inevitable as the repetition compulsion, each new discovery within the body of psychoanalysis, from Klein to Kohut, resulted in the splitting off of its founder and his or her adherents to form new training institutes through which to promulgate the new ideas.

The professional literature contains many admirable and thorough descriptions of the various psychoanalytic theories of the mind. They have been contrasted and compared in such well received books as Ruth Munroe's (1955) *Schools of Psychoanalytic Thought* and Greenberg and Mitchell's (1987) *Object Relations in Psychoanalytic Theory*. However, these and similar endeavors, which successfully explicate and elucidate the various systems of psychoanalytic thought, do not provide the reader with a vivid picture of the unique way each theoretical perspective illuminates its select portion of the clinical material.

Often the differences between theoretical systems seem more semantic than substantive (e.g., the difference between Freud's notion of transference and Sullivan's concept of parataxic distortion), but the substantive clinical differences may actually be obscured by the theoretical jargon. What would give life to these concepts is to see how they compare when applied to the same sample of clinical material.

My experience teaching graduate psychology students at John Jay College of Criminal Justice of the City University of New York and the University of Denver's Graduate School of Professional Psychology confirmed this impression. At these institutions, I regularly taught courses in the various schools of psychoanalytic theory and therapy. To dramatize the range of diversity within the different schools of psychoanalytic thought, I used the device of having my students write papers analyzing the same clinical case from each of the various theoretical perspectives studied. This assignment brought home, in a most vivid and compelling manner, both the uniqueness and specificity of each theory, as well as their points of commonality and compatibility.

There have also been two notable published efforts in this direction. The first was "How Theory Shapes Technique: Perspectives on a Clinical Study," *Psychoanalytic Inquiry* (1987, vol. 7, no. 2), in which prominent analysts who identify with particular schools of thought addressed themselves to the process notes from a few sessions conducted by a psychoanalyst with a traditional ego psychology orientation. A second effort brought together another collection of analysts, each advocating a particular school of psychoanalytic thought, applying his or her perspective to the process notes from four analytic sessions conducted by a self psychologist. "How Theory Shapes Technique: Perspectives on a Self-Psychological Clinical Presentation" was published in *Psychoanalytic Inquiry* (1990, vol. 10, no. 4). While valuable contributions, both suffered from the same limitation: only a small sample of the clinical material was presented (no doubt due to the space constraints of the journal). Given the limited clinical data with which to work, and the space constraints they were under, the contributing authors were circumscribed in their ability to demonstrate the richness of the theoretical and technical insights that can be generated by their individual theoretical orientations. Furthermore, Silverman (1987) and Fosshage (1990), the analysts whose clinical summaries were discussed in the respective volumes, felt that the experience of recording their treatment sessions impacted both themselves and their patients and influenced the content of the recorded sessions. This is an analytic phenomenon akin to the Heisenberg uncertainty principle in physics: that the act of observing and recording a therapy session will necessarily influence both patient and therapist, resulting in a session that is different from one where the participants are not being observed.

This book utilizes a format that tries to compensate for the limitations that affected the two *Psychoanalytic Inquiry* volumes. In the process, other difficulties are doubtlessly incurred. This book offers the contributors a wealth of clinical material with which to work, and the space to elaborate the full extent of their ideas. Leading exponents of the various major psychoanalytic schools of thought apply their insights to the identical clinical case. As my teaching experience and the two volumes in *Psychoanalytic Inquiry* have suggested, this approach to comparing and contrasting systems of psychoanalytic thought provides an exciting forum for the lively exchange of technical and theoretical insights.

It might be argued that a single author should undertake to apply each psychoanalytic system to the clinical sample so that the chapters would adhere to a consistent organization and structure. However, the single-author approach would suffer from the same limitations that books comparing theoretical systems usually face. No single individual has been trained in all systems, and therefore his or her knowledge of the other systems is necessarily obtained second hand. When it comes to the clinical application of various psychoanalytic systems, this limitation becomes especially detrimental. Without having been trained and supervised in a particular therapeutic framework, one cannot hope to capture the subtlety and nuance that someone grounded in that framework can bring to the clinical material. The virtue of an edited volume is that practicing experts in each of the psychoanalytic systems would bring the full power of their technical and theoretical formulations to bear on the clinical case. What this book then lacks in consistency of voice I hope will be more than made up for by the depth and range of the insights into the case.

The success of this enterprise will to a large extent depend on the quality of the clinical material that the authors address. The clinical material I have selected is the case of Alexander Portnoy, from Philip Roth's novel *Portnoy's Complaint*. There is a variety of reasons for choosing a work of fiction, and this novel in particular, to serve as the clinical material for this book. First, the value of using a work of fiction is that the case is free from the theoretical biases that a practicing clinician would bring to the written summary of one of his or her own cases. A work of fiction is not the case of a Kleinian or a Kohutian analyst, but the work of a writer's imagination. Hence, whatever material is included or excluded from the case presentation is attributable to the mysterious motives of the author, not to any subjective valuation by the patient's analyst. Since the analyst is not real, we need not be concerned with the extent to which the clinical material is edited to present the analyst in a favorable light. Second, since the patient is not real, there is no need to disguise the material to protect the patient's anonymity. All too often in our clinical literature, the measures required to adequately disguise clinical material so distorts the case that it begins to resemble a work of fiction. Even though a work of fiction cannot be considered a true sample of clinical material, the object of study in this book is the particular psychoanalytic system of thought and not the particular patient under examination. The case only serves as the vehicle for the demonstration of the explanatory power of the theory. Since the contributing analysts are dealing with a literary text, they are employing the methodology of hermeneutic inquiry to the clinical material.

I have assigned *Portnoy's Complaint* to hundreds of graduate students by now and I have found it to be a rich and complex text that readily lends itself to examination by all of the various schools of psychoanalytic thought. An actual clinical case presentation by an analyst, which would contain sufficient information and detail for others to analyze, might run over a hundred pages. This would put a burden on the reader who must read an extensive report about the patient before ever progressing to the heart of the book. Furthermore, including such a written report in the volume would greatly increase the length of this volume and the cost of publication. By selecting such a well-known work of fiction for the clinical sample, it is my hope that most readers of this book will already be familiar with the character of Alexander Portnoy. Many readers may choose to return to Roth's novel to refresh their memories, although the chapter authors have included enough of the original material that this should not be necessary. For readers of this volume who are not already acquainted with Alexander Portnoy, let them be assured that making his acquaintance will not entail any hardship.

A benefit from using *Portnoy's Complaint* as the clinical sample is that the book is written as the free associations of a patient in analytic treatment, with no verbal intrusions from the analyst to direct the flow. Because of Roth's skill, we have a character who is vital and alive, with a colorful personal history and a conflicted sense of his own worth. Furthermore, it is a tribute to Roth's skill that his character still lives vividly in the minds of those who first encountered him twenty-five years ago.

One noteworthy problem for today's readers is that while Portnoy has not changed in the last twenty-five years, society has. The role of women in the United States today has benefited from the feminist critique of our society's values and norms in the years since Portnoy first appeared. Within the context of the Clarence Thomas–Anita Hill hearings, and the resulting increased sensitivity to issues of sexual harassment, Alexander Portnoy's treatment of women does not look amusing. Rather than the victim of his culture and his Freudian drives, many people now see him as a victimizer. For this reason, I decided to include a chapter written specifically from a woman's perspective.

In addition to the social changes of the last twenty-five years, there has also been an explosive growth in psychoanalytic theorizing that has changed the face of psychoanalysis. While Freud argued that *psychoanalysis* was a term that should be reserved to describe his theoretical and clinical system, today the term *psychoanalysis* is used almost generically, to refer to a host of systems that stress the centrality of relational motives as opposed to strictly intrapsychic ones. Twenty-five years ago, Roth had fewer theoretical options, besides the Freudian, for the patient Portnoy to select. The culture of the times was infused with Freudian thought and it was only natural for Portnoy, a Jewish, New York intellectual, to be conversant with Freud's ideas. Many of the theoretical perspectives addressed in this volume were either unknown or undiscovered when Roth wrote *Portnoy's Complaint*. It would be naive to assume that twenty-five years from now there won't be a variety of new systems of psychoanalytic thought that are unimagined today. But Alexander Portnoy will still be with us, and perhaps future theoreticians will make use of his case to demonstrate the unique insights and techniques offered by their new theories.

REFERENCES

Fosshage, J. (1990). Clinical protocol. *Psychoanalytic Inquiry* 10:461–477.

Greenberg, J. R. and Mitchell, S. A. (1983). *Object Relations in Psychoanalytic Theory*. Cambridge, MA: Harvard University Press.

Miller, J. P. and Post, S. L. (1990). How theory shapes technique: perspectives on a self-psychological clinical presentation. *Psychoanalytic Inquiry* 10:4.

Munroe, Ruth. (1955). *Schools of Psychoanalytic Thought*. New York: Dryden.

Pirandello, L. (1922). *Six Characters in Search of an Author*. New York: E. P. Dutton.

Pulver, S. E., Escoll, P. J., and Fischer, N. (1987). How theory shapes technique: perspectives on a clinical study. *Psychoanalytic Inquiry* 7:2.

Roth, P. (1969). *Portnoy's Complaint*. New York: Random House.

Silverman, M. A. (1987). Clinical material. *Psychoanalytic Inquiry* 7:147–165.

2

Freudian Perspective: Portnoy Psychoanalyzed*

Bruno Bettelheim, Ph.D.

THERAPY NOTES FOUND IN THE FILES OF DR. O. SPIELVOGEL, A NEW YORK PSYCHOANALYST

Asked to write a review of Philip Roth's *Portnoy's Complaint*, I attempted a satire instead. Only an interesting work of fiction permits and deserves to be made the substance of a satire — which suggests my evaluation of this book. I proceeded as if Roth's novel were what it artfully pretends to be: the account of what the hero told his psychoanalyst at the beginning of his treatment. This permitted me to intimate how a psychoanalyst may react to what his patient tells him; a subject that may be of some interest, particularly to psychoanalytic patients, but which is hardly ever touched upon in the literature. I also took this opportunity to suggest that uncontrolled sexual acting out, which is all too often

---

*This chapter was previously published in *Surviving and Other Essays*, by Bruno Bettelheim, published by Knopf in 1979.

9

mistaken for sexual freedom, is actually a bondage to sex that destroys it, for the hero ends up impotent.

The novel describes the hero's confusion about who he is and wishes to be—the consequence of his entire life not being ordered, enlightened, or enriched by a definite morality in regard to human, and with this also sexual, relations. Writing about the novel this way permitted stressing that the goal of psychoanalysis is the internalization of experiences as a step toward their integration, and then the achievement of a consistent morality in sexual as well as personal relations, since the two are closely interwoven in any intimate male–female relation.

For those who might not be aware of it, the name or central topic assigned by Dr. Spielvogel to each of the sessions at its end is the title Roth gave to that chapter of his book. It concludes with the hero's realization that engaging in sex any which way, and at completely disregarded expense to others, is not "living big," but a vacuous boast that can no longer serve to hide the emptiness of his life. This is the consequence of his having made sex a substitute for meaningful human relations. With this realization psychoanalysis becomes possible, and this is the author's conclusion—to which I fully subscribe. So the book ends with a last chapter, "Punch Line," consisting in its entirety of "So [*said the doctor*]. Now vee may perhaps to begin. Yes?" (p. 274/287).

Monday, the first hour: A troublesome—aren't they all?—new patient, thirty-three years old, raised in Newark, New Jersey. Typical petty bourgeois Jewish Orthodox background. He is highly intelligent, a compulsive talker, extremely narcissistic and exhibitionistic. He hides his intellectual arrogance behind ironic self-deprecation. He cannot stop the diarrhea of talk, because it is his way of denying his essential constipation—his total inability to give of himself. His working for the underdog (some kind of public relations work for the poor) is not only a denial of his own exploitativeness, but reflects his inner feeling that only the lowest and most miserable could possibly accept him.

He gave me no chance to explain what psychoanalysis is all about, claimed to be very familiar with it, and proceeded to show that he lacks even the slightest understanding. He seems to think psychoanalysis is a self-serving rattling-off of complaints and accusations leveled at others and oneself, instead of recognizing the serious introspection and contemplation it ought to evoke. He is capable of neither of the latter, because he feels he is so worthless that he cannot be serious about anything that touches him — not his own self, nor his parents, not those he cohabits with.

He wants to do everything himself without any relation to, or contribution by, another person, in a typical masturbatory phallic fixation. He permits no one, including me, to make any contribution to his life. Obviously he has spent years at his self-justifying ruminations, where even his self-criticism is meant only to show how shrewd and honest he is about himself. Mainly the self-criticism serves to let him go on exactly as before without internalizing his guilt to the degree that he would need to do something about it; it serves him to avoid any need to change. He is convinced that to rattle off in this way becomes psychoanalysis when he does it aloud with me listening.

Despite his long account of all that went wrong in his life beginning with infancy, there is absolutely no realization of his sickness — his complete inability to relate to other persons. How can he, when all he sees of the world is his own projections, which he is certain are true pictures of reality?

He sees psychoanalysis as one vast catharsis, without the need for any deeper insight or internalization. Everything is just one huge ejaculation. I doubt if he can establish even the minimal transference that would enable him to analyze. Probably his selecting me for an analyst typifies his unwillingness to give up his bondage to his Jewish past. I wonder if I should have insisted that he go to a gentile, American-born analyst. I may still have to transfer him to one.

In our brief talk before treatment began, I asked him why,

given his feeling that his troubles originate with his Orthodox Jewish background, he selected me, not only Jewish, but European-born, as his analyst. He could not understand my point, saying that no gentile analyst could ever understand him. He speaks as if the issue were finding an analyst whose sympathy and understanding are endless, as were his parents' — not his own coming to understand himself. His selection of me for an analyst suggests that deep down he does not want to transcend his own background, and so chose an analyst who will not alienate him from what he pretends to hate, but without which he feels there would be nothing left for him or his life. It remains to be seen whether we can overcome this handicap.

Since he thinks his need is to spill out, uninterruptedly, I shall let him, for a full week. Then we shall see if he can stop the spilling long enough for analysis to be possible.

He carries on as if to convince me that all the clichés of a spoiled Jewish boyhood are indeed valid: the overpowering, overindulgent, overprotective mother and the ineffectual father. Essentially the hour was one long alibi. I am to understand that if he cannot meet life, cannot relate to another human being, it's not because of how he construes things, but because of his parents and their ritual background, along with two specific traumata.

He is a master of the alibi, and like the clever lawyer he is, he plays both sides of the street. He blames his misery on both kinds of trauma: the physical (an undescended testicle) and the psychological (his mother's threat of desertion, and her scaring him by holding a knife in her hand to make him eat). He must be certain I will see him as the suffering victim, no matter what kind of theories I hold about physical or emotional trauma as causing behavior like his. Actually, it is not traumata, but only his disgust with himself, that forces him to defeat all those who love him (his parents, his sexual partners, etc.).

The tirade against his parents, especially his mother, is uninterruptable. A few times I indicated the wish to say something, but he only talked on more furiously. His spiel was like a satire on the complaints of most of my patients, and on the tenets of psychoanalysis: a satire on the dominating and castrating father, and a mother too involved in herself and her own life to pay much attention to her son. This extremely intelligent young Jew does not recognize what he is trying to do — by reversing the oedipal situation, he is trying to make fun of me as he does of everyone, thus asserting his superiority over me and psychoanalysis itself. His overpowering love for his mother is turned into a negative projection, so that what becomes overpowering is the mother's love for him. Overtly he complains that she would never let him alone, was all-intrusive — behind which lies an incredibly deep disappointment that she was not even more exclusively preoccupied with him. While consciously he experienced everything she did as destructive, behind this claim is an incredible wish for more, more, more. His is an insatiable orality which is denied and turned into the opposite by his continuous scream of its being much too much.

Even the most ordinary, everyday request from his mother, such as her reminding him to send a card on his father's sixty-sixth birthday, is experienced by him as the most unreasonable demand, forcing on him a life of guilt and indebtedness to his parents. Whatever the mother did for him was always too little; the smallest thing she requested was always too much.

After listening all day to the endless complaints of patients about mothers who were never interested in whether they did or did not eat, whether or not they defecated, whether or not they succeeded in school, it should have been refreshing to listen to an hour of complaints about a mother who did exactly all that — but it was not. It was so obvious that he felt cheated at not being given enough. No doubt he is tortured by memories of his past, and by his present inability to be a man and enjoy normal sex. But he certainly makes the most of it, and nowhere do I see any effort on his part to free himself of this bondage to the past. Obviously he expects my magic and that of psychoanalysis to do this for him.

An important clue, to be followed up later: he is fascinated by his father's constipation, which is so stark a contrast with his excessive masturbation and incessant, diarrhea-like talk. This seems like an interesting fixation at the phallic level, as though the father's constipation has made him so anxious about his own ability to produce that to compensate, he produces without interruption — whether by masturbating, talking, or intellectual achievement. If he does not learn to hold in and store, but continues this indiscriminate discharge, analysis will certainly fail.

If I were to give a name to this patient after this first hour, I would call him "The Most Unforgettable Character I've Met." This is not because the patient thinks this designation is true of his mother, as he sees her (as is so of everyone and his mother) but because, while he wishes to believe the foregoing, his major effort is to impress me with himself as "the most unforgettable character I've ever met." Poor soul. Instead of trying to get from me the help he so desperately needs, he tries to impress me with his uniqueness. Everything he accuses his mother of, he is himself, in the extreme. She exploited him because she loved him so much. He exploits everyone because he loves no one.

Tuesday, the second hour: Despite the same incessant stream of talk, little new material. Speculations arrived at by the end of the last hour seem borne out today. As a child, he masturbated, preferably on the toilet, in line with the father's constipation, which emerges ever more as a central experience leading to a negative identification. The father cannot let go. The son cannot hold anything in, or hold onto anyone. The father, out of incessant fear for the future, chose and stuck to his job of life insurance salesman. This influence is internalized by the son as fear about his masculinity. For this he finds only one defense: the excessive masturbation that seems to prove his body is working, but at the price of self-disgust. Because this patient wants not a penis that gives pleasure, but an instrument that expels its contents; he seeks a self-assurance that his masturbation cannot give him.

Otherwise it was a repetition of the first hour's contents. In the deliberately vulgar language of the patient, I would entitle this session "Whacking Off." He uses much obscenity to impress others and fools himself into thinking he is liberated, while actually he is expressing his loathing for himself.

Wednesday, the third hour: It becomes increasingly clear that this patient has read too much about psychoanalysis while understanding nothing — for example, about castration anxiety and the effect of seeing menstrual blood. What he does not see is how desperately he wishes he had a castrating father, and how deeply disappointed he is because what he encounters instead is only what he experiences as a castrating mother. But even as he complains of how castrating she is, he cannot help admiring her inner strength, which alone seems to sustain the entire family. One gets the feeling that he has to see her as castrating, because he needs to see her as being strong enough to protect him. It becomes also more clear that his true sickness is the refusal to recognize his parents' deep love for him, because that would mean the obligation to love them back, and later, other human beings. Instead, he clings to his vision of all human relations as exploitative power plays.

A characteristic memory: an athletic cousin, Heshie, got in a physical fight with his father. Although considerably the stronger, Heshie had let his father pin him down and then defeat him in physical combat. My patient wonders a great deal about this. He cannot understand why his cousin deliberately lost the fight. He cannot recognize what he unconsciously knows: that while the father was keeping his son from marrying the gentile girl he loved, which had led to the fight, the father's motive was deep love for his son. The cousin realized, consciously or unconsciously, that to be overpowered by the deep love of another for oneself is the greatest victory possible in human relations, even if outwardly it seems like defeat. My patient, unfortunately, is unable to consciously accept such concepts about love, and I fear he never will. If he could, it would mean his problems were over and his analysis done.

The fact that he never had the closeness that exists between Heshie and his father, that he can neither let go of nor enjoy the specific Jewishness of his background, that he denies what he craves — all this gives my patient the particular "Jewish Blues" that formed the leitmotif of this session.

Thursday, the fourth hour: The patient connects an incident of his exhibitionary masturbation on the bus to his having eaten unkosher food (lobster) for the first time. In his unconscious he thus recognizes the connection between oral and phallic anxiety, and how much of his sexual acting out is based on oral anxiety, like the baby who shows off his phallus. From here, his associations moved to reveal what an anxious person his mother really is — but he refuses to recognize it. He even mentioned her endless stories of how she tries everything once only to find that any venturing out into the world leads to immediate punishment, if not destruction. An explicit memory — the mother's first attempt to drive, which led to an accident and so much anxiety that she never drove again — still brings no realization of how anxiety-ridden she is. Such an insight would destroy his image of her as the all-powerful, castrating woman. He does not realize that what he identifies with in his mother is not her strength, but her abysmal fear of life.

From talking of his resentment at the feeling that he owes his parents something — to get married and provide them with grandchildren, or to be a success in life so that they can brag about their son, as their friends and relatives do about theirs — he moves to his sexual desire for gentile girls. This association seems to indicate that he can have sex only if it is sex that his parents disapprove of. He is so tied to them that he cannot feel he has a separate existence unless he does something to hurt them. Of course this does not work out, and even in the midst of having intercourse he is already dissatisfied, already longing anxiously for the next girl to have sex with.

Clearly his promiscuity is one big effort to keep satisfaction from his parents — and he makes certain he is punished for this by getting nothing that is meaningful to him. For all his reading of psychoanalytic literature, he does not see that his promiscuity, particularly with gentiles, is one big reassurance that he is not having incestuous relations with his mother. By keeping his women ever-changing and meaningless to him, he remains faithful to his mother — not because she won't let him go, but because he won't let go of her. Having enslaved himself to her, he projects the relation to see it as if she, or both parents, had enslaved him to them.

Another crucial memory: a fifteen-year-old boy was pushed too hard by his ambitious mother to perform, and he hanged himself. Pinned to his shirt was a telephone message he had taken for his mother: that she is to take the mah-jongg rules along when she goes out that night. My patient can see in it only the boy's obedience, and not the boy's lethal venom at his mother who dares to enjoy a game with her friends instead of doing nothing all day and night except cater to her son.

As is typical for patients totally unable to form any human relations, who complain endlessly of the deficiency of human relations in their childhood, he tries to provide for others what is, in fact, totally absent in his own life. This patient, it turns out, is assistant commissioner of the New York Commission on Human Opportunity, concerned in his work with improving the lives of others. In his professional life he tries to prevent the poor from being exploited, while all he chases in his personal life is the chance to sexually exploit others.

The worst part of it is that he, who is so lacking in ego and the capacity to give, who is so driven to act out his uncontrolled instinctual tendencies, thinks he is suffering from a deficiency of the id. At one point he tells me what he wants from me: to put the id back into this particular Yid. That is, he does not really want to analyze himself; he does not want to have to develop ego control over superego and id. All he wants of me is to rid him of all the pangs of conscience he still feels about his selfish and asocial behavior. This is how he conceives of the purpose of psychoanalysis. Indeed, he offers to pay me an even higher fee if only I could do that for him.

He recalls masturbating once into a piece of liver which was then eaten at the family dinner. He has no inkling that this shows an extreme sexualization of the oral stage. But most of his seemingly phallic sexuality is really nothing but a screen for his fixation at the oral stage — this shows in his incessant demand to be given to. All the giving by both parents was not enough to fill him up. At least the girl he calls "The Monkey" understood him well. According to him she cried out against him, this great humanitarian whose job it is to protect the poor from their landlords, while his own sexual enjoyment comes from sexually degrading this girl who really seems to have fallen in love with him. She seems to have hoped their relationship might help her out of her own sexual, moral, human morass.

How wise Freud was to impose the sexual abstinence rule, and the rule against patients' reading in psychoanalysis. This patient uses his reading of Freud to masturbate with. Having no intention of analyzing himself, he wants me to do everything for him, as he expected and actually received from his mother, without his having to do anything for himself.

The only enjoyment he seems to get out of sex is in cunnilingus. Like his incessant talking and his pleasure in four-letter words, so with his preference for this perversion — all indicate that he was so intensely satisfied by the oral pleasure his mother provided, that he cannot conceive of its coming from anything else. He is, I am tempted to say, crazy in his efforts to wring oral satisfaction out of sex. In the language of the patient, this session exemplifies his "Cunt craziness."

Friday, the fifth hour: He begins the session by referring to Freud's paper on the misuse of sex to degrade the partner; this leads to memories of his sexual relations with some upper-class gentiles. He recognizes that his feelings of Jewish inferiority and his resentment of anti-Semitism are why he cannot find sexual satisfaction except through seducing his gentile partners into practices that to him are degrading. He induced The Monkey, who did not mind fellatio or even enjoyed it, to have lesbian sex with a prostitute — at which point, he was through with her. His excuse for setting that up is that The Monkey had hinted at it, and she had — since she really loved him, she tried to please him in every way. She had felt unworthy of him, felt that though she gave all she had, tried everything she knew, it never seemed to be enough. So she tried to suggest her readiness to do whatever else might satisfy him. Her offer to do anything he might want of her was then used by him to exculpate himself to me, to convince me and himself that it is really her fault that he so degraded her that she wants to kill herself. All his life it is always the same desperate story: unable to love anybody, including himself, he cannot believe that anybody — his parents, The Monkey — could do anything out of love for him.

Since he has never known true empathy for anyone, he cannot see that those "nice" gentile girls had sex with him precisely because he lived up to their stereotyped notions of the dirty, sex-crazed Jew. His forcing them into what they view as perverted sex proves to them that they were right about Jews in the first place. They selected this highly intelligent, thus seemingly very worthwhile, Jew because being specially admirable, he threatened their image of Jews as inferior beings. But if even this very bright, nice, concerned Jew wants nothing so much as to degrade them in sex, then their initial image of the "dirty" Jew is again confirmed.

And my patient does his best to oblige. Still thinking he degrades only them, he degrades himself even more. This mutual exploitation extends also to what the pair use each other for: to defeat their parents. For my patient the worst thing he can do to his parents is live with a gentile girl. Sleeping with a Jew is probably the worst thing these girls can do to their parents. How these neurotics always find each other! How they help each other act out their neurosis so there is no need to face it! His sex experiences certainly seem like an illustration to Freud's "The Most Prevalent Form of Degradation in Erotic Life."

Saturday, the sixth hour: Were I to see my patients only four or five times a week, as do my American colleagues, and not six times as I learned it in Vienna, this patient's story might have developed very differently. Last night, going over the notes taken up to now, I came close to deciding that this patient's narcissistic self-involvement, his deep oral fixation, his inability to relate, and so forth, all would make analysis impossible, and I had pretty much decided to tell him so at the end of today's hour. I hoped that the shock might, later on, permit him to seek out another analyst; I planned to suggest a gentile one. With a gentile it's possible this patient might begin to analyze, instead of misusing the psychoanalyst as a prop to get rid of his guilt, while continuing to destroy all who have positive feelings for him.

If this session had taken place on Monday, probably nothing would have changed. Maybe the fact that this was a Saturday, the Sabbath, had something to do with it; this I shall find out later. Anyway, today was entirely different. Instead of regaling me with his sexual successes — in masturbation, cunnilingus, and fellatio — the patient finally became a bit more human in recounting his sexual defeats, all by Jewish girls. This began with the patient's recalling how he admired Jewish men like his father, with his Sunday morning ball game, and how he wished to identify with such men but could not, because he wanted even more then to possess his mother. He had to run from his girlfriend The Monkey because as soon as he had gotten a girl to the point where no further degradation was likely to occur, all her attraction was gone for him. Unable, as always, to respond when the love of others for him was so obvious he could no longer deny it, the patient's only solution was to run away. Blaming women for trying to put him in bondage—though all he really wishes is to see them in bondage to him, with his having no return obligation—the patient fled to Israel, the mother country.

There unconsciously (but so close to consciousness that I feel analysis may begin after all) he realized that if he was no longer a Jew in a gentile world, if he could no longer use that excuse to justify his whole pattern of demanding and receiving without ever giving, then he was nothing—and he could not even manage an erection.

In desperation he tried to seduce a kibbutz girl by reversing the methods he had used with his gentile girls. He had degraded gentiles, and their debasement had made them extremely attractive to him, but also useless. Here instead it was he who submitted to debasement, particularly when the girl told him what should have long been obvious: that his self-degradation is the more despicable because he is a man of such high intelligence. He reacted to this by inviting her to have intercourse with him. Then, blaming others as always, he tried to pin his sudden impotence on his mother, claiming the kibbutz girl reminded him of her. He believed it to be the oedipal (but genital) attachment that made him impotent, while it was really his oral attachment, his wish to remain the suckling infant forever.

The long-suffering Jewish mother who lets herself be blamed for everything is willing to thus serve her son. He will never have to feel guilty about anything he might do, because he can always blame it on her. And in a way he can; but not as he thinks. He can blame his mother for letting him believe that whatever he wants, he must immediately be given. This—the central theme of his life—he screamed out at the kibbutz girl: "I have to have" (p. 270/283). It was she who finally told him that this belief of his— that he has to have what he wants, whatever it may cost the other—is not valid.

In a fantasy of being judged for his crimes, he realized, at least for a moment, that blaming his mother will not get him off, cannot justify his behavior to others. This raised the hope that analysis might just succeed. So, instead of dismissing him, as I had planned, I said, "Now we may perhaps begin." Only the future will tell if I was not too optimistic.

One more thought: He is very clever at presenting himself, and right after the first session I had the uneasy feeling that he wants to impress me as the most unforgettable patient I ever had. What if all he said so far was carefully prepared and selected? His determination not to permit me to interrupt with questions or interpretations suggests the possibility that he was afraid that any interference might throw him off his apparently stream-of-consciousness-like talk, because actually it was a carefully prepared story, designed to impress me. What if all he presented as the outpourings of his unconscious and preconscious, of his id and superego (the self-criticism, the fantasy about his being judged) were conscious ego productions? Was he trying to test me in order to find out whether I am smart enough not to mistake an essentially literary production for an effort at analysis?

If all this was so, did I do the right thing not to insist on interrupting him, or on directing his associations, and not to tell him at the end of the last session that it is time to stop being a man of letters so that, through analyzing himself, he might finally become a man? Again, we shall see.

But even if what has happened so far was not more than an effort to tell a good story, it is significant that it is "The Monkey" who emerges as having the greatest dignity. Though born desperately poor, social success means nothing to her. Having been married to one of the richest men of France meant nothing to her. When she felt used by him, she left him without another thought. Though aspiring to culture, she is not at all impressed by its trappings, nor by being invited to the mayor's mansion, because what is important to her is to be with the patient, not to attend a formal dinner. This she made clear by having sex with him within view of the mayor's house, not caring what others might think of her or what she did there, while he was deathly afraid of how all this might look to others. He, as always, involved only in himself, did not recognize that she was not motivated by any hedonist impulsiveness, but by the anxious question: "Are you taking me to the mayor's reception because you love me and want me near you, or because I am ornamental and therefore useful in your social climbing?"

What view can he have of himself as a person and as a Jew if social and sexual honesty, that is, if true humanity — in his eyes — resides only in the poor "Monkey"? Is it just another case then of the self-hating Jew living "In Exile"?

3

Ego Psychology Perspective: An Ego Psychological Analysis of *Portnoy's Complaint*

Elliot Adler, Ph.D.

In some ways, the initial sessions of an analytic treatment afford a psychoanalyst the best perspective for taking stock of the unique individual with whom one is setting out on an inevitably arduous journey of exploration. While the full significance of most of the things a patient reveals to us remains obscure for a long time, the personality or character style of the patient often stands forth in the clearest light. Transference has yet to force its way to the forefront of our attention, and the patient's self-presentation is relatively free of the increasingly passionate bias that will eventually obscure the analytic field.

In these sessions we are hearing Alex tell Dr. Spielvogel his story for the first time. We may safely presume that he has been telling himself a version or versions of this story for quite a while, so naturally we take care to understand what he wants us to be impressed with in his story, the spin he attempts to put on events, memories, and experiences. We are particularly interested in the way he conceives of his problem, and his expectations and fantasies of how the treatment will provide a cure.

A few things seem clear enough. Alex wishes to portray himself as a *victim* in the widest sense of the word. He is a victim of his mother's intrusive, controlling, and aggrandizing seductiveness, of his father's constipated impotence, of his girlfriends' longings for love and protection, even of his own impetuous penis. Additionally, the considerable weight of his personal ideals and moral ambitions are experienced as an oppressive external presence in his life. Hence the ubiquitous complaining tone of his narration. Explicitly or implicitly, the point of nearly every episode seems to be that somebody or something is making his life unusually difficult.

We are aware, however, that a powerful undercurrent in this turbulent sea of complaint is a rush of self-exculpation. Through his complaining, he appears to be defending himself against a veritable riptide of guilt and remorse. He has let down his parents, he has abused and abandoned his girlfriends, he is incapable of love, he is/has a selfish prick, and so forth. Though we are prepared to discover in the course of the analysis that both his complaints about others and those about himself have more than a little validity, we must be more immediately mindful that such a passion for blaming does not constitute the most desirable atmosphere in which to conduct an analytic inquiry. Generally speaking, such blaming constitutes a manic defense against searingly painful experiences of depression, guilt, shame, and remorse. Infused with sadomasochistic and narcissistic gratifications, such self-scrutiny is transformed into a parody of honest self-reflection and yields none of its salutary benefits.

Indeed, it is a very self-conscious young man who reveals himself in these sessions, one who listens searchingly to his own narrative voice with an ear to screen the nuances of his performance, unwilling, we might surmise, for his listener to catch him unawares. Inevitably, he anticipates, formulates, and answers the analyst's unasked questions. He presents himself rather as an acolyte bent on proving to his mentor how capable he is in playing the role of patient/analyst in a solipsistic display of professional mastery. He appears to have done his homework as well, quoting Freud's *Collected Papers* aptly, for the most part. We may wonder to whom his performance is ultimately addressed, an anal retentive analyst/father whose withholding silence he fears will reflect constipated inadequacy, or to an admiring and delighted analyst/mother, awed and cowed by his precocious display of brilliant insight and titillated to have such a promising patient/son?

For the moment, Alex makes remarkably few explicit demands on Dr. Spielvogel. In these early sessions he appears more than content to tell his story, almost reveling in an opportunity to display his formidable intellect, humor, and bawdy passion. No doubt such charms will wear thin soon enough. Already, on occasion, one feels an impatient urge to wrestle him off the stage in order to allow some room for the analyst's thoughts. But we must admire Dr. Spielvogel's forbearance in allowing things to unfold, especially as Alex continues to reveal important genetic and dynamic material. It would be all too easy to be nettled into some display of irritable impatience at Alex's flamboyant style, ignoring the genuinely poignant elements in his story. Clearly he uses his intellect and wit to control the analytic hour, creating a dazzling facade blending ironic charm and self-abasement to soften the nastier contours of his intention. He is, nonetheless, a remarkably clever fellow. There is no need to deprive him of all recognition of this fact, especially as these gifts could prove formidable allies to the treatment if the analysis succeeds in freeing them from service to neurotic ends.

As to his penchant for psychoanalytic interpretation and speculation, this may prove a mixed blessing. On the one hand, he does have a gift for applying theoretical ideas to his own experience in ways that are often plausible and persuasive. Eventually, as an outcome of treatment we would hope that he will develop a reliable capacity for objective self-analysis. And yet, without considerable working through of characterological traits and ingrained defenses, the self-analytic function is almost

always corrupted by tendentious intentions that serve largely re-
sistive purposes. Unfortunately, the more plausible a patient's
formulations, the more subtle the resistant elements tend to be. In
general the analyst is wise to avoid the twin dangers of dismissing
the patient's ideas and speculations out of hand, or alternatively,
of giving too much credit to the patient's claims to self-knowledge.
Insight, like anything else, is only useful in context, and even a
valid interpretation compromised by ulterior motivation — like
damp gunpowder — will not fuel explosive results.

The crucial question from an ego psychology point of view is
not what current theories Alex holds about his emotional problems, nor what characterological traits are most in evidence, but
what potential he manifests for self-understanding down the line.
Early in an analysis one can only make educated guesses, for ego
strengths and weaknesses are always a matter of degrees, which
we possess no instrument to calibrate. Alex's self-consciousness,
for example, though a defensively distorted mode of self-awareness, presumes an ego capacity for differentiated self-observa-
tion. His view of the object world also seems relatively uncontaminated by primitive, projective–introjective processes, except
when deeper anxiety situations are mobilized and a frantic
unalloyed hostility toward women — those "bitches" and "cunts" —
breaks through. Alex's descriptions of his important love objects
are vivid and genuinely poignant, even if broadly drawn and
colored with excessive ambivalence. This implies a capacity for
empathy and compassion that dilutes the off-putting impact of
his incessant exhibitionism. In any case, his childlike narcissistic
claims, which he usually reports with ironic, self-mocking humor,
lack the cold malignant edge that would argue for making these
features our primary diagnostic focus.

Alex himself often seems to be making a case for the view that
he loves his penis to the exclusion of any other object or human
being, but I was not persuaded. I sensed that he was struggling to
deny to himself, as well as to the analyst, how pained and guilty

he felt about his breakup with The Monkey. From this perspective, his assertion of an exclusively phallic narcissistic position is a refuge from mourning and loss and therefore an aspect of his shaky manic defenses. Naturally, all such initial assessments involve subtle clinical judgments that may have to be largely amended upon further experience.

Though the most crucial diagnostic thinking during initial sessions of an analysis relates to the capacity of a patient to use psychoanalytic therapy as a way of changing his or her life, it is always illuminating to formulate some understanding of the immediate events and forces that have driven the patient to take the fateful step of arranging for a consultation with the psychoanalyst. It is rare that such action is taken lightly out of intellectual curiosity. Even though it is rarely consciously articulated, such a step represents a tacit acknowledgment that the individual sees little hope of working things out on his or her own. The deeper understanding of the decision therefore yields entrée into the patient's core unresolvable conflicts.

Alex, not atypically, has consulted the analyst in the wake of a failure in his adult love life — the precipitous breakup and flight from a relationship with a woman whom he derisively refers to as "The Monkey," and a subsequent humiliating and frightening breakthrough of crudely sadomasochistic impulses as he struggled to reestablish his equilibrium after fleeing to the Promised Land. It is significant, however, that after his return to the States, in the period before calling the analyst, Alex began reading Freud's *Collected Papers*. This could be meaningfully looked at as a spontaneous attempt to get psychological help, an effort at self-analysis with a little assistance from the immortal Father of Psychoanalysis himself. Indeed, much of what we have been hearing in these initial sessions is more comprehensible and less bizarre when viewed as the fruits of this solitary labor. He specifically quotes Freud's famous statement used to summarize a common oedipal compromise formation, "Where such men love

they have no desire, and where they desire they cannot love."
This aphorism summarizes so succinctly his own cumulative
experiences with love that we suspect it functioned in his mind
like a well-timed interpretation, mobilizing him to contact Dr.
Spielvogel.

For all Alex's keen appreciation of the enormous improbability
of his union with The Monkey, we must not be fooled into
denigrating the profound emotional importance of this event.
For, by his own admission, the brief interlude in New England
represented the only time in his life he has been able to experience
the gratifications of mature love; that is, deep tenderness and
longing in the context of a sexually gratifying relationship:

> . . . the apprehension aroused by the model-y glamour, the
> brutish origins, above everything, the sexual recklessness — that all
> this fear and distrust had been displaced by a wild upward surge
> of tenderness and affection.[p. 184/197]

Paradoxically, this woman, who from one perspective must have
seemed the woman of his dreams, served to expose, with
devastating inevitability, the utter futility of his most cherished
fantasies.

In making a dynamic assessment, occasions of exceptional
happiness are as interesting as the catalogue of failures, humiliations, and remorse that strew the pathway of a neurotically
compromised life. I take it as a truly hopeful sign that Alex seems
genuinely disturbed and puzzled by this experience. Why, he asks
himself, with this particular woman at this particular time, has
love blossomed so fleetingly? Active curiosity about such psychological enigmas are requisite for forging a working alliance aimed
at dynamic exploration and discovery.

The relationship's beginnings were inauspicious, to say the
least, a crude pickup encounter on Lexington Avenue in Manhattan. The Monkey responded to his overture with a provocative
challenge "What do *you* want?" When his reasonable response,

"To buy you a drink," met with sarcastic rebuke, his escalation to "To eat your pussy, baby, how's that?" (p. 157/169) presumably was sufficiently reckless to carry the day!

Alex is initially astounded to find a beautiful woman who is as sexually adventurous as the women of his masturbation fantasies. Indeed, her direct, no nonsense, eat and be eaten attitude toward erotic pleasure has the unadorned directness of masturbatory fantasy. And yet—to his chagrin—Alex cannot fully enjoy his "good fortune." He is beset both by intrusive guilty fantasies of retaliatory disaster (venereal diseases, violent attacks), and an almost perverse unwillingness to accept The Monkey on the exclusively sexual level she offers. While aware of the absurd irony of his almost immediate impulse to educate this woman, he rationalizes his didactic compulsion as some high-minded Jewish affliction. He fails to recognize that this highly ambivalent impulse betrays both a longing for a more complete communion with a sexually yielding woman and a compulsive need to establish his unquestioned intellectual superiority and sadistic dominance. (We recognize in this belated effort to elevate a defensively degraded love object the already developed strategy he had adopted in adolescence toward his father.) For all his purported fascination with feminine orifices and their mechanics, uninhibited sex can engage his interest for but a brief time without evoking feelings of repulsion and dread.

Alex and The Monkey quickly cement their unlikely alliance by forging an implicit contract—she will provide an education in erotic abandon in exchange for an intellectual and moral one— propelled by a modern variation of a classic Pygmalion fantasy. Almost immediately, however, this fragile romantic premise is rendered by an underlying sadomasochistic structure. Alex's sadism, stirred and quickened by The Monkey's profound masochistic enticement, breaks through. From a narrowly psychosexual point of view The Monkey's entrance into Alex's life may have seemed a unique opportunity for liberating the chronically inhibited and frustrated areas of his psyche. Perhaps for a less profoundly conflicted man, it might have genuinely held such promise of restored health, not via a psychoanalytic process involving the interpretation of resistances and the gradual integration, renunciation, and sublimation of archaic desires but through a Dionysian course of sensual abandon and fulfillment! Like any good clinician, The Monkey did a careful diagnostic inventory in their first meeting, cleverly drawing him out about his deepest, most inhibited desires and fantasies. Alex's subsequent plea to his analyst to "make me *whole*" (p. 36/46) is congruent with The Monkey's implicit offer to restore his full potency.

It is in the nature of neurotic conflict that it is relatively oblivious to the fortuitous therapeutics of everyday life. Pregenital erotic desire, fueled by an amalgam of primitive sexual, aggressive, and narcissistic aims, and shaped by the unbearable psychic dangers of the archaic reaches of emotional life, typically generates fantasy derivatives involving crude patterns of excitement and discharge. Marked by the developmental character of their origins—immature cognition, elemental emotional intensity, and irrational (primary process) modes of representation—they are confined within interpersonal paradigms defined by poorly differentiated self and object representations. It is not surprising then, that highly charged scenarios and fantasy derivatives prove abhorrent to the adult's advanced emotional and moral sophistication.

It is, of course, a specific tenet of Freudian psychoanalysis that the earliest wishes of childhood are never entirely supplanted or erased by later development. Often they lay dormant, to be reanimated only when specific dynamic conditions prevail in adult life. Ideally, however, their energies find successful integration with the more mature striving of the self, augmenting the intensity of conscious investments by forging symbolic linkages to unconscious sources of fantasy and energy.

In the case before us, an intermediate situation holds sway.

Some of the wishes (or their derivatives) are active and conscious, though poorly integrated within the overall fabric of Alex's moral outlook. From a structural perspective, this reflects a moderate failure of superego integration. The more aggressivized sadomasochistic longings, however, are blocked from unmediated conscious expression—before his defensive breakdown in Israel, that is—and find their outlet erratically in disguised, symptomatic, or compromised actions, fantasies, and attitudes. As they infiltrate different areas of his personality, the impact on his functioning varies considerably. For instance, these fantasies seem to have achieved a degree of relatively successful sublimation in the work arena. Here, as the Assistant Commissioner of Human Opportunity he can be the righteous defender of the weak and helpless, directing his sadism against the hypocritical and powerful. These same inclinations, however, prove enormously debilitating in intimate relations with women, where urges to dominate and degrade play havoc with bonds of affection, undermining reactive urges to elevate and idealize.

Furthermore, this pregenital sadism seems a necessary condition of his potency. For unless his women are degraded objects (emotionally, intellectually, or physically) he is overcome by castration anxiety, and regressive threats of engulfment. Each important love in his life has been given an objectifying title— The Pumpkin, The Puritan, and The Monkey—as if to defuse the latent menace of their feminine power. One task that must be addressed in a thorough analytic inquiry is to identify and to learn as much as possible about the forces that conspire to keep such infantile imperatives so central in Alex's life, undermining more mature concerns and ambitions. The answer to such questions is never simple, as the role of any element in a personality is a function of a very complex and shifting constellation of internal and external forces, mediated by certain relatively stable structural configurations. Patients resist knowledge of these wishes and forces, as their integration inevitably requires confronting feelings of shame, depression, and anxiety, as well as undermining preferred (i.e., relatively safe) sources of gratification.

Thus, despite Alex's cumulatively disastrous experience with women, he still vainly attempts to cast his problem as one of heroic resistance to parental and societal expectations, an assertion of the macho prerogatives of unfettered testosterone. Yet he has every reason to be fully aware that his true state is one of growing isolation, desperation, and emotional impotence. We should not be overly surprised at these inconsistencies in self-awareness, as they are such predictable manifestations of unconscious conflict. That he is increasingly unable to maintain these compensatory fictions, and is preconsciously aware that fixations on pregenital erotic aims (phallic narcissistic, oral and anal sadistic) secure a regressive avoidance of genitality accounts for his consultation with the analyst at this time.

A contemporary ego-psychological understanding of genitality embraces more than the notion of subsuming the sexual drive under the aegis of the genital organ. It includes the ego's responsibility to the broader psychosocial obligations that arise from a satisfying genital union with the beloved. This may involve nurturing the beloved as well as any potential offspring of their union. Alex seems terrified of confronting these obligations of a loving relationship or of actively aspiring to a paternal identity, other than in romanticized fantasy. He expresses this succinctly by complaining that he does not feel "intact" as a man, and plaintively prays for his analyst's help in fulfilling his manhood. "Bless me with manhood! Make me brave! Make me strong! Make me *whole!*" (p. 36/46).

It will be one of the first goals of the analysis to transform this melodramatic supplicant at the shrine of psychoanalysis into a working patient pursuing the anxiety-filled task of facing the deeper "realities" within his internal world that truly undermine his courage. Before this can be accomplished, the analyst will have to inform him in a timely and tactful fashion that his complaining serves a number of avoidant functions, not the least of which is to keep him from taking seriously his own often penetrating insights into his dilemma.

Despite Alex's histrionics we cannot disregard the specificity of his plea for the analyst to make him whole. At the manifest level, of course, he is speaking metaphorically of his recognition that something is missing in his life and character. Yet in his choice of metaphor, we recognize a more literal reference to a bodily representation of damage, a transparent allusion to the floating testicle that disappeared inside his body cavity with the onset of puberty. Heard in this way, his plea implicitly condenses the memory of an adolescent anatomical trauma with an adult sense of failure at consolidating a mature masculine self.

That this shocking and mysterious disappearance was an occasion of enormous castration anxiety would appear incontrovertible. It is as if the portentous knife, which once his mother employed to enforce compliance with her feeding schedule, had found a terrifying re-embodiment in the surgeon's scalpel hanging over his testicular abnormality, warning him to curb the ferocious appetites of adolescence. The enduring imprint of this internal psychological situation, which condenses the pregenital imperatives of autonomous defiance toward an invasive and controlling mother, and the oedipal rebellion against the phallic father will provide the dynamic context to a number of central organizing themes in his life. It stands as an example of how adolescent development results in a reorganization of preoedipal and oedipal conflict giving rise to the unique, highly condensed compromise formations that mark a personality with its richly idiosyncratic stamp.

It is virtually impossible to do justice in summary to the psychological complexity that emerges from this development. What follows is an attempt to trace some of the dominant trends and a few of the interrelationships in Alex's material, although such attempts often result in hopelessly reductive portraits.

Increasingly, Alex's desperate measures to ameliorate castration anxiety and castration depression give dynamic focus to a number of enduring and embarrassing emotional preoccupations: shame over inadequate genital endowment, awe of his father's large penis, mortification at his mother's teasing belittlement, guilt over masturbatory excess, and dread of exposure and punishment for his sexual fantasies and actions.

Much of his compulsive exhibitionism can be viewed as a species of compensatory magic aimed at disproving/forestalling an unconscious belief in his own castration. (Unconscious fantasies of being a feminized castrate and being threatened with castration as a punishment represent no contradiction.) His mother's hysterectomy, which he associatively connects to images of a butchered chicken with its extractable entrails and egg (gonad), and the dripping (menstrual) blood of koshered meat, makes real to him the horrifying image of a woman "hollowed-out" by surgery. He can never again "look her in the eye" (a displacement upward) without dread, and he flees to the elegiac ballfield of memory, with its reassuring security of clearly prescribed role performances. How comforting to prove one's manhood in this neatly ritualized sport, rather than in disturbing and messy intimacy with a woman's bleeding body!

Alex's associations also suggest that he has not succeeded in forging an unconscious identification with a powerful paternal phallus (his father, it seems, can't wield a baseball bat), a fantasy that might have ameliorated his shame and diminished his dread of potential feminization. Internalization of the paternal phallus (i.e., as an unconscious fantasy) often serves as a talisman magically assuring confident triumph over the menacing oedipal and preoedipal maternal imago that is imbued with such power to control, stimulate, gratify, and disappoint. This development is typically associated with a measure of sadistic denigration of femaleness, which helps suppress increasingly shameful dependent longings and largely unconscious urges toward re-fusion, en route to a securely integrated masculine identity. The familial recognition Alex received for his intellectual precocity represents the one uncontaminated pathway for the expression (and sublimation) of phallic narcissistic tensions, without which he might have had to resort to an overtly homosexual solution to his conflicts. Nevertheless, despite this inflated sense of mental prowess (i.e., an unconscious mental phallus), he still looks down on his shriveled member as a poor tool woefully ill-suited to satisfying voracious female passions.

In his aggressive and sadistic demeaning of women as dumb "cunts" we recognize an anxiety-filled impulse to deny (to castrate) the unconsciously feared phallic attributes of the woman, by subjugating them to his phallic will. Within a more comprehensive psychodynamic context this violent imperative will be viewed as serving a number of purposes. On the one hand, it represents a regressive animation of the archaic imago of the phallic woman in an attempt to ward off the castration anxiety stimulated by the terrifying imago of a butchered, vaginal mother. On yet another level, his deep attempt to deny passive erotic response to the brutally potent, castrating father (the negative oedipal) compels him to act out a reversal of his wished for and feared submission to the father with each of his girlfriends in succession. In this compromise formation, the vindictive and betrayed father is simultaneously a punisher and an object of passive desire, while the girlfriend is assigned the masochistic role of sexually degraded, castrated object. Thus when Alex first "risks everything" by masturbating next to the golden *shikse* under the eyes of a Polish bus driver, he is giving first expression to this enormously dangerous and exciting bisexual scenario that will continue to inform his erotic life. From this point of view, still another way of hearing his overdetermined plea to the analyst to make him whole is suggested. It is as an unconscious erotic invitation: "Fuck me and fill me with your potent phallus!"

Thwarted in his effort to form an alliance with his father, Alex is eternally in thrall to that "most unforgettable person" of his childhood. His early conviction that Sophie Portnoy could transform herself into his schoolteachers, is echoed by an unconscious belief that each of his girlfriends is about to transform herself into Sophie Portnoy. Projectively, he invests this imago—the ubiquitous preoedipal mother—with the intention of unmanning him in word and deed, in order to manipulate, entrap, and devour him. His most reliable weapon in this frantic battle to preserve an independent masculine self in the face of a woman's engulfing enticement is his mental phallus. Thus he pridefully displays his intellect to evoke awe and admiration in women's eyes, just as he *cuttingly* directs his wit at any woman who arouses anxiety. Various stratagems are evident to ward off this danger, including choosing his women from the class of women least likely to evoke associations to his mother, *shikses*.

Compounding his urgent need to denigrate women to protect an autonomous masculine self is a corollary failure to establish an esteem-enhancing identification with his father vis-à-vis the world at large. He consciously devalues his father's social status and finds specific evidence in his chronic constipation of suppressed rage and ignominious submission to the will of exploitive WASP executives in the company hierarchy. This bowel inhibition assumes emblematic significance as a symbol of the shameful suppression of instinctive desire and the dangers of holding in one's "shit." It also renders his father's impressive "*shlong*" limp and lifeless in Alex's eyes, the vestigial organ of a domesticated mammal.

Undoubtedly there was an element of wish fulfillment in this attribution, as if Alex was reassuring himself that he need not be afraid or envious, though he paid for this reassurance by depriving himself of an idealized identificatory figure. There is also a large measure of retaliatory vengeance as well. For an important predisposing motive underlying this devaluation of his oedipal rival is his lingering and bitter disappointment that his father had not been willing to blunt the willful thrust of his mother's childrearing practices nor even to lend support to his own feeble effort to defy his mother's tyrannical control. "Why did he let her get away with this?" "And why didn't he stop her!"

In this context it is important to emphasize that his ultimate view of his father as the passive victim of the exploitive WASP establishment is a later construction, modeled on his own abject surrender to his mother's coercive ways. Not only has his father failed to thwart the mother's intrusive efforts to control Alex, but he has (in Alex's eyes) foresworn his natural right to be his wife's primary object of admiration, by making his academic achievements a family glory. This oedipal capitulation incites contempt while stimulating Alex's grandiosity. The glory of this oedipal victory is probably exaggerated in order to efface the stinging memory of his own earlier ignominious defeats at his mother's hands.

We must bear in mind that at this point in the analysis we are hearing a highly elaborated retrospective view of his childhood. We have every reason to expect his views will change in significant ways under the influence of the intrapsychic changes set in motion by the emergence and analysis of a transference neurosis. Though we cannot—and should not—anticipate with any conviction the direction these changes will take, there is significant evidence that Alex's tendency to systematically denigrate his father's stature in his narrative history may disguise a more formidable and menacing vision of an earlier paternal figure, the superpotent castrating father of the primal scene.

Though we can trace through Alex's history a hunger for a suitably powerful masculine identificatory figure (most notably his heroic cousin Heshie and his uninhibited friend Arnold Mandel), it is ultimately the WASP executive whose picture hung on his parents' wall, who comes to embody the truly empowered adult male. Though to his mind he can never, as a Jewish male, be fully confident in his manhood, he pursues a vindictive strategy of revenge by seducing *shikses* who are/could be the daughters of his father's purported tormentors. Alex partially rationalizes his intentions, and through this oedipal displacement succeeds in combining two incompatible aims: he restores his father's honor and power (and by extension, Jewish honor for their collective social impotence), and he humiliates these powerful rivals through sexual conquest and degradation of their daughters.

But this secret phallic victory at the expense of the powerful WASP father cannot be enjoyed, as it is fraught with all the guilt, anxiety, and shame of his earlier masturbatory conquests. Hence his anxiety and embarrassment when confronted with a situation where his boss, Mayor Lindsay (the prototypical WASP), is about to meet the provocatively erotic Monkey. On this occasion, Alex's expressed irritation with her "open door policy" (i.e., symbolically an open sexual invitation to an intruder who embodies paternal retribution) as he arrives at her apartment, barely conceals his fury at her easygoing ways, though he quickly hides this rage behind a mask of supercilious disdain for her defects of education. We may surmise that he is beset by an unconscious dread of being unmasked as an aggressive oedipal usurper and receiving the talion retribution he knows he deserves. (In this connection it is worth recalling that his brief idyll of uninhibited love for The Monkey flowered only when they left New York City for a weekend, and his defensive contempt returned on the drive home as they approached the city limits. Also when registering at the inn, he spontaneously employed the alias of his adolescent friend, Arnold Mandel!) The Monkey, sucking him off on a bench outside Gracie Mansion, tangibly and intuitively understands the reassuring meaning of this act; Alex still has his penis and she craves it above all others.

A more fateful denial of/encounter with the phallic father whose fearsome potency presumably has butchered and bloodied the formidable Sophie Portnoy's internal organs so badly, occurs in the erotic denouement of their tempestuous relationship, the episode with the whore in Rome. The threesome with the big-chested Lina is, of course, the perverse culmination that has been foreshadowed from the beginning, when the recollected scene — and imaginatively embellished detail of eating a banana while watching another couple's fornication — provides the eponymous act from which The Monkey derives her nickname. The encounter sours (as with many perverse scenarios, the pleasure of enactment is less keen than the fantasied anticipation) when The Monkey finds herself having to watch while Alex fornicates with the whore. Furious at being left out, she accuses Alex of degrading her and turning her into a lesbian, ultimately threatening to kill herself unless Alex makes her an honest woman.

That this perverse scenario represents an enactment with the aim of undoing Alex's passive exclusion in the primal scene, is extremely likely. Understood in this way, we realize that the big-chested whore is the sexually available mother, while The Monkey is cast in the despised and dreaded role of the passive little boy who can only participate by orally submitting to the phallic father (i.e., eat his banana). When Lina returns with her real-life little boy and offers to invite a male friend to screw the signora, the frame of illusion and unreality necessary to safeguard the defensive transformation of his primal-scene anguish is torn away. The madonna/whore split, strategically central to Alex's defensive adaptation, along with the transformation of passive into active, has been irremediably sundered and the relationships underlying defensive premise is shattered. This whore *is* a mother and the "whore-y" girlfriend *wants* to be a mother. To compound his distress, the father is trying to reclaim his rightful place in the primal bedroom. Alex flees from the primal scene to the promised land where "everyone is Jewish" even the whores and hoods. Here there is no possibility of splitting off and displacing the incestuous portent of the oedipal objects. Alex cannot escape.

In a final desperate effort to regain an active masculine stance after his break with The Monkey, reactive sadistic impulses toward women break through with almost manic abandon in his actions as well as his thoughts. Thus when Naomi, the strapping young sabra (who "looks like" his mother and "could be" his sister) belittles his proudest professional achievements, he is driven to attempt to overpower her sexually. In the ensuing combat, to assert his shaky prowess on a physical level, he desperately summons deeply archaic oral and anal sadistic impulses to contaminate and infect the feared vagina. Failing to dominate or degrade her, he is devastatingly exposed as a whining, pleading, and passive little boy whose pee-pee is an object of derisive contempt to the "big" woman who stands over him.

Thus we see that at the core of Alex's ubiquitous conflictual behavior is a *struggle over passivity*, whether in the guise of a passive dependent longing for fusion with the preoedipal mother, or a passive masochistic submission to the oedipal father. Conquest and domination define a vulnerable masculinity largely fueled by reactive phallic narcissistic, anal, and phallic sadistic strivings. His unconscious feminine identification and latent homosexual wishes are defensively repressed, while incestuous oedipal wishes are guiltily expressed with the help of isolation and displacement. As analysis proceeds, this underlying motivational structure of infantile desire, defense, anxiety, and guilt will be interpretively revealed, and Alex will be in a better position to pursue inhibited ambitions congruent with his ego ideal.

Of course, even if this initial dynamic formulation proves essentially correct, the outcome of the treatment will be determined in the mastery and interpretation of the transference rather than by the clarity of the analyst's conceptualization. Naturally, the major struggle we can anticipate in this treatment will revolve around Alex's intolerance of any passivity with regard to the analyst. This intolerance should become the focus of a good deal of exploration and analysis, touching upon all the dynamic issues outlined above. However, no matter how much latitude the analyst gives him, the interpretive process itself will inevitably become embroiled in the defensive conflict that is at the heart of the patient's neurosis. Dr. Spielvogel's interpretations will necessarily come to represent either menacing phallic intrusions (i.e., the activity of the analyst's mental phallus) or suffocating coercive feedings, and Alex will find more or less subtle strategies to ward off and neutralize the anxiety and rage they evoke in him. Narcissistic and sadomasochistic paradigms are already abundantly evident in the interaction with the analyst. They will become increasingly animated in the transference–countertransference interplay that has to be worked through for the analysis to become a transformative experience rather than an intellectual exercise. If all goes well, Alex will gradually begin to forge less ambivalent identifications with Dr. Spielvogel and eventually be able to approach the work of analysis, *and of his life*, with a seriousness and self-respect that thus far have eluded him.

4

Mahler's Developmental Perspective: The Hatching of Alexander Portnoy

Judith Hanlon, Ph.D.

When Alex consults Dr. Spielvogel he is a tormented, guilty, and anxiety-ridden man with multiple problems, both symptomatic and characterological. Twice impotent with women (the immediate precipitant for his seeking help), he is in general severely crippled in love. He has had a series of short-lived relationships and cannot make a commitment. Women for him are degraded and objectified, or idealized, perfect, and pure. He is addicted to masturbation and to sadomasochistically tinged sexual encounters, and suffers a persistent dread of reprisal for these activities, particularly in the form of intense castration anxiety. Paralleling his incapacity to love others, Alex is defective in self-love, seeking always to make himself over, to live down his past, to become someone else. His sense of maleness is fragile and in need of constant shoring up.

This chapter explores the role of separation–individuation problems in Alex's pathology. Although phallic and oedipal issues are obvious—he is intensely preoccupied with his penis, he is impotent with a woman who looks like his mother, and so forth—

I argue that these are built on earlier difficulties in the process of establishing a separation. Like any patient, Alex can tell us far more about his later childhood, his adolescence, and his present life than he can about his first three years when the major achievements of separation–individuation occurred. Further, we know that the residua of the separation–individuation phase have not persisted unchanged but rather have been carried through, interpreted, and transformed in complex ways throughout his development. Nevertheless, from his present presentation, from his narrative, and from his description of his family we can infer difficulties in the preoedipal period, difficulties that have shaped and colored Alex's subsequent oedipal, latency, and adolescent phases.

The overriding and persisting importance of the early omnipotent mother in Alex's psychic life is announced on the first page. He begins his story with a description of his ubiquitous and magical mother who transforms herself every day when he goes to school into each of his teachers, transforms herself back, and flies home and in through the window in time to serve him milk and cookies. She is there at the end of the book as well in only slightly disguised form, that of the red-haired sabra, looming over him, looking down at

. . . this what? This *son*. This *boy*! This *baby*! [p. 269/282]

And she is everpresent in the pages in between, as we understand her to be in Alex's consciousness. Sophie Portnoy, we learn, is so powerful that she can accomplish *anything*—she makes jello with peaches suspended in it in defiance of the law of gravity, and has *radar*—even before radar!—that enables her to warn all the women in the building to take in their laundry at the first drop of rain.

The persistence of this larger-than-life maternal image reveals a less-than-optimal separation. Alex decries his endless childhood "which I won't relinquish—or which won't relinquish me!" (p. 271/284). Indeed, he is stuck in the past, and, in particular, he is unable to give up his mother. Although 5-year-old Alex's fantasy is of his mother following *him* to school, we can read in it his own wish to stay close to *her*. As an adolescent, he cannot be as daring and independent as his friends Mandel and Smolka, so attached is he to his mother's care, to "cream of tomato soup heating up on the stove . . . [and] freshly laundered and ironed pajamas" (pp. 172–173/185). And perhaps one reason for his failure to commit himself to a woman as an adult is that he cannot relinquish his own mother. At the same time he seems to be desperately struggling to get away from this dangerous, potentially engulfing figure, choosing as an adult *shikse* women who are (on the surface) her opposite, and trying to keep his visits down to once a month— a struggle against "imponderable odds" (p. 34/44). Alex's conflict calls up the picture of the rapprochement toddler, alternately clinging and pushing away, wanting to be united with and at the same time separate from the mother (Mahler et al. 1975). His ongoing difficulty achieving "optimal distance" (Mahler 1971, p. 413) suggests a troubled early separation–individuation period. He seems to have been caught in a protracted separation struggle throughout his life.

Because the maternal image is so powerful, so idealized, and so all-important to Alex, he tries to counter it by degrading and objectifying women. Hence, his girlfriends are The Monkey, The Pumpkin, and The Pilgrim. At 33 he tells Dr. Spielvogel that "while everybody else has been marrying . . . and having children," he has been "chasing cunt" and "still cursing himself for speaking not a word to the succulent pair of tits that rode twenty-five floors alone with him in an elevator" (pp. 99–100/110–111). The Monkey, we learn, has a very low opinion of herself, and simultaneously, a very high opinion of Alex, the reverse of Alex's internal psychic situation of persisting, infantile idealization of his mother. The ménage à trois of Alex, The Monkey, and Lina the prostitute serves to degrade the two women and to dilute their emotional power. But Alex cannot escape the pull of the longed-for idealized maternal figure. He meets Naomi, red-haired and Jewish like his mother, and idealistic, pure, healthy, and powerful. Within minutes of picking her up he thinks of marrying her, and a few hours later he declares his love. When she rejects him he must reduce her again: "Now let's fuck," he tells her. When she refuses, he tries to force her, attempting to overpower the woman who to him is so powerful.

Mahler and colleagues (1975) describe how the rapprochement toddler often uses splitting to cope with the struggles and longings of separation. To protect the good object, the image of the longed-for, erstwhile, all-good symbiotic mother is kept separate from that of the ambivalently loved, potentially castrating, and engulfing "mother after separation." Mahler and colleagues emphasize the importance of reconciling and integrating these good and bad images and of attaining more realistic views of self and other. Optimally, this is accomplished during the rapprochement subphase (15 to 25 months) and consolidated during the fourth subphase of separation–individuation called *on the way to emotional object constancy* (approximately the third year). Alex has failed to achieve this integration; he cannot get women in perspective. As an adult his internal world contains a longed-for idealized woman, a castrating, engulfing one, and as a defense against both of these, a view of woman as degraded and devalued object.

It is not hard to see where Alex's separation went awry. His is a mother who threatens abandonment when he disobeys. Although he tries to be the best little boy imaginable, he tells Dr. Spielvogel, "there is a year or so in my life when not a month goes by that I don't do something so inexcusable that I am told to pack a bag and leave" (p. 12/22). Alex tries to be stoic on such occasions, telling himself he doesn't care, but with the door double-locked behind him, he is ultimately reduced to terrified and desperate begging for forgiveness. And in the most overt way imaginable, Sophie Portnoy withdraws her love when he defies her, saying, "I don't love you anymore, not a little boy who behaves like you do" (p. 13/23). When Alex asserts his will by refusing to eat she brandishes a kitchen knife! Later she becomes enraged at the thought of her adolescent son eating junk food — *chazerai* — instead of her home-cooked meals, and she warns him that he risks dire illness for this practice. To keep him close she paints the outside world as dangerous and life-threatening:

> "Alex, polio doesn't know from baseball games. . . . I don't want you running around, and that's final. Or eating hamburgers out. Or mayonnaise. Or chopped liver. Or tuna. Not everybody is careful the way your mother is about spoilage. . . . You don't begin to know what goes on in restaurants" [p. 32/42–43]

Sophie's wish that Alex should never separate is clearly and inexorably communicated: "Will you leave me, my baby-boy, will you ever leave Mommy?" she asks. He replies, "Never, never, never, never" (p. 67/78).

As if all this fear-inducement weren't enough, Alex is dealt a heavy dose of guilt. Usually, this takes the form of being made to feel responsible for his father's health problems. After every argument, Alex braces for the inevitable *whispering*:

> "Alex, he didn't have a headache on him today that he could hardly see straight from it?" She checks, is he out of earshot? God forbid he should hear how critical his condition is, he might claim exaggeration. "He's not going next week for a test for a tumor?" [p. 23–24/34]

But Jack Portnoy, we learn, has been "going for" this test for as long as Alex can remember.

Mahler and her co-workers (Mahler 1971, 1972, Mahler et al. 1975) have emphasized the crucial importance of maternal availability and attunement in the establishment of the child's separate self. The mother must adapt to the child's rapidly changing needs during this delicate process. Initially, during what Mahler calls the normal *autistic* phase, in which the infant's experience is purely physiological and inwardly directed, and the *symbiotic* phase, during which the infant begins to dimly perceive the mothering half within an omnipotent dual unity, the mother must empathize with nonverbal bodily cues toward alleviating states of need, hunger, and tension.[1] As the infant progresses through the subphases of the separation–individuation phase, the mother must relinquish the gratification of symbiotic oneness and not only accept but also encourage the child's steps toward breaking away. In the *differentiation* subphase, she must allow for the baby's pulling back from her hold, climbing off her lap, and crawling. During *practicing* the infant is exhilarated with developing new skills and exploring the expanding environment, but still needs the emotionally attuned mother in close proximity to return to as "home base" for "refueling." The mother's emotional availability and sensitivity are especially vital during the sensitive rapprochement period, when the infant's growing cognitive capacities have made him or her painfully aware of being small, alone, and vulnerable, creating in the infant an ambivalent wish to undo the separateness he or she has achieved.

---

1. The existence of these two phases preceding that of separation–individuation has been questioned by recent infant observational researchers. Fred Pine, one of Mahler's collaborators, has even questioned the usefulness of the notion of an autistic phase altogether. However, the assumption that the infant has experiences during these early weeks and months that are *relatively* inwardly focused and boundaryless — perhaps in the course of the same day as he has many other experiences — seems to hold, and hence, so does the need for this kind of maternal responsiveness [see Pine (1981, 1985) and Stern (1985)].

Pine (1981, 1985) also offers a reconceptualization of the notion of phases. Noting that a child can be in several phases at one time, for example in the second year he/she can be in the anal phase, the separation–individuation phase, and the phase of basic gender identity, he concludes that the phase concept cannot refer to the *totality* but only to significant *moments* of the child's experience. A phase, according to Pine, is a period of critical formative events in a particular line of development. In this chapter, I use the term *phase* in Pine's sense.

Mahler and colleagues (1975) have found that, beyond being consistently attuned and available, the mother must actively demonstrate

> her willingness to let go of the toddler, to give him, as the mother bird does, a gentle push, an encouragement toward indepen- dence . . . [which] may even be the *sine qua non* of normal (healthy) individuation. [p. 79]

With the continued availability and encouragement of the mother during the rapprochement subphase, the child is able to gradually give up the omnipotence and control of symbiosis, replacing it with confidence in his/her developing capacities and an increasing sense of autonomy. As Settlage (1980) describes it

> He needs her affirmation of him in his changing and expanding sense of self and identity, her validation of his continuing importance to her, of his developing skills and abilities, of his urges and feelings and their acceptability and manageability, and of the continuity of his old and new self in her eyes. A too sudden deflation of his sense of omnipotence and control tends to evoke the grandiose view of the self and the idealization of the omnip- otent parent, the narcissistic defenses described by both Kohut (1971) and Mahler (1971). [p. 84]

Alex describes to Dr. Spielvogel his mother's hysterical and destructive responses to his efforts at separation in his later childhood, adolescence, and even adulthood. Sophie is not likely to have responded much more appropriately during his formative first three years. Alex probably did have an adequate symbiotic experience. Sophie, we know, was highly invested in her perfect child. True, this investment was a narcissistic one, probably resulting at times in her misreading *his* cues as *her* wishes. Still, she must have relished the closeness and unity of symbiosis when she could most experience him as part of herself. And Alex seems

to have accomplished the basic task of differentiation without
major problems as well; certainly there is nothing psychotic in his
thinking, nor do we know of any severely regressive experiences
of merger and loss of self. But as Alex increasingly became an
individual in his own right, as he learned to crawl, walk, talk, and
play, Sophie's response must have been highly inconsistent. On
the one hand, his developing mastery and skill would have been
narcissistically gratifying to her—she would have basked in the
accomplishments of her "brilliant . . . beautiful" (p. 87/98) "Albert Einstein the Second!" (p. 2/12). On the other hand, when he
moved too far away or went against her wishes she would have
tried to stop him by frightening him with her endless "watch-its
and . . . be-carefuls" (p. 33/43) or by threatening him with
abandonment, as she did later in banishing him from the home.

The result is that Alex has grown into a very accomplished
man—he is New York City's Assistant Commissioner of Human
Opportunity—but one with a shaky sense of separateness and
selfhood. Having had inconsistent mothering during the difficult
rapprochement crisis, he has tried to fall back on the narcissism,
grandiosity, and omnipotence characteristic of the earlier subphases, but he cannot get away from an underlying feeling of
insufficiency. He pleads for his mother's recognition so that he
can recognize *himself*, but all his achievements still cannot earn
him status as a separate individual:

> "Mother, I'm thirty-three! I am the Assistant Commissioner of
> Human Opportunity for the City of New York! I graduated first
> in my law school class! Remember? I graduated first from every
> class I've ever *been* in! At twenty-five I was already special counsel
> to a House Subcommittee—of the United States Congress,
> Mother! Of America! If I wanted Wall Street, Mother, I could be
> on Wall Street! I am a highly respected man in my profession, that
> should be obvious! Right this minute, Mother, I am conducting
> an investigation of unlawful discriminatory practices in the
> building trades in New York—*racial discrimination!*". . .

> Anyway, Sophie has by this time taken my hand, and with hooded
> eyes, waits until I sputter out the last accomplishment I can think
> of, the last virtuous deed I have done, then speaks: "But to us, to
> us you're still a baby, darling." [pp. 109–110/120–121]

Fred Pine (1979) has distinguished between lower and higher
level pathology of separation–individuation. The former has to
do with ties to an *undifferentiated* other. The latter involves the
relation to a *differentiated* other but is tied to the separation–individuation process. Alex's problems seem to be of the higher-level
kind. He *has* differentiated, but his separation is fragile and
fraught with conflict. Threatened with his mother's rage and
withdrawal for moving away from her, he has been unable to
achieve that hallmark of successful separation–individuation, the
consolidation of object constancy—the ability to hold internally
an emotionally sustaining image of the object in times of
aloneness (Mahler et al. 1975). (Alex's fantasy of his mother
following him to and from school is one attempt to deal with this
lack.) For Alex, separation brings enormous anxiety, guilt, and
conflict. These in turn create an intense but terrifying wish to be
reengulfed. It is this regressive wish that makes love so dangerous
to Alex, and it is against this wish that his failure to commit and
his control and degradation of women are meant to defend.

At one point, in spite of himself, Alex begins to "feel something. Feel *feeling!*" (p. 190/203) with The Monkey. At this
moment he is reminded of a poem by William Butler Yeats,
which he recites to her, in which a great bird swoops down upon
a girl:

> A sudden blow: the great wings beating still
> Above the staggering girl, her thighs caressed
> By the dark webs, her nape caught in his bill,
> He holds her helpless breast upon his breast. [p. 191/204]

The association is telling, revealing Alex's view of love as an
enveloping, an overpowering. In spite of the sex reversal—the

bird in the poem is the male — we can recognize Alex's own fear
of and longing for surrender to an overpowering object.

If Sophie Portnoy has made it hard for Alex to separate, then
Jack Portnoy certainly has not helped. And as theorists of early
development have emphasized, the father's role in differentiation
is crucial (Abelin 1971, Greenacre 1966, Kaplan 1978, Loewald
1951, Mahler et al 1975). Louise Kaplan describes it well:

> Fathers play a decisive role in the crisis of the second birth. Even
> before the crisis, both sons and daughters turn to the father for an
> alternative to the intense passions of the mother–infant dialogue.
> The special excitement associated with the father is observable as
> early as six months of age . . . *A father is the centrifugal force that pulls
> mother and child out of the orbit of oneness.* [1978, p. 219, emphasis
> added]

For the already differentiated child the father is needed as
protector from the potentially overwhelming, reengulfing
"mother after separation" (Mahler 1971, p. 416).

Alex tells Dr. Spielvogel that his father is barely a presense in
his early years; he is "a man who lives with us at night and on
Sunday afternoons. My father they say he is" (p. 44/54). When
he is at home, Alex sees a man so powerless that he cannot
achieve that earliest and most basic of human accomplishments,
moving his bowels, this in contrast to Alex's omnipotent mother,
who can do anything.

> Her ubiquity and his constipation, my mother flying in through
> the bedroom window, my father reading the evening paper with a
> suppository up his ass . . . These, Doctor, are the earliest impres-
> sions I have of my parents, of their attributes and secrets. [p. 3/13]

Jack Portnoy, Alex tells Spielvogel, works day and night for a
big insurance company, Boston & Northeastern Life, canvassing
the slums, performing the incredibly invaluable task of giving

people "an umbrella for a rainy day"—only Alex knows that people laugh at him in the slums. He is aware, too, that his father, as a Jew who cannot rise up in the company, is exploited. He tries in vain to turn his father into someone he can idealize. At the age of 8 he discovers to his great sadness and disappointment that his father cannot hit a baseball, cannot even hold the bat right. As a college student, Alex attempts to raise his father's intellectual level via an anonymous subscription to *Partisan Review*, but when he returns home for vacation the journal is nowhere to be found, discarded as "*junk*-mail by this schmuck, this moron, this Philistine father of mine!" (p. 7/17).

Alex sees a father who lives in servitude to his company and to his family, which only increases his own fears of weakness and submission. If only his father could break free so, via an identification, could he. Projecting his own wish for liberation as well as his immense hostility toward his mother, Alex develops the pleasurable fantasy that his father is carrying on an affair with an aging cashier at his office.

The fantasy expresses, too, Alex's wish that his father be masculine and potent. Alex needs a strong father not only to help him separate, but also to help him establish his own masculine identity. According to Mahler and colleagues (1975), gender identity has its beginnings during the separation–individuation phase, although it is not ultimately consolidated until the phallic phase.[2] In the children they observed identification with a father or older brother facilitated an early beginning and proved crucial in the continuing consolidation of a male identity.

---

2. Boys have been observed to mirror their fathers in play and bodily movements as early as late in the first year (Kaplan 1978). During the practicing subphase, at around 12–14 months, the upright position and perhaps an advance in zonal libidinalization facilitates the pleasurable visual and sensual exploration of the penis. The discovery of the anatomical sex difference occurs in some children as early as 16–17 months, but most often occurs in the 20th or 21st month, during the peak of the rapprochement subphase (Mahler et al. 1975).

At the same time as the boy must identify with his father to establish a male identity, he must "disidentify" with his primary object, his mother (Greenson 1968). These two phenomena — disidentifying with the mother and counteridentifying with the father — form a complementary series and reinforce each other. The personalities and behaviors of both parents play an important role in this process. The father must be available and suitable as an object of identification and idealization. The mother must allow her son's autonomy, respect and enjoy his phallicity, and, of major importance, must relinquish ownership of his body, particularly his penis (Mahler 1971, Mahler et al. 1975).

Alex is doubly hampered in this double process. His father, only minimally available in his early years, is insufficient as a figure of identification. His mother is intrusive, controlling, and discouraging of his autonomy, as we have seen. She has failed to give up control of his body. Treating him as a narcissistic extension, she behaves as if his body were her own, failing to observe appropriate boundaries. Alex describes her intrusiveness and overinvolvement with his body:

> For mistakes she checked my sums; for holes, my socks; for dirt, my nails, my neck, every seam and crease of my body. She even dredges the furthest recesses of my ears by pouring cold peroxide into my head. It tingles and pops like an earful of ginger ale, and brings to the surface, in bits and pieces, the hidden stores of yellow wax, which can apparently endanger a person's hearing . . . but where health and cleanliness are concerned, germs and bodily secretions, she will not spare herself . . . [p. 10/20]

Alex recalls that during his toilet training his mother would tickle his penis, ostensibly to get him to urinate. During his adolescence, thinking he is occupying the bathroom because he has diarrhea (actually he is masturbating), Sophie demands that he show her his stool: "Alex, I don't want you to flush the toilet. I want to see what you've done in there. I don't like the sound of this at all. . . . Was it mostly liquid or was it mostly poopie?" (pp. 20–21/30–31).

Unable to feel in possession of his own body, unable to disidentify with an overintrusive mother, and unable to establish a firm male identification with his father, Alex is shaky in his sense of maleness. He feels like a mama's boy. Only somewhat sarcastically, he tells Dr. Spielvogel what a mystery his heterosexuality is altogether:

> The mystery really is . . . how I made it into the world of pussy at all, *that's* the mystery. I close my eyes, and it's not so awfully hard—I see myself sharing a house at Ocean Beach with somebody in eye make-up named Sheldon. [pp. 124–125/136]

Trying to fill in for his limited father, Alex seeks out male identifications—his cousin Heshie; the men in the Sunday morning baseball game; his brother-in-law Morty. Alex loves to accompany his father to the shvitz baths—a safe place without goyim and women—and he is particularly delighted to observe his father's genitals, their concreteness providing him with clear relief and reassurance:

> I . . . eye with admiration the baggy substantiality of what overhangs the marble bench upon which he is seated. His scrotum is like the long wrinkled face of some old man with an egg tucked into each of his sagging jowls. . . . And as for his *shlong*, to me, with that fingertip of a prick that my mother likes to refer to in public as . . . my "little thing," his *shlong* brings to mind the fire hoses coiled along the corridors at school. *Shlong*: the word somehow catches exactly the brutishness, the *meatishness*, that I admire so . . . [pp. 48–49/58–59]

In the context of Alex's layered problems, his compulsive masturbation is an overdetermined symptom. On one level it defends against intense castration anxiety, which breaks through repeatedly in his terror of having acquired cancer or venereal disease. His masturbation reassures him of the intactness of his penis. At the same time it shores up his sense of power; through a fantasy in which the woman begs for what "no girl in recorded history has ever had," it undoes his feelings of smallness and need.

> "Oh shove it in me, Big Boy" cried the cored apple . . . "Big Boy, Big Boy, oh give me all you've got," begged the empty milk bottle . . . "Come, Big Boy, come," screamed the maddened piece of liver . . . [p. 17/27]

At its most basic level, however, Alex's masturbation is an act of autonomy, affirming his very existence as a separate individual. The slammed bathroom door behind which he masturbates is his desperate attempt to create a much-needed boundary. His penis is his "battering ram to freedom. . . . all I really had that I could call my own" (p. 31–32). After masturbating, Alex comes back to the dinner table to hear his father saying

> "I don't understand what you have to lock the door about. That to me is beyond comprehension. What is this, a home or a Grand Central station?" ". . . privacy . . . a human being . . . around here *never*," I reply, then push aside my dessert to scream, "I don't feel well—*will everybody leave me alone?*" [p. 19/29]

After dinner he is back in the bathroom again, masturbating furiously.

Like his masturbation, Alex's actual sexual encounters when he gets older, far from being true expressions of relatedness, serve to reinforce a threatened self. Alex puts sexuality in the service of solving earlier, fundamental, nonsexual problems—existence, separateness, selfhood, and power.

That Alex has serious problems on a preoedipal level does not preclude oedipal ones as well. In fact, his preoedipal vulnerabilities have set him up for an exacerbated oedipal crisis. The inadequate separation and poor boundaries in his relationship with his mother have only increased the incest threat. We have seen the early bases for his especially intense castration anxiety: early fear of reengulfment and difficulty claiming full possession of his own body have interfered with his overall sense of bodily integrity, increasing his vulnerability to later castration anxiety. He has been made to fear disease and bodily harm in response to acts of self-assertion, and this has been easily transformed into an exaggerated fear of castration in response to sexual transgression. Alex's father's limitations as a strong alternate figure have played a role as well; as he provided inadequate protection from the engulfing early mother, so he would be viewed as providing an insufficient barrier to the incest threat. And Alex's early difficulty disidentifying with his overwhelming mother and forming a positive identification with his father have provided a shaky basis for a healthy resolution of his oedipus complex.

Because Alex's problems are complex and deep-rooted, his treatment will be long and arduous. Some of its major themes are laid out in the first session. Like Alex's life, in which, as he says it, there is "nothing but self," his session is a one-party event, a masturbatory, self-involved reverie. Fearful of his own need, weakness, inadequacy, and potential aloneness in relation to a *separate* other, Alex cannot let Dr. Spielvogel exist in the room as a real person. He attempts to control, amuse, entertain, and overwhelm, but not to relate. Alex avoids the responsibility of a separate person for his plight. His narrative is indeed a complaint, an infantile wallowing, culminating in his final

Aaaaaaaaaaaaaaaaaaaaaaaaaaaaaaaaaaaaaaaaaaaaaaaaaaaaaaaaa-
aaaaaaaaaaaaaaaaaaaaaaaaaaaaaaaaaaaaaaaaaaaaaaaaaaaaaaaaaa-
aaaaaaaaaaaaaaaaaaaaaaaaaaaaaaaaaaaaaaaaaaaaaaaaaaaaaaaaaa-
aaaaaaaaaaaaaaaaaaaaaaaaaaaaaaaaaaaaaaaaaaaaaaaaaaaaaaaaaa-
aaaaaaaaaaaaaaaaaaaaaaaaaaaaaaaaaaaaaahhhh!!!!! [p. 274/287]

Spielvogel's intervention, "So. . . . Now vee may perhaps to begin. Yes?" (p. 274/287) is in keeping with a developmental understanding of Alex's problems. A perfect retort to Alex's regressive, narcissistic posture, it seems to address the fact that no true exploration or interaction *has* begun. Spielvogel injects himself as an object into the session, countering Alex's inarticulate wail with an implicit call for separation, work, and responsibility.

This chapter has focused on the role of separation-individuation difficulties in Alex's psychopathology. Alex is a man who seems never to have gotten past a fixation on an overwhelming, overpowering, idealized, and perfect, or, alternatively, engulfing and dangerous maternal image. Struggling to achieve some degree of power over and independence from women, he has avoided commitment and degraded the women he has become involved with, but, paradoxically, this has also kept him his mother's boy. Sophie Portnoy, narcissistically invested in Alex but unable to recognize him as a separate person, has clearly fostered these developments. Jack Portnoy has provided a weak alternative to her and an inadequate figure for identification. Alex's separation–individuation pathology is of the "higher level" kind, according to Pine's (1979) classification; he is clearly differentiated, but enormous anxiety and guilt accompanying separation have made his separation shaky and created an ambivalent wish for reengulfment. Alex has sexualized his preoedipal problems in his compulsive masturbation and sadomasochistically oriented sexual encounters. Although he came to therapy largely because of his impotence, he senses that his life is empty and he is stuck.

It is fortunate that Alex has decided to enter treatment. One hopes that his therapy will help him resolve these basic developmental issues, enabling him to achieve a true sense of autonomy and a firmer sense of self.

REFERENCES

Abelin, E. L. (1971). The role of the father in the separation-individuation process. In *Separation-Individuation: Essays in Honor of Margaret Mahler*, ed. J. B. McDevitt and C. F. Settlage, pp. 229-252. New York: International Universities Press.

Greenacre, P. (1966). Problems of overidealization of the analyst and of analysis: their manifestations in the transference and counter-transference relationships. *Psychoanalytic Study of the Child* 21: 193-212. New York: International Universities Press.

Greenson, R. R. (1968). Dis-identifying from the mother: its special importance for the boy. *International Journal of Psycho-Analysis* 49:370-373.

Kaplan, L. (1978). *Oneness and Separateness: From Infant to Individual*. New York: Simon and Schuster.

Kohut, H. (1971). *The Analysis of the Self*. New York: International Universities Press.

Loewald, H. W. (1951). Ego and reality. *International Journal of Psycho-Analysis* 32: 10-18.

Mahler, M. (1971). A study of the separation-individuation process and its possible application to borderline phenomena in the psychoanalytic situation. *Psychoanalytic Study of the Child* 26:403-424. New York: Quadrangle

———— (1972). On the first three subphases of the separation-individuation process. *International Journal of Psycho-Analysis* 53:333-338.

Mahler, M., Pine, F., and Bergman, A. (1975). *The Psychological Birth of the Human Infant*. New York: Basic Books.

Pine, F. (1979). On the pathology of the separation-individuation process as manifested in later clinical work: an attempt at delineation. *International Journal of Psycho-Analysis* 60:225-242.

———— (1981). In the beginning: contributions to a psychoanalytic developmental psychology. *International Review of Psycho-Analysis* 8:15-33.

———— (1985). *Developmental Theory and Clinical Process*. New Haven: Yale University Press.

Settlage, C. (1980). The psychoanalytic understanding of narcissistic and borderline personality disorders: advances in developmental theory. In *Rapprochement: The Critical Subphase of Separation-Individuation*, ed. R. F. Lax, S. Bach, and J. Alexis Burland, pp. 76-100. New York: Jason Aronson.

Stern, D. (1985). *The Interpersonal World of the Infant*. New York: Basic Books.

5

Lacanian Perspective: A Lacanian Analysis of *Portnoy's Complaint*

Gerard J. Pape, Ph.D.

LACAN'S VIEW OF LITERARY CRITICISM AND THE PSYCHOANALYSIS OF ARTISTS

To write a Lacanian analysis of *Portnoy's Complaint* is a contradiction in terms. First of all, one cannot psychoanalyze a work of art or a character in a work of art, or the author of a work of art, according to Lacan. Yet there are references in Lacan's writing to works of art. But the artwork serves to show how literature is pathological and, thus, is about psychoanalysis, not the reverse. Lacan's analysis of Poe's "The Purloined Letter" is perhaps the best known example. We also have his work on de Sade's "Philosophy in the Bedroom" and on Joyce's *Finnegans Wake*. One must note, however, that these contain more structural analysis than content or clinical analysis. Lacan knew that many artists demonstrate structural truths about the unconscious, *jouissance*, desire, symptoms, and the *"objet a"* and he gave credit to artists for working with the veiled *"objet a"* — the sublime object that causes desire and that desire seeks as well.

Such an approach is not the same as pretending that a character in a book is one's patient. *Portnoy's Complaint* is Philip Roth's humorous parody of a psychoanalysis, and what may appear to be the content of a psychoanalysis is really a refusal of a psychoanalysis. Whose refusal? Philip Roth's? Alexander Portnoy's? Both? The psychoanalyst Spielvogel says of Portnoy: "Many of the symptoms can be traced to the bonds obtaining in the mother-child relationship" (p. i/i). Of course, this is Roth enjoying making fun of a type of psychoanalysis that believes it has all the answers to life's most complex problems. In a very real sense, the whole text of *Portnoy's Complaint* can be seen as one big joke at the expense of psychoanalysis, with the "Punch Line" on the last page: "So [*said the doctor*]. Now vee may perhaps to begin. Yes?" (p. 274/287). This ending to the novel is meant to be a big joke at the expense of psychoanalysts who don't listen, don't understand, and who say little or nothing.

From a Lacanian viewpoint, there is another possible interpretation. Could Spielvogel have taken all Portnoy's previous material to be the narcissistic narrative of Portnoy's ego and so, in essence, could the analyst be saying something to the effect of, "Now that you've gotten all that off your chest, let's really begin the treatment." In other words, Portnoy's psychoanalysis has not yet begun. Spielvogel could have listened to all of Portnoy's material as preliminary to the treatment, and it is not until the end of these preliminary sessions that Spielvogel feels that Portnoy may be ready to begin his analysis.

PORTNOY AND THE REAL

In Lacanian terms, the "Real" in psychoanalysis is a matter of "truth or consequences." If we don't tell the truth in analysis, the consequence is that the death drive within us wins out, leaving us at the mercy of our symptoms. Analysis is thus an encounter with the Real of trauma, loss, and lack that the analyst helps the patient to confront. One of Lacan's criticisms of American ego psychology and psychoanalysis was that, by virtue of its focus on the ego, its defenses and resistances, and so forth, the patient might dance around the Real, never truly encountering it except as symptoms.

This is especially true of the obsessional patient who, by way of his obfuscating—focusing on time, money, rules and regulations, and so forth in the analysis—attempts to put off the encounter with the Real indefinitely. Lacan described this as the obsessional waiting for the death of the Master (Lacan 1977, p. 99). The obsessional patient tries to wait out the analyst, hoping to avoid the terrifying encounter with his own death drive, his own *jouissance*.

Jouissance may be defined briefly as the enjoyment or satisfaction that is "beyond the pleasure principle" (Freud 1920). *Jouissance* is a type of "enjoy-meant," that is, the satisfaction of the drives at the level of the body and the satisfaction of enjoyed meanings at the level of language. Ellie Ragland-Sullivan (1991) explains:

> The dialectic of the drive concerns satisfaction derived from feeling whole, not the objects aimed at themselves. But, and here is the catch for the treatment, satisfaction is achieved by repeating what already makes us sick, by clinging to the excess *jouissance* that links desire to death.

The Lacanian analyst has various strategies for helping the patient have the requisite encounter with the Real. The most important of these requires a cutting short of the analytic session. When the patient strays into the realm of imaginary narrative, the session is cut short. "Imaginary" may be described as an intoxication with such issues as who's right/who's wrong, who's a good mother/who's a bad mother, who's a good father/who's a bad father, who's guilty, and so forth. All these are imaginary in the sense that they leave the patient in a kind of hall of mirrors in which he or she is a prisoner of his or her own imaginary beliefs and identifications at the level of narcissistic myth and illusion. The patient identifies too much with his or her own personal myths, getting stuck in issues that have no resolution and that are, in fact, an avoidance of the reality of trauma, lack, and loss. This "getting stuck" represents an impasse in the treatment, knots of "enjoy-meant," that is, enjoyed meanings linked to *jouissance*.

It is the task of the analyst to effect displacements or shifts of *jouissance*, to help the patient out of his or her impasse. Primarily, however, it is the ethical responsibility of the patient to speak the truth and to not give up on his or her desire. This *ethics of psychoanalysis* implies that the patient must find the courage and the will to speak the truth, even as it is terrifying to gaze into the abyss of the Real and to not give in to society's demands for conformity and adaption as a pseudo-solution to the problems posed by symptoms and impasses in the Real.

With regard to the character of Portnoy, there are several points in the novel where Portnoy comes close to confronting the Real of his symptoms. Most of the time, however, he is lost in the imaginary of his family myths and stories. Portnoy loves talking about Mama and Papa and all their problems. He likes to complain and present himself as the long-suffering victim of his intrusive, seductive mother and his guilt-producing, impotent father. In fact, one might imagine that if Portnoy were in analysis with a Lacanian, he might have many, many short sessions. These short sessions are not punishments by the analyst but an effort by the analyst to effect shifts in "enjoy-meant," to displace *jouissance*. As he goes on and on with his tales of compulsive masturbation and of mother concerned about the state of his feces, his enjoyment in his symptoms is unmistakable. Endless tales of his parents' stupidity and their attempts to evoke guilt are told with incredible showmanship and narcissistic enjoyment. An ego psychologist might well see Portnoy's sense of humor as only an ego strength—which it is, ironically—while at the same time being a manifestation of frozen libido or death drive. Portnoy surely loves his symptoms, and he does love to talk about them. In fact, he loves his symptoms more than himself (Lacan 1975).

But there are traces of the Real that intrude into his narrative. In telling of his father, Portnoy says,

> But what he had to offer, I didn't want — and what I wanted he didn't have to offer. . . . Why must it continue to cause such pain? . . . Doctor, what should I rid myself of, tell me, the hatred . . . or the love? Because I haven't even begun to mention everything I remember with pleasure — I mean with a rapturous, biting sense of loss! [pp. 25–26/36]

These little bits of "rapturous" loss, what Lacan called the "*objet a*," that try to fill the hole of loss appear to Portnoy as "memories of practically nothing — and yet they seem moments of history, as crucial to my being as the moment of my conception" (p. 26/36). These *objets a* are representations of pure loss for Portnoy, unconscious intrusions of discontinuity into his otherwise seamless narrative. When Portnoy's mother speaks of "a real fall sky," or his father of "good winter piney air," these are pieces of "enjoy-meant" surfacing. But without the help of an analyst to keep him on track, Portnoy is off again on his imaginary narratives: whom his mother should have married, feeling guilty about his hard-working father, his mother's hypochondriacal worries about him, and so forth.

There is another intrusion of the Real, when Portnoy speaks about his life as "living . . . in the middle of a Jewish joke!" (p. 35/45). The "joke" is a crucial manifestation of the unconscious:

> Is this the Jewish suffering I used to hear so much about? Is this what has come down to me from the pogroms and the persecution? from the mockery and abuse bestowed by the *goyim* over these two thousand lovely years? Oh my secrets, my shame, my palpitations, my flushes, my sweats! [pp. 35–36/46]

Portnoy is describing the effects in the Real on his body and being of two thousand years of inherited Jewish suffering.

TRANSFERENCE

The Lacanian definition of transference as the "supposed subject of knowledge" is relevant. Portnoy puts Spielvogel in the place of the Other, the unconscious subject of truth (which he lacks), the one who will provide him with the requisite unconscious knowledge that will free his desire. He is asking Spielvogel to fill his lack, to make him whole, to make him a man. Portnoy expresses in the transference his wish that Dr. Spielvogel might free his desire:

> Bless me with manhood! Make me brave! Make me strong! Make me *whole*! Enough being a nice Jewish boy, publicly pleasing my parents while privately pulling my putz! Enough! [p. 36/46]

All the while, supposedly, Spielvogel knows how to do this, Portnoy not realizing that there is a lack or gap in the Other, a lack that the analyst himself will eventually come to embody if the analyst does not try to fill it, a lack that the patient must encounter as an impasse, as that which resists representation. Portnoy's appeal to Spielvogel in the transference is also a demand for love: "If you love me, give me the knowledge I lack." Portnoy wants Spielvogel to say "enough" to his symptoms and to thus provide the words that Portnoy himself lacks, words that would truly effect a shift in the way in which Portnoy enjoys himself.

But the patient must find his own words for his symptoms. The analyst's words will not do, as locating the precise signifiers that constitute the patient's impasse is not accomplished when the analyst bypasses the patient's inability to speak by substituting his own words. Ironically, Portnoy, who seems to speak volumes, cannot find the words to truly speak about his symptoms, what causes his suffering, what keeps him "pulling my putz." The way the analyst directs Portnoy's treatment can help effect a shift in *jouissance*, though it would be up to Portnoy—not the analyst—to find the words to talk about his symptoms. For Lacan, the symptom, as elaborated in his seminar XXIII, Le Sinthome (1975), is much more than just a disorder of behavior, affect, or thought, as in *DSM-III*: "Each person's number one symptom is an attachment to the repetitions of jouissance by which Lacan redefined Freud's death drive." What is at stake in the psychoanalytic clinic is "analyzing the particularity of unconscious desires that underlie his or her symptoms as enigmatic cause" (Ragland-Sullivan 1991). The symptom both gives us consistency and keeps us enslaved to *jouissance* and Other desire.

PORTNOY'S SYMPTOM

Lacan reworked Freud's concept of castration. Castration anxiety as organ anxiety is certainly experienced by males on the imaginary level as a fear of loss of the penis, but that is only a part of the larger gender question of "What am I?" For Lacan there are three types of castration and it is castration that constitutes desire (Ragland-Sullivan 1992). One type, the most primordial, is the cut that effects the loss of symbiosis with mother. The second is castration due to the effects of language. The third is how *jouissance* itself is castrated (i.e., limited and rigidified) by the particularity of a given subject's traumatic history leading to the specific constitution of a fundamental fantasy, the *objet a*, and the drives.

Portnoy as an obsessional subject is constituted by the traumatic fact that his mother acts aggressively, like a traditional male, while his father is passive and submissive, like a traditional female. Portnoy notes that there is a "mix-up of the sexes in our house" (p. 40/50). Portnoy admits that as a child, the question of whether he was a male or a female, was not so clear: "I am so small I hardly know what sex I am" (p. 43/53). Again, on the imaginary level, Portnoy identifies penis size with masculinity. Mother speaks of Portnoy's penis as a "little thing." The urinary flow of his little penis is a "sis," something he identifies with a girl, like his sister. It is crucial to him that even if his father acts like a woman, he must have a big penis, a "*shlong*," impressive in its "brutishness . . . *meatishness*" (p. 48/59). Portnoy feels "shame and shame and shame and shame" (p. 49/59) for his smallness, his inadequate masculinity. He calls himself "Alex the little prick . . . Alexander the Great," (pp. 62–63/73).

Portnoy's price for being "Alexander the Great," "being carried . . . like the Pope through the streets of Rome" (p. 88/99) is that he must "stay with mommy forever and ever." He will always remain mommy's little baby, her little boy with his "little prickling." For Portnoy, it is quite exciting for mother to ask him, "Well, how's my lover?" (p. 96/107). Indeed, his mother's seductiveness feeds his fantasies of impossible *jouissance*.

As an obsessional subject, Portnoy's symptom is *jouissance*, itself. While superficially it appears that Portnoy desires many women, what is really the case is that he has substituted sexual fantasy and the desire for *jouissance* for desiring a woman. Portnoy's "endless fascination of these apertures and openings! . . . Tits and cunts and legs and lips and mouths and tongues and assholes!" (pp. 102–103/113–114) is a desire for *jouissance* itself, not a desire for any particular woman. Portnoy states that, as far as women are concerned: "I have desires—only they're endless. . . . *want. And* want! *And* WANT! . . . You see, I just can't stop!" (p. 102/113). Portnoy's "desire continually burning within for the new, the wild, the unthought-of and . . . *the undreamt-of*" (p. 100/111) can never be satiated, for "it seems to make no difference how much the poor bastard actually gets, for he is dreaming about tomorrow's pussy even while pumping away at today's!" (p. 101/112).

Portnoy's sexual fantasies include desires for unlimited *jouiss-*

ance. However, he refuses to give women what satisfies them, seeing himself as under their demand. Lacan's characterization of the obsessional's question "Am I alive or dead?" is with regard to desire. The obsessional's relentless search for *jouissance* is actually an attempt to wipe out desire, in order to escape the mother's desire. The obsessional identifies with the mother's body, wanting to be the object of desire, like a woman.

This lack of sexual desire for a woman is Portnoy's way of "trying to free from bondage nothing more than my own prick" (p. 251/264). Indeed, Portnoy fantasizes that if he only has sex with "Thereal McCoy," he will escape his mother's desire by finding the perfect *shikse* woman who will free his desire by being the embodiment of his male sexual fantasies. Portnoy proposes several versions of "Thereal McCoy," including such women as The Monkey, The Pumpkin, and The Pilgrim. Each sexual encounter ends as disillusionment as a missed encounter. He asks, "*So why did I let her go?*" (p. 217/230) and "Why didn't I marry this beautiful and adoring girl?" Perhaps he let them go because they weren't "Thereal McCoy" (i.e., mother). Portnoy admits, "I don't seem to stick my dick up these girls, as much as, I stick it up their backgrounds." Getting to fuck *shikse* girls is a bit of revenge on behalf of Portnoy's father, who worked and was exploited by a WASP insurance firm: "A little bonus extracted from Boston & Northeastern, for all those years of service, and exploitation" (p. 240/254). Thus, Portnoy is less interested in fucking the *shikses* as in "fucking over" those fathers of the *shikses* who fucked his father over socially and economically. "Fucking" is not really about sex for Portnoy; it's about *jouissance*.

It is not until the utter failure of Portnoy's missed sexual encounters with the various *shikse* women, his disillusionment with sex, and his utter inability to love a woman and father children that Portnoy decides to visit Israel, where he has his most sustained encounter with the Real. Portnoy tries to convince himself that there is no such thing as real love, that all is "weakness . . . convenience and apathy and guilt. . . . fear and exhaustion and inertia, gutlessness plain and simple" (pp. 103–104/114–115). He mocks the romantic love of "marriage counselors and the songwriters and the psychotherapists" (p. 104/115). Not for him, this "bullshit" love. He asks of his sexual activity, "*Why* should it end! To please a father and mother? To conform to the norm?" (p. 102/113). He is referring to his parents' demand that he provide them with grandchildren, something he is unable to do.

THE LAW AND THE DRIVE

Portnoy is obsessed with the question of whether to break the law and whether his father broke it in his marriage. On the one hand, father represents an identification with duty itself: "Rules . . . you obey without question, regardless of how idiotic they may appear" (p. 78/89). Father is committed to "duty, discipline, and obedience . . . self-control, sobriety, sanctions" (p. 79/90).

Portnoy goes on at length about the idiocy of Orthodox Jewish dietary law. Indeed, the question of what one should or should not eat obsesses him. As for the goyim, "They will eat *anything*" (p. 80/91). The goyim will "*do anything* . . . what they want they take . . . [they] know absolutely nothing of human boundaries and limits" (pp. 80–81/91). This theme of "eating" and what one should or should not eat can also be found in the book when father invites the *shikse* cashier home to eat a real Jewish meal. Portnoy's mother seems to accuse father of sexually "eating" the *shikse*. Portnoy becomes confused about his own "hot" wishes to "eat his sister's chocolate pudding." All of these references to eating food concern incorporation as manifestation of the oral drive — not food *qua* food.

Symbolic order law, as represented by the Orthodox Jewish dietary laws, is infiltrated by the oral drive and obscene sexual enjoyment, which is confirmed by an impasse in the Real for

Alex with regard to his father, as a faulty figure for identification, a symbolic father whose "no" to incestuous union with the mother is weakened by his own passive, masochistic femininity, and by his likely sexual transgressions with *shikses*. For Alex, father's affair with the *shikse* woman "is like some piece of heavy furniture that sits in my mind and will not budge — which leads me to believe that, yes, it actually did happen" (p. 84/95).

Alex's mother's preoccupation with what Alex eats, her insistence that if he does not eat what she says to eat, he will die of some dread disease, only adds layers of meaning to "eating" as a key signifier for him. He ultimately identifies with an image of himself as slave of his mother's oral commandments that he translates as sexual. He is "a lapper of cunt, the slavish mouth for some woman's hole. Eat!" (p. 270/284).

It becomes clear that all of Portnoy's frenzied attempts to free his penis from bondage only serve to confirm that he is mother's slave, that he feels compelled to fulfill mother's desire: "Eat!" As an obsessional seeking *jouissance*, Portnoy has given a sexual meaning to his mother's command "Eat!" that may be translated as "I am eating (incorporating) a woman" as fulfillment of the oral drive.

Portnoy cannot face the alternative. To truly face separation from mother is to experience in the Real, heartrending feelings of lack and loss. When he thinks back on mother's hysterectomy, he is greatly disturbed by the fact that "where I was conceived and carried, there now is *nothing*" (p. 67/78). Portnoy feels that he is nothing. In essence, *Portnoy's Complaint* is the story of a failed psychoanalysis — failed, because Portnoy really does not want to lose his relationship with his mother. He can't bear it. In a moment of lucidity, he tells Spielvogel,

> All I do is complain . . . and I'm beginning to wonder if maybe enough isn't enough. I hear myself indulging in the kind of

ritualized bellyaching that . . . gives psychoanalytic patients such a bad name. . . . Is this truth . . . or is it just plain *kvetching*? [p. 93/104]

PORTNOY'S OTHER ANALYSIS?

As mentioned, it is in Israel that Portnoy comes closest to an encounter with the Real. Portnoy actually has some awareness of his proximity to the Real when he says "other patients dream— with me, *everything happens*. I have a life *without* latent content. The dream thing *happens*!" (p. 257/270). What is the "dream thing"? It is the dreamed of, fantasized sexual encounter with "Thereal McCoy." But he does not recognize her as such. Portnoy says of Naomi, "the resemblance between this girl and the picture of my mother in her high school yearbook is something I do not even see" (p. 259/272). When Portnoy encounters Naomi, he immediately falls in love with her, offers to marry her, have children with her, and so forth, something he has been totally unable to do with all his *shikse* women he has lusted after so intensely.

Naomi recognizes the falseness of Portnoy's imaginary love, his fantasy that with her he will have the impossible *jouissance* that was promised, but never delivered by mother. Instead of returning his demand for love with her own, she gives him sterner stuff—truth. First, she lets him know what she thinks of his position in the symbolic order as Assistant Commissioner of Human Opportunity in New York City:

> "Your job is to make such a system appear legitimate and moral by acting as though justice, as though human rights and human dignity could actually exist in that society—when obviously no such thing is possible." [p. 262/275]

Portnoy's father's law or authority is a sham, saturated with the obscene enjoyment of himself with the *shikse* woman, and of

Portnoy with his mother. There is no justice, no consistent right or wrong in this family. The basic law for Portnoy is "*Jouis!*" that is, "Enjoy!"

Portnoy, as father's only son, desperately tries to save the law and the social, familial order inherited from father. Like father, he identifies with the role of being a suffering and oppressed person. As Assistant Commissioner of Human Opportunity, he tries to fill up the hole in the Other, the inconsistency, the lack, the injustice, and so forth. He tries to prop up the symbolic father, to infuse meaning into an already indecipherable script. His task is in the realm of the imaginary, to make justice, law, and human rights magically appear where they do not exist. Above all, he must not expose the lack, loss, and failure in society, father, and in himself. In this sense, Portnoy tries to embody the male norm, to put on the garb of normal masculinity by identifying with law and the social order. It is Woman, as represented by Naomi, who exposes this *semblant* or semblance. Thus, she becomes Portnoy's symptom, his castration. He is utterly impotent with her.

In the novel, Portnoy proposes sex as the answer. Sex as the answer is accepting the Other's demand that one enjoy oneself, the neurotic solution. This is what the obsessional does so he can avoid Woman, that is, desire. However, Portnoy cannot enjoy himself when confronted with "Thereal McCoy." In the face of an encounter with the sublime object of his desire, he is impotent. (Similarly, the only reason King Oedipus could have sexual relations with his mother was because he did not know she was his mother. This is the punch line to the Freudian oedipal drama.) Where Portnoy thought to find something familiar, that is, the by now hackneyed Freudian myth of how all little boys want to sleep with their mothers and kill their fathers, instead he finds something far more monstrous and farcical. Behind the great tragedy is a joke. Portnoy's worst fear that he is guilty of incest and parricide is a joke because it is based on a fantasy of impossible *jouissance*. Of course, physically, incest is possible, and it tragically can and does happen. *Jouissance* is another matter. Imaginary fantasies fall impotent before the impossible of the Real: the impossibility of denying castration and of having the perfect symbiosis with mother, the impossibility of the perfect sexual relationship, the impossibility of finding *the* perfect woman or man, the impossibility of embodying in a unitary and noncontradictory identity what it means to be a woman or a man. The farce or the joke lies in mistaking the imaginary drama for the real tragedy—denying the Real of impasse, we get caught up in imaginary fantasies and scenarios, believing that sex or anything else is the answer.

Naomi gives Portnoy a further encounter with the Real when she says:

"You are the most unhappy person I have ever known. You are like a baby. . . . The way you disapprove of your life! Why do you do that? . . . You seem to take some special pleasure, some pride, in making yourself the butt of your own peculiar sense of humor. I don't believe you actually want to improve your life. Everything you say is somehow always twisted, someway or another, to come out 'funny'. . . . Everything is ironical or self-depreciating" [p. 264/277–278]

Naomi rightly understands the *jouissance* in Portnoy's symptom of self-depreciation, the enjoyment he experiences in degrading himself. She is right to wonder if he actually wants to improve his life. The "enjoy-meant" that Portnoy gets in making his whole life into a kind of joke is a real knot for him, an impasse of frozen *jouissance* and dead meanings that no amount of *"kvetching"* will change. However, it is also clear that Naomi herself is as castrating as Portnoy's mother and that she enjoys criticizing him, too. Furthermore, it does Portnoy no good to be analyzed by Naomi. She speaks to him from the position of the supposed subject of knowledge; thus, she is another master, like his mother. However, Naomi did do one rather Lacanian intervention that might have helped Portnoy. When he persisted in his self-depreciating, she cut their meeting short and left.

PORTNOY'S NAME

When Portnoy tries to convince Naomi to be his wife and to mother his children, she asks, "What is the *matter* with you? Is this supposed to be humorous?" Portnoy protests, "*Why not me?* I carry the family name!" (p. 263/276). Naomi is not impressed by Portnoy's credentials in the symbolic order, neither his family name nor his position as Assistant Commissioner of Human Opportunity. She counsels him: "You should go home" (p. 268/282). Portnoy hears this advice on the level of the Real as a command to go back to his mother, to admit that he is not a man. "This *son*! This *boy*! This *baby*! Alexander Portnoise! Portnose! Portnoy-oy-oy-oy-oy!" (p. 269/282).

What is the meaning of these various names? Son, boy, and baby are all clear enough with regard to his inability to separate from mother. But what of "Portnoise"? It is a curious name that contains some meanings relevant to Portnoy's symptoms and identity. In French, *port* means to carry, or a carrier of, and *noise* refers to an idiomatic phrase, '*chercher noise à quelqu'un,*" meaning, trying to pick a fight or dispute with someone. Putting these names together, Portnoy's name suggests "a carrier of attempted fights or disputes." The reference may be to Portnoy's carrying not just the family name, but also the burden of his parents' disputes. The "noise" that Portnoy heard as a child might well have been the sound of his parents fighting. When Portnoy visited with the *shikse* Pumpkin, he was astonished to find that not all families used words as "bombs and bullets" (p. 221/234), again suggesting the noisy nature of his parents' disputes.

The last one of Portnoy's names, "Portnoy-oy-oy-oy-oy!" suggests Portnoy as a carrier of family and cultural suffering. The heritage of thousands of years of persecution of the Jewish people and the suffering of Portnoy's father, in particular, are embodied in Portnoy's name, and hence his identifications and symptoms. Portnoy is thus the carrier of a heavy burden of unhappiness — the unhappiness in his parents' marriage, the suffering of his father as an exploited Jew in the world, and the heritage of the Jewish people as persecuted and annihilated over the centuries. Thus, Portnoy's complaint is not just for himself. He complains on behalf of his family and on behalf of centuries of oppressed Jews, not to mention that he hears and represents the complaints of oppressed minorities in New York.

While attempting to have sex with her, Portnoy jokes to Naomi that he is another sort of carrier, a carrier of venereal disease, and that he intends to "change the future of the race." Portnoy finally also becomes a carrier of Woman's complaint against Man. His superego accuses him of degrading The Monkey, Mary Jane Reed, and he is sentenced to a case of impotence.

Instead of understanding the real reasons for his impotence, he misrecognizes and concocts an imaginary narrative of guilt — thinking that because he had a ménage à trois with The Monkey and Lina, an Italian prostitute, he is being "punished" with impotence. Portnoy fantasizes the police saying to him, "You better come on out and pay your debt to society" (p. 273/287). Indeed, Portnoy's name does imply that he will be a carrier of "debt to society," but not for the crime of imaginary incest, of trying to attain impossible *jouissance.*

He carries the far more onerous burden of the failures of his family and of being Jewish. This Real burden marks him with suffering symptoms and frozen "enjoy-meant" that do not allow him to overcome the impasses in his life — an inability to free his desires from those of his mother, and an inability to free himself from the debt of his father's failure as husband, father, and Jew, and Portnoy's own burden of being born Jewish, and thus being placed in the difficult position of historical victim of injustice, and at the same time feeling obligated by Jewish law to root out injustice in the world.

At the end of the novel, Portnoy's psychoanalysis seems to end in failure or impasse; paradoxically, it is only in the doctor's punch line that a new beginning by way of a psychoanalysis oriented toward confronting the Real of trauma, lack, and loss may be possible. By not allowing Portnoy to endlessly retell his stories and his jokes, perhaps *jouissance* as the inertia in death drive (repetition compulsion) may be budged and Portnoy may begin to unknot his own impasses. "So [*said the doctor*]. Now vee may perhaps to begin. Yes?" (p. 274/287).

REFERENCES

Freud, S. (1920). Beyond the pleasure principle. *Standard Edition* 18: 3–64.
Lacan, J. (1975). *Le Sinthome* [Seminaire XXII]. Unpublished.
_____ (1977). *Ecrits*, trans. A. Sheridan. New York: W. W. Norton. (Original work published 1966.)
Ragland-Sullivan, E. (1991). On "The Direction of the Treatment and the Principles of its Power": A critique of Lacan's essay. *Analysis*.
_____ (1992). Personal communications.

6

Object Relations Perspective: Alexander Portnoy in Search of Self

Joseph Newirth, Ph.D.

Portnoy's Complaint (Roth 1969) is an epic tale, similar to Homer's *Odyssey*, of a man searching for his identity and his place in the world. Both Odysseus and Alexander Portnoy are on journeys among people, places, and events of their times. Odysseus' hubris at Troy, his pride and grandiosity, offended the gods. His adventures are a mythic account of his development of self, of compassion, empathy, and a clearer inner vision. At the end of his journey, the mature Odysseus joins with his father and son in order to reclaim his home and reunite with his wife. However, Roth's hero does not find his home, nor is he able to reunite with his family. Alexander Portnoy is the alienated son of America, the disenfranchised son of immigrants. He cannot be at home in the modern *shtetl* of Newark, in the upper middle class environs of New York, in white Anglo-Saxon Protestant America, or in Israel. In his book, Roth challenges the simplistic notion of America as a melting pot, just as he challenges the simplistic notions of the psychoanalytic drive theory. How are we to understand Portnoy's alienation, his cynicism, his despair, his

obsession with sexuality, and finally his impotence? These symptoms and character traits reflect both the narcissistic crisis of our time (Lasch 1978) as well as core concerns in the debate between the psychoanalytic theories, which remain loyal to Freud's metapsychology and suggest that the critical issue is the need to civilize or sublimate sexual impulses, and the object relations and self psychology theories, which focus on the internalization of patterns of relationship between self and other as the critical psychological issues. In this chapter, I present a relational view of Portnoy's dynamics, an understanding of Portnoy's character in terms of relational theory (Mitchell 1988), and suggest ways in which an analyst with an object relations orientation might approach a patient presenting similar life situations and symptoms.

THE CLASSICAL PSYCHOANALYTIC VIEW OF PORTNOY'S PATHOLOGY

The analyst in Roth's novel is silent; his introduction and his final ironic comment suggest that he represented, or perhaps was a caricature of a classical Freudian analyst. From the perspective of classical psychoanalytic drive theory, Portnoy's pathology is understood as an unresolved oedipal struggle. He is both fixated on his sexual wish for his mother, and is simultaneously involved in a compulsive, defensive flight from his attraction to her. His character pathology and his symptoms are explained as the expression of and a defense against these oedipal wishes. Dr. Spielvogel, in classical psychoanalytic tradition, defined Portnoy's difficulties as the outcome of an unresolved oedipal struggle in which his "strongly-felt ethical and altruistic impulses are perpetually warring with extreme sexual longings" and are a result of "the bonds obtaining in the mother–child relationship" (p. i/i). His obsession with sexuality, his compulsive masturba-

tion, and his need to be with non-Jewish women can all be understood as flights from this sexual attraction to his mother.

Portnoy's need to invite Lina, the Italian whore, to join him in bed with his girlfriend, The Monkey, can be understood as both a defense against his wish to have intercourse with his mother, "She is a whore, not my mother," and a simultaneous fulfillment of his wish, "Here is my mother, the other man's woman, finally I have her, I am the victor." This act could also be understood as a way in which Portnoy was able to turn his passive experience of the primal scene, watching mother and father have intercourse, into an active experience in which he is watched. He makes his girlfriend into the passive observer in his attempt to master the early oedipal trauma and become the sexually potent member of this newly created family.

From a classical drive theory perspective it would be argued that the fulfillment of this oedipal wish led to a deeper, more pathological regression that was extremely frightening because it brought him closer to the danger of literally having sex with his mother. Because of this fear, Portnoy, like Oedipus, had to flee, this time to Israel. The classical analyst would see in this behavior the expression of a compromise between the oedipal wish and the defense against it. Could there be a better place to find his Jewish mother, or to find someone that would fulfill mother's desire for him to marry a "nice Jewish girl," than in Israel? But to be in Israel and impotent, is Portnoy's final flight from his oedipal wish. Freud's (1918) case of the Wolf Man may suggest an alternative explanation of Portnoy's impotence; in this case Freud suggests that a deeper component of the oedipal wish is to replace mother in intercourse with father through an act of self-castration. From this classical perspective the silent analyst's final ironic comment, "Now vee may perhaps to begin. Yes?" (p. 274/287) can be understood not simply as the punch line in a Jewish joke, but as reflecting an implicit transference interpretation. It would seem that his assessment of Portnoy as a phallic, exhibitionistic, and masochistic character, who shows off his sexual prowess and then asks to be castrated by the analyst, led him to wisely avoid taking on the transference role of the punitive mother.

My presentation of a classical interpretation of Portnoy's dynamics rests on the impulse-defense organization of the mind, with the analyst's primary function being that of broadening the patient's awareness of his unconscious motives. In contrast, the relational approaches focus less on the exploration of motives and more on the way the patient comes to understand and generate his/her experience of and in the world.

EARLY FAILURE IN THE HOLDING ENVIRONMENT: THE FALSE SELF ORGANIZATION

Object relations theory and self psychology parallel other contemporary historical, cultural, and philosophical movements of this half of the twentieth century in which relativity and contextual approaches to understanding have replaced the nineteenth century's emphasis on truth and linear explanations of causality. In conjunction with these changes in the implicit models of the mind there have been radical shifts in the metaphors used to understand and discuss the analytic process from those of the classical models that emphasized the physical property of objects and liquids to these contemporary models that emphasize the process of storytelling, literary criticism, and hermeneutics. In his discussion of the social constructivist view of the psychoanalytic process Irwin Hoffman's (1992) emphasis is on the analyst's inevitable participation in the construction of the patient's narrative and a view of the analytic process that focuses on the development of new experiences within the analytic relationship. The patient's difficulties in experiencing himself as the subject, agent, and author in the center of his/her evolving life story becomes a defining characteristic of psychopathology from the relational perspective.

From a developmental perspective relational theorists have emphasized the importance of the parent's early attunement to the developing infant's experience of the world. This is carried into the analytic realm through an emphasis on processes of attending to and elaborating the patient's experience as opposed to interpreting and translating the patient's experiences into theoretical and genetic explanations. A great deal of attention is placed on understanding the patient's experiential world, particularly how the use of language has impacted on and represents the patient's development. D. W. Winnicott (1971) has discussed this process of empathic attunement as the holding environment that parallels the view of the analyst as a container (Bion 1977) or as a mirroring self object (Kohut 1984). In the following discussion, I will highlight Portnoy's phenomenological experiences both to illustrate the listening process of a relational analyst as well as to show how the selectivity, framing, and punctuation of experience organizes a relational view of the analytic process. This empathic perspective should be contrasted to that of the classical analyst who maintains a more objective perspective that focuses on the discovery of the patient's motives.

Winnicott and his followers would understand Portnoy's difficulties as reflecting an early failure in the development of a true self structure and the predominance of the false self organization that was a result of early experiences of impingement and failures in the good-enough mothering function. Winnicott's views coincide with and elaborate Melanie Klein's work on the development of the paranoid position, the depressive position, the function of aggression in the development of the self, and the development of symbolic thought from concrete experiences. Relational theorists have focused on this internal self structure and the individual's capacity to organize experience. The relational analyst would focus on Portnoy's experience of himself as an object as dominated by false self experience and an inability to symbolically process experience. Portnoy's experience of himself as an object can also be understood as a failure in the development of an internal cohesive self (Kohut 1984) and the need for external, archaic self objects to maintain his fragile sense of cohesiveness and affective constancy. Portnoy's obsession with sexuality can be thought of as an example of a perversion (Khan 1979), an externalization and a concrete attempt to force a mirroring or empathic response from objects in the environment. This can also be seen as an archaic form of self soothing, a means of providing an intense, pleasurable, and focused experience as a way of shutting out a hostile, controlling, rejecting, and persecutory environment. Portnoy's desperate need to be left alone, to soothe himself through masturbation, reflects his need for a holding experience, an experience in which he can express control over his world and escape from the constant impingements and manipulations that he experiences.

These early failures in the holding experience, in being empathically mirrored, and in the development of a cohesive self are reflected in his inability to refer to himself as a subject, as an individual, as an agent, and instead to only experience himself as an object. This phenomenon of his experiencing himself as an object, as a thing, is seen in his frequent references to himself as one of a class of objects, the class of sons of Jewish mothers. The relational analyst would resonate with and facilitate the expression of the great pain that is embedded in his rageful statement to the analyst:

What do we want? . . . *To be left alone!* If only for half an hour at a time! Stop already *hocking* us to be *good!* *hocking* us to be *nice!* Just leave us alone, God damn it, to pull our little dongs in peace and think our selfish thoughts — stop already with the respectabilizing of our hands and our tushies and our mouths! Fuck the vitamins and the cod liver oil! Just give us each day our daily flesh! And forgive us our trespasses — which aren't even trespasses to begin with! [p. 121/132]

The analyst would experience Portnoy's desperate need to be alone, to comfort himself, to feel that his body was his own; to comment on the difficulty of feeling so manipulated that not one body part, not one opening was truly safe from efforts toward being made respectable.

It is the analyst's ability to experience and express these affects and to respect the patient's beginning sense of wholeness, unity, and centeredness that defines his/her function as a mirroring selfobject in the transference. The relational therapist would hear Portnoy's words and understand his sense of desperation, his need for self soothing, and his real need for self delineation and definition. In focusing on the early deficits in development, the relational analyst expands the view of what is transformative in psychoanalysis to include experiences of mirroring, holding, and containing that had been missing in the early developmental matrix of self-object relations. The therapist's empathic understanding would initially be communicated through nonverbal means and only later through statements that would be resonant with his developing subjective experiences. As Portnoy's therapist, I would try to help him recognize the absence of experiences of private space and time, of any feelings and experiences that were simply his. These early failures leave the individual vulnerable to fragmentation, extreme affective lability, severe anxiety and depression, an inability to maintain a consistent affective tone, and a compulsive need for archaic selfobjects to stimulate and consolidate the self. As the treatment proceeds the early focus of the treatment is on the development of a holding environment in which the analyst's understanding of Portnoy's experiences from his inner perspective would be verbalized; the emphasis would be on developing the patient's capacity for self experience as opposed to explaining his hidden motives.

THE DEVELOPMENT OF THE FALSE SELF

Winnicott (1975) has written about infants and children who are exposed to early failures in the holding environment in which their early life is dominated by impingements as opposed to a responsive holding experience. In this situation the caretakers were unable to respond to the infant's evolving needs and rather impose their schedule and plan on the emerging individual. A consequence of early experiences of impingement and the failure of the early holding environment is the development of the false self in which the individual organizes his/her experience as a response to being acted upon by other people. The concept of the false self, which Winnicott developed, is an extremely useful way of describing the repetitive relational schemata that an individual uses to organize his relationships with others. In the false self organization the individual experiences him/herself as an object, as one who is powerless to affect the inevitable criticism and attack, and as one who experiences a world in which he/she is an alien. As an object rather than a subject (true self), the individual remains at a distance, dissociated from experiences of hurt, humiliation, and persecution. Winnicott's writings have focused on the absence of and the development of subjective experience. Portnoy is in this distant, schizoid position; he is an observer of his experience, a false self, and an object rather than the subject of his experience.

In Israel, Portnoy meets a sabra, Naomi, who initially enacts with him his repeating drama of being criticized and humiliated by women. However, she then finds her own voice and describes the self-hatred that is embedded in his schizoid stance as an observer and as an object rather than as a subject. This repetitive enactment represents a false self schema and a primitive enactment of his relationship with his mother in which he alternatively enacts the sadistic humiliating role and the masochistic role of the object of the attacks. Naomi accurately describes Portnoy's cynical and hostile humor, and interprets it as his way of both enacting this repetitive (transference) relationship and as a means of remaining unaffected, an impersonal object, a false self who is a long way from being able to grieve for his past injuries (Miller 1981). Naomi says to Portnoy:

"The way you disapprove of your life! Why do you do that? It is of no value for a man to disapprove of his life the way that you do. You seem to take some special pleasure, some pride, in making yourself the butt of your own peculiar sense of humor. I don't believe you actually want to improve your life. Everything you say is somehow always twisted, some way or another, to come out 'funny.' All day long the same thing. In some little way or other, everything is ironical, or self-depreciating.[p. 264/277–278]

Portnoy's repetitive construction of this sadomasochistic relational paradigm is both a means of protecting himself from the early traumas of impingement, safeguarding his nascent true self, and a way of maintaining a connectedness and sense of self in the world. To understand Portnoy's experience of himself as a false self, and as an object, we have to look at his early experiences of self and the experiences of how he was experienced in his relationship with his parents. Our self experience is a function of both how we are acted upon and how we are experienced in others' fantasies. He experienced himself as either the greatest little boy that ever lived or as the worst and most rejected child. His view of himself seems to be related to the family's idiosyncratic and strange way of referring to him in the third person. This way of speaking is not simply an ethnic version of English, but rather emphasizes a quality of his being experienced not as an individual who exists in the external world but rather as his parents' internal fantasy; he is not Alexander an external subject, but rather an impersonal object, a primitive omnipotent fantasy expressing gratification for his parents' needs. As the object of this internal omnipotent drama everything that Portnoy did was a volitional act; every success is an act of will and every failure is a result of his evil choice. This attribution of omnipotence is an aspect of a primitive, paranoid organization of behavior; it is impersonal and it emphasizes splitting and magical control of the environment, it ignores context, compassion, personal limitations, and mixed feelings.

Portnoy's words reflect his experience of living in an impersonal and paranoid environment:

What *was* it with these Jewish parents, *what*, that they were able to make us little Jewish boys believe ourselves to be princes on the one hand, unique as unicorns on the one hand, geniuses and brilliant like nobody has ever been brilliant and beautiful before in the history of childhood—saviors and sheer perfection on the one hand, and such bumbling, incompetent, thoughtless, helpless, selfish, evil little shits, little *ingrates*, on the other! [p. 118/129]

The same theme of the choice between perfection and intolerable evil is again echoed in Portnoy's words. Here, too, the idiosyncratic use of the impersonal third person emphasizes both his status as one of a class of objects (the false self organization), and his real sense of terror that he would be thrown away and forgotten like a useless object or thing.

"—a little boy you want to be who kicks his own mother in the shins—? . . . But what am I going to do with a child who won't even say he's sorry? Who won't even tell his own mother that he's sorry and will never never do such a thing again, *ever*! What are we going to do, Daddy, with such a little boy in our house!" [pp. 121–122/133]

This sense of being an object, of being in the impersonal realm, a member of a class and not an individual, is a critical part of the false self experience; it leads to the patient ultimately experiencing himself in the world in a hopeless and powerless way. This sense of hopelessness and powerlessness becomes the hallmark of the early development of the paranoid position. In the paranoid position, aggression and control are initially experienced as outside of the self, and the self is experienced as passive to the push and pull of the environment, as well as to any external aggression. The successful mastery of the paranoid position leads to the development (Winnicott 1975) of personalization, the experience of living within one's body as a subject or agent, and a realization of the capacity to understand and operate

within the limitations of time, space, and reality. This struggle
for psychosomatic unity, to be a subject, an agent who can
comfortably negotiate the world, is a significant aspect of the
movement from the grandiosity (positive or negative) and the
alienation of the false self organization in the early paranoid
position. An example of this movement from grandiosity and
alienation was expressed by a patient who after many years of
analysis was beginning to feel less hopeless and powerless. She
corrected me in my descriptions of her depressed moods that I
had previously consistently described as "feeling like shit." She
said that she "did not feel like shit, rather she felt like dust." Shit,
she said, was once alive and she felt as if she were "inert and not
even decaying and dead." Similarly, another patient as he was
moving from the passive paranoid position (Newirth 1992) to the
active paranoid position in which he was beginning to experience
himself as potentially hopeful and powerful said, "I used to feel
like nothing, I don't feel like something, but I no longer feel like
nothing." For these patients as well as for Portnoy the false self
organization reflects a minimally related schizoid, dissociated,
deadened, and insignificant adaptation to the world in which
their primary self experience is that of extreme alienation,
powerlessness, and hopelessness. This schizoid or narcissistic
organization represents a developmental failure in the early
(passive) paranoid position and not a defense against the sexual
and aggressive wishes of the oedipal stage.

THE PARANOID POSITION AND THE
DEVELOPMENT OF SYMBOLIC PROCESS

Object relations theory conceptualizes the false self organization,
the self as an object, as a failure in the resolution of the paranoid
position. The paranoid position (Klein 1975) represents ways that
the individual organizes his/her relational paradigms, dynamic
themes, and cognitive or symbolic processes. The paranoid

position first develops in infancy and represents the earliest organizational efforts of the child as well as ongoing relational schemata that human beings use to organize their experience of self and objects in the world. It develops in order to master the intense confusion and experiences of annihilation arising out of the impact of the environment and the flood of impingements from the inner world on the individual. In the paranoid position the world is organized through processes of splitting experience into segments and dichotomies: things are either good or bad, male or female, object or subject, and are broken up into smaller manageable units. The relational themes and actions of the paranoid position define the individual in terms of grandiosity, dominance, cruelty, and aggression. The following questions reflect these paranoid themes: Is this in my control or is this outside of my control? Who is dominant and who is submissive? Am I the greatest person in the world or am I nothing?

In the paranoid position, thoughts, fantasies, words, and actions are all experienced as equivalents; that is, the person in the paranoid position experiences the world concretely and not symbolically. The achievement of the depressive position and the acknowledgment that one can genuinely have an impact on people who are important allows the individual to develop the capacity to experience self and other both as subjects and as objects, as beings with inner experiences who are able to act in a directed fashion in the external world. The achievement of the depressive position allows for the development of empathy and compassion because the recognition of one's inevitable hurtfulness or ruthlessness (Winnicott 1975) leads to the desire to make reparation (Klein 1975) and act in a personally caring, loving way.

Portnoy's words describe his experience of being an alien in an unwelcoming land and of his anger, cynicism, and hopelessness of ever being recognized as a subject with real inner value. During college Portnoy attempted to flee from his family, to transform himself and be one with the dominant world of WASP

America. However, he quickly learned that it cannot be so simply achieved; his unresolved paranoid rage and his lack of an inner identity (subjective self) stood in his way. His experiences again suggest early failure in the resolution of the paranoid position, which has left him in the position of acting on either the sadistic or masochistic aspect of the paranoid organization. This active component of the paranoid position involves the individual's struggle with aggression, whether he or she is in control or whether the other is in control.

Portnoy's words are a profoundly painful statement of his sense of powerlessness and his resolve to find a way, to act, to have revenge on the world that has so rejected him:

> Look, we ate our meals with that radio blaring away right through to dessert, the glow of the yellow station band is the last light I see each night before sleep — so don't tell me we're just as good as anybody else, don't tell me we're Americans just like they are. No, no, these blond-haired Christians are the legitimate residents and owners of this place, and they can pump any song they want into the streets and no one is going to stop them either. O America! America! it may have been gold in the streets to my grandparents, it may have been a chicken in every pot to my father and mother, but to me, a child whose earliest movie memories are of Ann Rutherford and Alice Faye, America is a *shikse* nestling under your arm whispering love love love love love! [pp. 145–146/157]

Again, Portnoy gives voice to his deeply felt experience of alienation, powerlessness, and his wish for revenge. His wish for revenge can be understood as part of the early expression of sadism and ruthlessness, which are developmentally normal attempts to gain control over the world in which he feels powerless and hopeless.

> And that was the heart of my boyhood, four years of hating Tojo, Hitler, and Mussolini, and loving this brave determined republic! Rooting my little Jewish heart out for our American democracy!

Well, we won, the enemy is dead in an alley back of the Wil-
helmstrasse, and dead because I *prayed* him dead—and now I want
what's coming to me. *My* G.I. bill—real American ass! The cunt
in country-'tis-of-thee! I pledge allegiance to the twat of the
United States of America—and to the republic for which it stands.
[pp. 235–236/249]

For Portnoy to move beyond the paranoid position, he would
have to be able to acknowledge that he has seriously hurt someone
of importance and to make reparations to that person. His
parents' inability to allow him the expression of the most minimal
angry and destructive feelings, to both recognize that they can
survive his anger and allow him the opportunity to make
reparation, were the developmental deficits that limited him in
this area. The treatment needs to become focused on a fluid
development of themes of aggression, destructiveness, sadism,
and masochism. These themes would be enacted in their various
permutations in order for the patient to be able to experience and
internalize these themes. The Monkey's overwhelming experience of rage at having to play a part in Portnoy's enactment of his
sadism is quite understandable and reflects an inevitable transference paradigm. In this therapeutic paradigm, Portnoy would
make the analyst feel that he has been denigrated as the analyst
attempted to provide Portnoy with a wished for gratification. In
this example The Monkey is both the mechanism through which
he finds revenge and the proxy for his need to be cruel; what was
done to him he is now able to do to another. Through the process
of projective identification, the analyst would begin to experience
emerging sadistic and controlling thoughts toward the patient and
toward others. There would be a regression to a paranoid mode
in both the transference and countertransference experience. The
task of the analyst would be first to process and accept his or her
discomfort with the sadistic and paranoid fantasies, and second,
to facilitate the movement of these anxiety-provoking fantasies

into a more symbolic frame through the use of transitional experiences.

THE DEVELOPMENT OF SYMBOLIC EXPERIENCE

Kleinian theory involves an epistomological or cognitive theory in which the world is first experienced as containing disconnected, concrete objects, and then with the development of the depressive position, the individual develops the capacity to experience the world symbolically. The capacity to use symbols is critical (Segal 1981).

> [It] governs the capacity to communicate, since all communication is made by means of symbols. When schizoid disturbances in object relations occur, the capacity to communicate is similarly disturbed: first because the differentiation between subject and object is blurred, second, because the *means* of communication are lacking since symbols are felt in a concrete fashion and are therefore unavailable for purposes of communication. . . . Words, for instance, whether the analyst's or the patient's, are felt to be objects or actions, and can not be easily used for purposes of communication. [p. 57]

Winnicott's development of the use of transitional experiences as an aspect of working within the countertransference can be seen as clinically extending Isaacs (1943/1973) early observations on the nature and function of fantasy as well as Bion's (1977) extensive work on linking, attacks on linking, and on the development of thought processes. Winnicott uses the concept of transitional objects, transitional phenomena, and transitional experience to describe the development of the individual's capacity to infuse external experience with subjective, personal meaning, and also to develop a sense of agency. Winnicott (1971) has differentiated his definition of fantasies into those that represent the experience of an individual who is a passive object in a world in which he feels himself a victim (paranoid position), and those in which the person has achieved the status of a subject and can experience him or herself in the world as an active agent who is capable of creating inner experiences, dreams, and fantasies in the outside world.

The experience that Portnoy presents to his analyst reflects a profound statement of a developmental failure; he is incapable of using symbolic processes and can only experience the world as a series of external events over which he has no control. He experiences the world as a passive object who is buffeted and victimized by external events. In the following statement, Portnoy uses the cynical, hostile depreciating voice of the false self organization to cover up his experience of inner emptiness and hopelessness.

> Dreams? If only they had been! But I don't need dreams, Doctor, that's why I hardly have them — because I have this life instead. With me it all happens in broad daylight! The disproportionate and the melodramatic, this is my daily bread! The coincidences of dreams, the symbols, the terrifyingly laughable situations, the oddly ominous banalities, the accidents and humiliations, the bizarrely appropriate strokes of luck or misfortune that other people experience with their eyes shut, I get with mine open! Who else do you know whose mother actually threatened him with the dreaded knife? . . . maybe other patients dream — with me, *everything happens*. I have a life *without* latent content. The dream thing *happens*! Doctor: *I couldn't get it up in the State of Israel!* How's *that* for symbolism, *bubi*? [p. 257/270]

From the perspective of relational theory, being impotent in Israel is not a symbolic experience, as Portnoy's hostile challenge to his analyst suggests. It is a concrete experience, an icon, and another example of how Portnoy, because he has not developed the capacity for inner symbolic experience, uses action as a substitute for thought. One can look at Portnoy's life and his narrative as a series of "sound bites," or enactments rather than symbolic experiences and discourse. He experiences himself as a character in a movie he did not write or direct, and one that he cannot stop. Portnoy is correct: he lacks dreams and an inner symbolic and fantasy life. He is simply involved in the repetitive enactments of his own life without ever being able to internalize his experiences and take control over his destiny. M. Masud Khan (1979) discusses the patient's need for a witness to his or her life experience in order to help process the external repetitive events into inner, personal, and symbolic experience. Being impotent in Israel is not a bad joke as Portnoy presents it; it is a very highly charged experience representing the convergence of failures in his self development. Being sexually impotent is first a concrete manifestation of his overall experience of himself as impotent and powerless; it is a concrete expression of that which he cannot put into symbolic discourse. Second, it is a concrete expression of his experience of being a homeless and alien Jew; not only is he without a home, but he cannot even find a home in a place where other Jews have been able to find one. In working with Portnoy, the analyst would need to approach these experiences from the perspective of developing the capacity to use symbolic processes and focusing on the emergence of transitional experiences and the capacity to use illusion.

One of the most difficult tasks in working with narcissistic and schizoid patients like Portnoy is the recognition that their use and experience of language is as concrete external events as opposed to subjective and symbolic experiences. Words are experienced from a paranoid perspective as serving purposes of attack, defense, humiliation, and submission. Thus, in the paranoid position, there is a failure to recognize that one is a subject and not simply an object. A subject is an autonomous agent who has inner feelings and experiences. This recognition of the mutuality of subjectivity allows for a recognition of mutual concern and caring, which initiates a shift in the organization of relationships as well as in the dynamic themes and the capacity to use language symbolically. This shift is not simply a matter of learning how to speak abstractly, but a recognition and identification with the other's inner experience (Winnicott 1971).

Portnoy's brief experience with Kay Campbell's father caused him to recognize this difference between his concrete, objectified experience of language, and the mutually subjective symbolic language that was rare in his experiences.

> Did I have a good night's sleep? . . . Why, yes! I think I did! Hey—did you? "Like a log," replies Mr. Campbell. And for the first time in my life I experience the full force of a simile. This man, who is a real estate broker and an alderman of the Davenport town council, says that he slept like a log, and I actually *see* a log. *I* get it! Motionless, heavy, *like a log*! "Good *morning*," he says, and now it occurs to me that the word "morning," as he uses it, refers specifically to the hours between eight A.M. and twelve noon. I'd never thought of it that way before. He wants the hours between eight and twelve to be *good*, which is to say, enjoyable, pleasurable, beneficial! We are all wishing each other four hours of pleasure and accomplishment. Why, that's terrific! Hey, that's very nice! Good morning! And the same applies to "Good afternoon"! And "Good evening"! And "Good night"! My God! The English language is *a form of communication*! Conversation isn't just crossfire where you shoot and get shot at! Where you've got to duck for your life and aim to kill! Words aren't only bombs and bullets—no, they're little gifts, containing *meanings!* [pp. 220–221/234]

FAILURE IN MUTUAL IDENTIFICATION: THE IDEALIZING TRANSFERENCE

Portnoy's brief experience with Mr. Campbell reflects a moment in which he experienced the possibility of a mutual identification with an idealized self object (Kohut 1984). Mr. Campbell was someone that he could admire, merge with, and whose strength and confidence he could experience. This experience of merger or identification with an idealized object is an important way for Portnoy to fulfill a previously unfulfilled need that had left him severely damaged and vulnerable. Portnoy's hunger for and disappointment in his father as an idealized selfobject with whom he could have identified, and merged with his strength, is reflected in the following powerful statement:

> Christ, in the face of my defiance—if my father had only been my mother! and my mother my father! But what a mix-up of the sexes in our house! Who should by rights be advancing on me, retreating—and who should be retreating, advancing! Who should be scolding, collasping in helplessness, enfeebled totally by a tender heart! And who should be collapsing, instead scolding, correcting, reproving, criticizing, faultfinding without end! Filling the patriarchal vacuum! Oh, thank God! thank God! at least *he* had the cock and the balls! Pregnable (putting it mildly) as his masculinity was in this world of *goyim* with golden hair and silver tongues, between his legs (God bless my father!) he was constructed like a man of consequence, two big healthy balls such as a king would be proud to put on display, and a *shlong* of magisterial length and girth. And they were *his*: yes, of this I am absolutely certain, they hung down off of, they were connected on to, they could not be taken away from, *him*! [pp. 40–41/50–51]

Heinz Kohut (1984), in writing about failures in early experiences of the father as an idealized selfobject, discusses the increased valuation of the penis, either one's own or another's. In Kohut's discussion, it is clear that the penis becomes an icon, a concrete representation for the strength of the father.

Jessica Benjamin (1991) presents a model of the development of a strong sense of self and the experience of a healthy sexuality through a relationship that is extraordinarily similar to Kohut's descriptions of the idealized self-object relationship. Although her focus is on the development of a strong subjective identification in women, her thesis is equally applicable to men. Benjamin's concepts are related to the concepts of internalization of good and bad objects during the formation of one's identity. Benjamin points to the importance of the young person's identification with his or her father as an individual who is both able to be desired and is desirable as a sexual subject. She believes that

> a confirmed recognition from the father—"Yes, you can be like me"—helps the child consolidate this identification and so enhances the sense of being a subject of desire. In contrast, the lack of recognition and the denial of the identificatory bond damage the sense of being a sexual subject, and lead the individual to look for his or her desire through the other, and consequently to masochistic fantasies of surrendering to the ideal other's power. [p. 289]

This description of surrender to the other's sexual power is a critical theme in Portnoy's relationships, and one that reached its masochistic zenith in his brief relationship with Naomi in Israel.

The complexity of the processes of mutual identification are suggested in the following quotation in which each parent fails to provide the young Alexander with an undegraded image of manhood. Portnoy's own words capture both his need for and the failure in the process of mutual identification with his father.

> "Do you want to make a nice sis?" she [mother] asks me—when I want to make a torrent, I want to make a flood: I want like he [father] does to shift the tides of the toilet bowl. "Jack," my mother calls to him, "would you close that door, please? Some example you're setting for you know who." But if only that had been so, Mother! If only you-know-who could have found some inspiration in what's-his-name's coarseness! If only I could have nourished myself upon the depths of his vulgarity, instead of that too becoming a source of shame. Shame and shame and shame and

shame — every place I turn something else to be ashamed of. [p. 49/59]

Portnoy's masochistic and sadistic use of sexuality can be understood as a failure in his identification with his father, and his father's failure in being an idealized selfobject. His repetitive concrete enactments of expressions of male power represent disintegration products of his failed masculine identity. He frequently confuses himself with his father; he has not differentiated himself from his father in his mind. Moreover, Portnoy can only think in terms of sexual experiences. He apparently hopes that his father will admire him and recognize his power through his penis and through concrete sexual acts. The confusion between self and other and his use of sexual experiences as substitutes for paternal strength is clearly expressed in the following confused memory:

> A terrible act has been committed, and it has been committed by either my father or me. The wrongdoer, in other words, is one of the two members of the family who owns a penis. . . . Now: did he fuck between those luscious legs the gentile cashier from the office, or have I eaten my sister's chocolate pudding? . . . But *is* that me — or my father hollering out his defense before the jury? Sure, that's him — he did it, okay, okay, Sophie, leave me alone already, I did it, *but I didn't mean it* . . . "That's right, Sophie, I slipped it to the *shikse*, and what you think and don't think on the subject don't mean shit to me. Because the way it works, in case you ain't heard, is that I am the man around here, *and I call the shots!*" And slug her if you have to! Deck her, Jake! Surely that's what a *goy* would do, would he not? . . . Poppa, why do we have to have such guilty deference to women, you and me — when we don't! We mustn't! Who should run the show, Poppa, is *us*! [pp. 86–87/96–98]

Portnoy also is expressing an early version of the relational theme of sexuality as dominance, and the gentile woman as the route to emancipation, an identification with the power of the American man through a merger with the object of desire, the woman's genitals.

For many patients promiscuous sexuality represents failures in identification and concretized attempts to find the parent with whom to identify through the other's sexuality. This repetitive sexual behavior changes as the patient develops an idealizing self-object transference with the analyst in which there is a merger and mutual identification with the strength and power of the analyst as a new selfobject. The real relationship with the analyst sets the limits on the patient's capacity to experience himself as a powerful and confident individual who can utilize the projective and introjective identifications that are a necessary part of the treatment. Successful treatment of Alexander Portnoy would involve his development of a positive identity as a man who can experience himself as potent, sexual, and desirable without experiencing guilt, shame, or sadomasochistic related-ness. This sense of identity is both an aspect of becoming a subject rather than an object and the related capacity to experi-ence the world and the self through symbolic and transitional experiences. The subjective experience of identity rests on the individual's capacity to use symbolic, inner experiences as ways of organizing the self in the world of objects and subjects. The subjective or cohesive self is a representational organization; it is a critical internal fantasy (Isaacs 1943/1973) through which one organizes experiences in the world. The developmental and clinical aspects of this process rest on the processes of mutual identification and recognition.

In his discussion of the processes of mutual identification, Harold Searles (1979) emphasizes the importance of the child's capacity to symbolically care for and heal the parent's pathology as well as the parent's identification and idealization of the child. Portnoy's frustration at being unable to give to his father, to provide him with love and gratitude, is quite palpable, suggesting that his sense of impotence is partly a function of the failure in his ability to give to, affect, and reach his father. Portnoy's lifelong, frustrated desire to give his father the love, gratitude, and admiration that would allow for a mutual recognition and identification is expressed in the following words:

> In that ferocious and self-annihilating way in which so many Jewish men of his generation served their families, my father served my mother, my sister Hannah, but particularly me. Where he would be imprisoned, I would fly: that was his dream. Mine was its corollary: in my liberation would be his — from ignorance, from exploitation, from anonymity. To this day our destinies remain scrambled together in my imagination, and there are still too many times when, upon reading in some book a passage that impresses me with its logic or its wisdom, instantly, involuntarily, I think, "If only he could read *this*. Yes! Read, and understand — !" Still hoping, you see, still if-onlying, at the age of thirty-three. [pp. 6–7/17]

Like Icarus, Portnoy's fate was determined by father's failure to lead the way. The profound failure in mutual identification would need to be dealt with in the analysis as the analyst allowed himself to become involved in processes of mutual identification.

CONCLUSION

The relational analyst would be prepared to develop new experiences within the analytic relationship in addition to the use of interpretation. Transferences and countertransferences are thought of as representing both old and new affective relational schemes: opportunities for the development of an understanding of the past, for the development of a new sense of subjectivity and self-directedness in the present, and ideals, goals, and dreams to organize the person's life as it moves toward and creates the future. The relational analyst would understand

Portnoy from the perspective of early developmental failures in the areas of subjectivity, the capacity to use symbolic processes, and the development of an identity and ideals. The transference and countertransference would initially be dominated by a holding and emphatic mirroring experience. A more paranoid and hostile relational paradigm would emerge in which issues of dominance, humiliation, and power would develop. Through the development of this regressed paranoid transference–countertransference relationship, Portnoy would develop the capacity to move beyond repetitive concrete enactments into the use of symbolic inner experience. Finally, the analysis would develop into an idealizing transference with the analyst as an idealized selfobject. Portnoy would then be able to both identify himself with this idealized analyst and feel recognized as a capable, potent, and desirable man. The emphasis in this treatment would be on the growth of Portnoy's capacity to be in relationships and to experience himself as a cohesive, successful, and potent person.

REFERENCES

Benjamin, J. (1991). Father and daughter: identification with difference — a contribution to gender heterodoxy. *Psychoanalytic Dialogues* 1:277–300.

Bion, W. R. (1977). *Seven Servants: Four Works By Wilfred Bion*. New York: Jason Aronson.

Freud, S. (1918). An infantile neurosis. *Standard Edition 7*. London: Hogarth.

Hoffman, I. Z. (1992). Some practical implications of a social-constructivist view of the psychoanalytic situation. *Psychoanalytic Dialogues* 2:279–286.

Isaacs, S. (1943/1973). The nature and function of phantasy. In *Developments In Psycho-Analysis*, ed. M. Klein, P. Heimann, S. Isaacs, and J. Riviere. London: Hogarth.

Khan, M. M. R. (1979). *Alienation In Perversion*. New York: International Universities Press.

Klein, M. (1975). *Envy and Gratitude*. New York: Delacorte Press/Seymour Lawrence.

Kohut, H. (1984). *How Does Analysis Cure?* Chicago: University of Chicago Press.

Lasch, C. (1978). *The Culture of Narcissism*. New York: W. W. Norton.

Miller, A. (1981). *Prisoners of Childhood*. New York: Basic Books.
Mitchell, S. A. (1988). *Relational Concepts in Psychoanalysis*. Cambridge, MA: Harvard University Press.
Newirth, J. (1992). An object relations perspective: the paranoid position and the development of identity. *Psychoanalytic Psychology* 9:289–298.
Searles, H. F. (1979). *Countertransference and Related Subjects*. New York: International Universities Press.
Segal, H. (1981). *The Work of Hanna Segal: A Kleinian Approach to Clinical Practice*. New York: Jason Aronson.
Winnicott, D. W. (1971). *Playing and Reality*. New York: Tavistock (Methuen).
———— (1975). *Through Paediatrics To Psycho-Analysis*. New York: Basic Books.

7

Interpersonal Perspective: The Analyst's Participant-Observation with the Special Patient

Irwin Hirsch, Ph.D.

It feels fitting to me that I write this chapter. Though I have always read a great deal of fiction, some of it qualitatively better than *Portnoy*, this still remains the most thoroughly enjoyable novel I have ever read. I first read *Portnoy's Complaint* in 1969, after it was published. Philip Roth is five years older than I but our lives at the time had very much in common. Indeed, our life history also had a number of points in parallel. He articulated my personal experience better than anyone had done to that point and did so with hilarious humor. His wit is this book equals that of the two most profound comics of my generation, Lenny Bruce and Woody Allen. Roth touched on many personal truths for me and helped me laugh at myself. That is a wonderful combination of experiences and I am indebted to him for it. I reread *Portnoy* some twenty-three years later in preparation for writing this chapter. Though my own life has changed significantly, I believe I laughed just as much. The experience could not have possibly been as profound the second time around and was distant from some of the issues of relatively young adulthood or very pro-

107

longed adolescence, but the psychological wisdom is still formidable.

I would like to share an anecdote. Shortly after reading *Portnoy*, I was having a quiet dinner at a luncheonette on the Upper East Side of Manhattan, a block or two from my own office. Five yards down the counter was Philip Roth and I stared throughout the meal. I knew intuitively that he was on his way to see his analyst, for the district is the home of many practitioners. Extremely curious to see who was this Spielvogel, I followed Roth to a townhouse that indeed was a psychiatrist's office. The name on the doorbell was German or Austrian and indeed had two parts to it, like Spiel and Vogel. I had never heard of this analyst nor did he especially appeal to me from the way he was presented in the novel (I am a very different sort of analyst than the prototypical Freudian blank screen, Spielvogel), but the experience left me feeling even more a part of Roth and his exposition.

I begin this chapter with a summary of the interpersonal approach to psychoanalysis, and then examine the personality of Alexander Portnoy and discuss how I would work with Portnoy in contrast with how Dr. Spielvogel did.

INTERPERSONAL PSYCHOANALYSIS

Harry Stack Sullivan was the American "psychoanalytic pioneer" who helped shift the emphasis from drive discharge to interpersonal relations as the basic building block of human personality. He is not unique, in that most deviation from this basic classical Freudian position has rotated around that same issue. As more early psychoanalytic correspondence gets published, it is clear that Sandor Ferenczi in particular is a major forerunner of both interpersonal theory and the British object relations school. However, it is evident that Carl Jung, Alfred Adler, and Otto Rank also broke with Freud on the fundamental question of the primacy of sexual and aggressive drives and drive derivations. In contemporary times, relational or nondrive psychoanalysis may be overtaking classical Freudian psychoanalysis as the dominant point of view. The term *relational* is an umbrella concept, under which a number of somewhat different psychoanalytic perspectives exist. Interpersonal psychoanalysis, object relations theory, and self psychology are the three dominant subthemes. These positions are different from one another in a variety of important respects. However, each pays minimal attention to drives and emphasizes historical and current relationships with others, and the internalization of those relational configurations, as the key to understanding why people are the way they are.

Interpersonal psychoanalysis, for many, is connected with Sullivan and has probably been the most criticized and/or ignored of the contemporary developments in psychoanalysis. For one, Sullivan's theory represents the only significant psychoanalytic orientation that was not initiated by an analyst who was originally trained as a classical Freudian analyst. This lack of credentials has always hurt his credibility as well as that of the interpersonal school in total. In addition, many have believed that his theory of human development gave short shrift to the intrapsychic world of the individual and that Sullivan's only interest was in the observable relations between people. Some have read him as being positivistic, a variation of American behavioral psychology. These criticisms have some basis, although others have found clear reference to an internalized self in his writing (e.g., his concept of personification). If indeed there is an internalization of one's history of interpersonal relations and expectancies that are dominated by these intrapsychic configurations, the basic psychoanalytic notion of unconscious motivation must be part of the picture. Sullivan was reluctant to focus on speculation about what was inside. He believed that this has led to reification of posited structures and this in turn had led to theory dominating over observation. He was more comfortable with what could be

seen between people and believed that this vantage point mini-
mized an overly abstract and theoretical approach to understanding people.

Regardless of whether or not Sullivan himself sufficiently
emphasized the inner world of the individual, unconscious
process, and the analysis of transference, it is clear that some of
his early colleagues did and that most contemporary interpersonal
analysts do so. Clara Thompson, Sullivan's closest colleague,
more than anyone else, made the effort to integrate Sullivan into
mainstream psychoanalysis. She was classically trained in the
United States and much of her writing is an effort to place
Sullivan in a historical perspective and adjust his sometimes
arcane concepts to more traditional thinking. Her work cannot at
all be interpreted as antithetical to notions of unconscious
motivation. She wrote significant pieces on the concepts of
transference and countertransference, comparing the classical
and interpersonal meanings of these key concepts. She facilitated
the evolution of interpersonal psychoanalysis, which, like all
points of view, has changed over years. The writing of the leading
interpersonal thinkers such as Edgar Levenson and Benjamin
Wolstein, as well as the relational theorist Stephen Mitchell, can
clearly be seen as extensions of Clara Thompson's elaboration of
Sullivan. Unfortunately, many analysts still associate interpersonal psychoanalysis only with Sullivan and have never read the
interpersonal literature beyond his basic writing. It is not unusual
to see "new" ideas developed in the field that are almost exact
replicas of interpersonal writing, without attribution to that
literature. Interpersonal analysts often live with the feeling that
the wheel is constantly being rediscovered (see Hirsch 1985).

In addition to a development theory that stresses relationships
over drive discharge, interpersonal thinkers developed a theory of
therapy that focuses upon the analyst as part of the analytic
process. The participant-observation model is a sharp contrast to
the blank-screen model. According to the former model, despite
every effort toward neutrality and objectivity, the observer

cannot help but become part of what is being observed. Just as the laboratory scientist effects the results of the experiment, based on personal bias (often unconscious), the analyst always unwittingly influences the psychoanalytic data of the patient. In the classical Freudian model of Spielvogel, the patient's biologically based drive patterns of libido and aggression are seen to spring forth as givens, quite independent of the analyst's participation. Similarly, child development is primarily a function of a prewired set of drive-related phenomena, with parental participation as a secondary factor. Biology and drives are more significant than psychology and relations with others. The interpersonal developmental model, like the psychoanalytic model, is one of mutual participation.

Freud's seduction theory is an excellent example. Freud originally believed that parental seduction was the cause of child and adult psychopathology as well as childhood sexuality. He then shifted his theory in the early part of the century and because of the shift, psychoanalysis developed along more biological and intrapsychic, as opposed to interpersonal, lines. If Freud had stayed with a modified or metaphorical version of the seduction theory, he would likely have continued to view childhood sexuality not as a biological given but as related to parental seductive feelings or interactions with the child. The interpersonal analyst sees the interaction with the significant others as the initiating factor. This interaction becomes internalized and woven into the fabric of developing personality. Freud viewed instinctual forces within the child as the basis for sexual (and aggressive) feelings toward the parents and toward others. The child as seething cauldron allows for relative innocence on the part of the parents and the analyst.

In the classical analytic situation, the patient's attribution of sexual or aggressive feelings to the analyst is inevitably interpreted as a distortion or a projection. The blank-screen analyst believes that he or she is not a participant but is only an observer. The patient is almost always viewed as inaccurate in attributions and everything reverts to the biologically based drives and their locus within the patient. The analyst does not have to ask if he or she is either initiating or otherwise participating in the patient's experience of the situation. From a classical Freudian perspective, countertransference participation is an error to be corrected. From an interpersonal point of view, countertransference enactment is unavoidable. It is a given that must be used to further the cause of the analysis.

Interpersonal psychoanalysis is in harmony with Freud's abandoned seduction theory. In the psychoanalytic situation, the patient and the analyst unconsciously influence each other. The analysts' participation is unwitting. Participant observation is not a prescription of what to do but a description of what inevitably occurs (Greenberg 1991) when any two people get together. One of the primary activities of the analytic inquiry is to clarify the nature of that unconscious interaction (Levenson 1991). The analysis of transference refers not only to what the patient brings to the analytic situation but to the participation of both parties (Gill 1982). The object of analytic inquiry is not the intrapsychic world of the patient *in vacuo* but the field of interaction between analyst and patient. The patient is the more dominant participator and the analyst the more recessive. The patient shapes the world, as all of us do, to conform to the past and to expectancies based on internalized past relationships (Mitchell 1988). This is the interpersonal version of the repetition compulsion. The analyst unwittingly becomes caught up in this system, since the observer cannot help but become part of the observed. Thus, the analyst can never really be a screen and is destined to analyze from within the patient–analyst system (Singer 1970).

One can never simply assume that the patient is projecting or distorting. The patient's observations are always seen as at least plausible and reality is not the exclusive property of the would-be objective analyst. From this point of view, there is no objective reality. Interpersonal psychoanalysis has evolved to a perspectivist or relativist philosophical position (Hoffman 1983). Because both parties participate, patient and analyst are seen to each have perspectives on truth or reality. These shared psychic realities (Wolstein 1975) are viewed as a more appropriate line to clarity of experience than the more authoritative interpretation. The latter is, more often than not, a declaration made by an objective party to a subjective one. It is more in harmony with the model criticized by Heinrich Racker (1968), as a relationship between a well or objective analyst and a sick or distorting patient.

Spielvogel, the Freudian archetype, does not seem to view either countertransference experience or the relational field as primary areas of inquiry. The study of the productive use of countertransference experience (Epstein and Feiner 1979) was developed by analysts of the interpersonal orientation and the object relations school. Spielvogel believes that his silence successfully maintains his neutral blank screen and that his attitudes and feelings are not unconsciously conveyed to Portnoy nor influence Portnoy.

An interpersonal approach suggests quite the opposite. Just as parents' unspoken attitudes and feelings have profound effect, the analyst often participates without knowing it. From a contemporary interpersonal perspective, psychopathology is a function of rigid loyalty to one's family (Searles 1979). This often dissociated love and loyalty maintains ties to the past, which may be in stark contrast to new experience and new relational configurations. Conflict is ever present but there is no conflict between id and ego or superego. Conflict reflects guilt over leaving behind the ties that bind one to past figures and forging a life that is separate and different in quality. Very often, the more pathological the history, the more rigid and disabling are the loyalties.

In a participant-observation model, the analyst unwittingly but inevitably enters the patient's world and therefore has the opportunity to facilitate new experience and separation from internalized family configurations. Despite efforts at neutrality and objective analytic distance, the analyst becomes caught in the web of the patient's old configurations. The analyst unconsciously acts out with the patient repetitions of the old while consciously working toward new and richer experience. The study of countertransference experience allows the analyst to see how the past is being repeated within the transference–countertransference matrix. If the analyst is viewed as outside of the field, the real risk is that mutual repetition remains unrecognized and unanalyzed. The tendency to interpret the patient's comments about the analyst as transference distortions closes off avenues of self and interactional examination. From an interpersonal viewpoint, the patient moves forward when he or she is optimally aware of initiating old patterns or repetitions, within and outside of the transference. The analytic relationship must break the pattern of repetition on the one hand, but it cannot do so without first becoming caught up in the repetition, on the other hand. This is why the analysis is believed to take place from within the system and why awareness of countertransference enactments is so pivotal to the interpersonal analyst.

The interpersonal school, perhaps more than any other perspective, is antagonistic toward notions of diagnosis and of clear prescriptions of therapeutic technique related to diagnosis. Sullivan's most famous phrase, "We are all more simply human than otherwise," captures much about an analytic attitude that focuses more on unique individuality than on categories derived from a medical model of therapy. Though Sullivan did speak of diagnostic entities and some interpersonal analysts still do, there is only minimal literature in this area.

Harold Searles (1979), strongly influenced by Sullivan's analytic work with schizophrenic patients, perhaps more clearly than anyone else in the literature has drawn similarities between psychotic and neurotic lines of development and experience. He believes that all individuals possess similar personal qualities to varying degrees and that the madness seen in hospitalized schizophrenic patients is quite within all of us. Individual

psychopathology reflects learned internalized interpersonal configurations and the patient's adaptation as well as adhesion to
consistent familial experience. Regardless of the nature or degree
of psychopathology, these patterns are visible in the transference
and can be worked with in the transference. The patient is viewed
as the architect of his or her world. Contemporary experience, the
transference relationship included, is ultimately shaped to conform to the patient's past experience with and expectancies of
others. Notions of will and existential thinking in general are
strongly reflected in the interpersonal paradigm. The contemporary interpersonal analyst is likely to devote considerable effort to
the patient–analyst relationship as a repetition of and perpetua-
tion of earlier experience. As Searles has made very clear, all
people strive to repeat their problematic history and therefore
love their own pathology. On the other hand, people are viewed
as striving toward self-actualization, and the tension between
these two personal aims, regardless of diagnosis, is universal.

The question of diagnosis is significant here. Most analysts, if
they were forced to make a diagnosis of Portnoy, would probably
call him narcissistic. This is of particular importance because
different analytic schools have very different ideas about how to
work with narcissistic patients, or even whether or not narcissism
is a clear diagnostic category in the first place. A very personal
revelation is pertinent here. I earlier referred to perceived
similarities between myself and Roth, particularly back at the
time of publication of *Portnoy's Complaint*. I had recently finished
my doctorate in psychology and was looking forward in two years
to begin psychoanalytic training. I wished to begin my own
personal analysis and consulted a rather traditional classical
analyst for that purpose. After our interview he told me that he
could not see me in analysis per se, since he viewed my problems
as basically not neurotic but narcissistic. Without going into
further detail, until I went for a second consultation elsewhere, I
feared I had no future as an analyst myself. Of course, I feared
much more; essentially I saw a loveless life ahead of me.

Spielvogel, to his credit, is intent on analyzing Portnoy despite his narcissism. This issue is relevant because historically, psychoanalysts have viewed individuals who are considered narcissistic as not analyzable. This belief started with Freud and the concept of the transference neurosis. The neurotic individual was seen as sufficiently related to others to engage intensely in the transference, while the narcissistic person was seen as too affectively withdrawn to do this. Psychoanalysis developed along a two-species line: diagnosed neurotics were analyzed and nonneurotics or those with too much narcissistic involvement were not. Little distinction was made between the most extreme form of narcissistic involvement like psychotic depression or schizophrenia and milder forms of the narcissistic characteristic such as I or Portnoy displayed. Interpersonal analysts were the only group of analysts that did not develop a special technique to work with narcissistic patients and that exclude them from analytic consideration. Object relations analysts in Great Britain and in South America have never excluded people as analytic patients based on diagnostic criteria, as have classical analysts, but the former have developed different techniques to work with nonneurotic patients. This is similar in spirit to the American self-psychologists. As an orientation, self psychology developed out of classical psychoanalysis with the express purpose of broadening technique to include work with nonpsychotic, narcissistic patients. For them, Portnoy would be a dream. Like the object relations analysts, the self psychologists purport to adhere to classical techniques for neurotic patients and their own revised technique for narcissistic patients. Diagnosis is thus pivotal in their thinking.

In essence, both schools believe that narcissistic patients suffer from early deficiencies and before analysis of transference in the usual sense can take place, the analyst must make up for these early deficiencies by providing a nourishing and somewhat gratifying analyzing environment. Self psychologists and object relations analysts speak somewhat differently about this but they agree that early deficiencies must be compensated by the analyst. Traditional classical analysts, by and large, write this off as supportive psychotherapy and maintain their analyzable versus nonanalyzable dichotomies. Interpersonal analysts, with their Sullivanian roots in working with schizophrenic patients, have not agreed with this distinction from the outset. There is no distinctive technique within interpersonal psychoanalysis that addresses clearly different modes of analysis with different diagnostic categories. Many contemporary analysts, following the lead of Searles (1979), Merton Gill (1982), and Edgar Levenson (1991), believe that acute attention to the transference-countertransference matrix allows for psychoanalysis to be applicable to a very broad range of patients. Clearly, Spielvogel was more of that mind in working traditionally with Portnoy than was the analyst with whom I originally consulted.

Narcissism, from an interpersonal perspective, indeed is a broad characteristic. The pure quality of narcissism is most widely known to be characterized by vanity, exhibitionism, arrogance, grandiosity, and self-absorption. The other person tends to be used to make the narcissist feel good, and well-being depends upon receiving a continuously adequate quantity of positive regard. The other is not usually viewed as whole person and is generally used as supplier of nutrients. The basis for this is an absence of a sense of inner strength or substance, an emptiness that leaves one vulnerable to annihilation. The extremely narcissistic individual does not generally feel a clear and meaningful sense of self at the core or center. How others view this individual is likely to be taken as a reading of the self. This is why the prototypical narcissist so desperately searches for positive regard. If admiration is not forthcoming, the result may very well be flight or deep depression based on confrontation with feelings of nothingness. Dependency is often profound but is not consciously experienced as such, for the feeling is much feared. Other people are important for the provision they supply and thus are fragmented as individuals. To be personally dependent or to feel conscious love for a whole other person is to risk annihilation.

As with all qualities, narcissism rarely exists in pure form and is always on a continuum. Everyone is narcissistic to some degree. If psychopathology is partially viewed as impairment of the ability to love, narcissism can be seen as an element in all problems in living. It is a way in which everyone protects him or herself from full presence with the other; it is a degree of personal inaccessibility. One of the more common, everyday forms of this is self-absorption. There are different modes of self-absorption. Among the more common are depression and dysphoric self-concern, ruminative or other ideational preoccupation, strong vanity and selfish pursuit of desires. These qualities exist on a continuum within people representing the highest to the lowest levels of psychological functioning. The interpersonal analyst tends to think of narcissism as descriptive of these personal qualities and not so much as a diagnostic entity. It characterizes ways people are with themselves and in their relational world. From this perspective, it is, therefore, possible to function quite outstandingly in one's work, as did our Portnoy, while at the same time being miserably unhappy and destructive to others in one's personal relationships.

In thinking of narcissism in this way, it is obvious that narcissistic characteristics cannot possibly emerge from one particular etiological source. From the perspective of many object relations and self psychology theorists, narcissistic characteristics are exclusively a deficiency disease. The interpersonal analyst is more likely to think in relativistic terms. Narcissistic personality traits are not all or none qualities and are likely to be multiply determined. For example, many people who exhibit strong narcissistic qualities come from families in which one or another parent was overinvolved, in contrast to depriving. In a family constellation where a parent infantilizes, overprotects, or overly admires the child, there may readily develop an overblown sense of self-importance and grandiosity. This may leave the individual somewhat unprepared for all of the rigors of life. They may expect to be equally loved and admired everywhere and have little sense of reciprocity in relationships. When others are less loving or less tolerant than the family, feelings of emptiness, depression, and insubstantiality may become acute. From this developmental pattern, the self-absorbed or inflated individual clings to his or her internalized family constellation as a way of maintaining a sense of comfort as well as providing the family members with what they require.

Many people who achieve a great deal in life come from backgrounds where they were overly indulged. They were viewed, as was Freud himself, as the most special child in the family and the primary source of familial pride and esteem. In many respects this is a wonderful message to be brought up with, for this specialness is often carried forward into the world and reenacted with other people and with institutions. It can make for a charmed life, where one continues to have the knack of getting what one wants from the world. This quality leads to trouble when separation issues are not resolved or when little is expected in return by the family. Analysts can easily fall into countertransference love with a patient who was so special to his or her family. Some people are blessed with the ability to be almost universally admired and respected. If this is not analyzed, as it often is not with some high-achieving patients, the analytic procedure is simply a repetition of the past. When the patient, despite being genuinely admired by the analyst, is sufficiently self-absorbed, it is more difficult for the analyst to feel this unambivalent countertransference love. Many have written of the analytic difficulty of coming face to face with patients who do not give or who do not reciprocate. Analysts can easily feel useless and deprived and talionically withdraw into personal depression as a way to self-nourish.

Another reciprocal reaction is anger and subtle forms of attack. This could take the form of excessive silence or harsh confrontation, depending on one's personal and/or theoretical bent.

When functioning best, the interpersonal analyst maintains an evenly hovering attention to both transference and countertransference experience and is able to use the latter to enrich the analysis. The interpersonal analyst, because of the way the theory informs, is unable to have the luxury of existing outside of the intersubjective field.

PORTNOY THE PERSON

Alexander Portnoy is too special to his mother and some of this is based on her own selfish possessiveness of him. To his mother, Portnoy is perfection. He is beautiful and brilliant in the same way I imagine Freud was to his mother. In comparison with his depressed and struggling father, Mrs. Portnoy's son is a god. He seems to have won his mother, over his only male rival, hands down. He hardly needed to do anything beyond simply existing. He was so nourished by his mother that he almost could not help but become brilliant. He was fed with all the nutrients that make one live up to inherited potential for intelligence: attention, attunement, verbal engagement, and consistent outpourings of love.

The best moments of mother's life were Portnoy's preschool years. They stayed home together and talked all day. She never noticed the time go by as she did her household chores and talked with her precious son. Portnoy's sister, like father, is bland in every way, in comparison. For mother, her daughter is ancillary, while her son is her whole life.

Mother is ubiquitous. Portnoy cannot move without his mother being there. Even his first grade teacher, whom he adores, is reincarnated as mother in an elaborate romantic fantasy. Mother is a far more competent person than father. She appears stronger in health and in character, less depressed and more lively and intelligent. One has the impression that were it she working instead of plodding papa, the family would be more economically comfortable. A boy can feel wonderful about himself when so thoroughly loved by such an able and strong woman.

Portnoy carries this feeling forward in life; he can do no wrong in the eyes of women and in his professional achievements. His brilliance is thoroughly nurtured and he is the smartest and most verbally clever wherever he is. Women admire him as his mother adored him. He expects this and he repeats his centrality and his specialness in his academic and professional life and with women. This is consistent until his fateful encounter with the Israeli women who view his narcissism as effeminate self-indulgence.

Portnoy has little personal sense of reciprocation in male–female relatedness. Women exist for his satisfaction and pleasure, not as entities in and of themselves. They are present to satisfy, desire, and admire him, like mother. They can be faceless and interchangeable, like sister. He is markedly dependent on women but not on a particular woman. Any one will do as long as she can adore him and is exciting sexually. Women can be exciting by virtue of their physical appearance or by possessing certain attributes, particularly social status. His interest in women has little to do with their personal qualities.

The down side of mother for Portnoy is the selfish power she has over him and the guilt she evokes regarding thoughts of separation. While it is enormously enhancing to be so loved and admired, mother's intentions are not only in her son's interest. Mother Portnoy wishes to possess her son entirely. He is so far superior to her husband that her desire for him is boundless. She does not want him to lead a separate life and to truly love another woman. This is her narcissism, though it takes the disguised form of giving to her son. In excessive giving she is also taking possession. Separation from mother produces profound guilt in the protagonist. He has thoroughly internalized his mother and everything that would make him his own unique person produces considerable conflict.

Portnoy's life is a struggle between being good for his mother and being bad as a way of shedding or gaining control over mother. He consistently struggles between being a good boy and a bad boy. Bad refers to independent strivings, which Portnoy needs to exaggerate in order to maintain some semblance of separateness. To be an overtly passive and dependent good boy is a death sentence. In his own life, his arch-goodness is exemplified by his memory of helping his mother and her friends sort out their mah-jongg tiles. He is a boy so good that he loses his boyness and acts like a girl. He is a preschooler doing the household chores with mother in her happiest moments. If he maintains his manifest goodness there are two logical consequences in his fantasy: suicide and homosexuality.

The ultimate good boy is his neighbor, Ronald. Ronald was so thoroughly dominated and castrated that when he committed suicide as an adolescent, he attached a note, pinned to his neatly pressed shirt, indicating that one of his mother's friends had called. The ultimate mama's boy nerd does the good-boy thing even as he finally tells his mother that he cannot take her any more. The only private place he can find away from mother is his death. Portnoy's homosexual fantasy has him living the life of a woman with his effeminate male lover on Fire Island. They cook and keep house just like mother. In this scenario, Portnoy is totally identified with his powerful mother. He is a woman, playing mah-jongg and cooking and gossiping just like mother and her friends.

If Portnoy is not bad and rebellious, he feels he cannot prevent one of the above configurations. His badness in adulthood takes the form of extreme efforts to take control of his mother through the sexual subjugation of women. His rebellion in adolescence is recordbreaking masturbation and sexual preoccupation. Even for an adolescent, Portnoy's masturbatory feats are impressive. His relationship with his omnipresent mother is eroticized. She is all over him. He masturbates profusely because he is overstimulated by her but also because it is his way of gaining control over his desire. He refers to his penis ("wong") as the only thing he could call his own. He takes it in hand to prevent his mother from taking it over entirely. Jerking off, as obsessive as it is for him, is largely an autonomous act. It both reflects living close to a sexy mom and not allowing mom to take charge of his sexual organ and his total self. Every time he masturbates or "fucks the family dinner," he is saying that he is both enmeshed in the family and stroking toward autonomy. If he stops for a moment, his sexuality and his personal center belongs entirely to mother.

It is the norm in the neighborhood for the mothers to refer to their sons as their lovers and this is brazenly and openly done in front of their dull, pedestrian, constricted husbands. By making sure his penis never leaves the grip of his fist, he is also helping to preserve his father as someone whose penis may be available for mother. Portnoy is not competitive with father. If mother desired father's penis, Portnoy would be able to ease up flogging his own.

As he gets older, Portnoy's badness continues along the same lines. He maintains his autonomy by using women to stroke or suck upon his penis. These women must be different from mother. They cannot be Jewish, for one, and they have to possess something toward which he strives. They may come from a higher social class, a radically different culture, or simply be extraordinarily beautiful or sexy. Portnoy repeats his specialness with each one of his women but he also turns the tables on them. He uses these women far more than they use him. Unlike mother, these women never control and dominate him. Portnoy exploits his women, takes all he can get from them and then leaves. It is an analogue to adolescent masturbation; each conquest like each independent stroke leaves him feeling a notch more free of mother's grip.

Portnoy enters analysis for a few good reasons. He recognizes that he is unable to love and that he treats women cruelly. He is afraid that he will spend the rest of his life in flight from mother and in relentless pursuit of sexual conquest. In addition to this very central fear, he also suffers from considerable guilt. I believe that he is genuinely guilty about the way he treats women but he is also neurotically guilty over not giving mother what she wants. At age 33, mother desires another Portnoy in the form of a grandchild. The good boy Portnoy who is reliable and compulsive and neat and clean, just like mother, is way overdue regarding this responsibility. He has done everything he was supposed to do in school and professionally to make mother proud, but in this realm he hurts her deeply. She views his serial pursuit of non-Jewish women as a rejection of herself. Indeed this is so but the good boy is in considerable conflict over continuing this. Portnoy finally begins analysis because he meets his "mother" in the form of two Israeli women, with whom he is impotent. In going to Israel, Portnoy is attempting to return to mother and do what a good Jewish boy should do. However, the Israeli women he meets are too close to mother, either by virtue of being very Jewish or by being very strong. The sexual virtuoso cannot perform. Sexual performance has saved him both from suicide and from homosexuality and now he has lost his erection and his primary source of perceived strength and autonomy. He enters analysis, desperate to regain his potency in the form of being a special patient, just like he was mother's special boy. I also believe that he begins analysis for the two other and more constructive reasons I noted. By the time he is ready to start therapy I think that Portnoy recognizes his tortured battle with guilt as well as his repeated inability to truly give to another. If he were only commencing analysis to regain his potency under the admiring eye of his analyst-mother, he would indeed be more thoroughly narcissistic than I view him as being.

So much to say about mother and so comparatively little to say about father. It is tragic for all concerned that Portnoy's mother loves him so much more passionately than she does her husband. If only father were more positively prominent, mother might have left little Portnoy alone somewhat more. Father stands out mostly in the negative. He is pictured as hard-working but barely successful; and that because he does the "shit work" that nobody else will do. "Shit" dominates father's life. He is perennially constipated and, when not working, inevitably on the toilet. He is always discontented either about his bowels or his work and has very little, beyond a reliability and a good work ethic, to give to Portnoy. Portnoy never had to struggle to defeat father and win mother's love. Father was defeated originally by his far stronger and more capable wife and by her idea of a son, even before Portnoy was born. Portnoy is in the sunlight and his depressed father is in the shithouse, from the moment Portnoy is a light in his mother's eye.

The interpersonal analyst does not necessarily view the oedipal struggle as the central theme in human neurotic development. There are some families in which this prototype indeed does seem to have significance and others where only a stretch would make the data fit the theory. Interpersonal analysts have been critical of Freudian theory as too strong a theory, leading to situations where actual unique experience is violated in order for the data to fit the strong theory. In Portnoy's family, mother and son are a pair, as are father and daughter. In many respects, Portnoy is more identified with his competent and spirited mother than with his depressed, bland father. I do not see active rivalry in the Portnoy family, for the ground rules and territories are clearly mapped out. Sister and father are muted in the background or in the bathroom, and mother and son are on stage together.

It is important for Portnoy to be different from father and to compensate for his defeated self. He assumes a somewhat negative identification with father; striving to be opposite to him as much as possible. Portnoy is a climber; he wants to be first in his class, an important man in New York City and the darling of all the women. He wants women from the upper echelons of WASP culture. Father slaved for the upper class Protestants and Portnoy wants to be accepted into their world and to sexually degrade their daughters. In part, he is trying to transcend father and, in part, gain revenge for his father. If Portnoy is viewed as a nonentity by a woman, as he was by the second Israeli woman, he is deflated and feels just like his flatulent, toilet-bound father.

Portnoy does not relate well to men. His esteem comes from his perennially being first in his class and from the love of women. There is virtually nothing in the novel that describes male to male relatedness in any way. It does not seem as if he had truly close friends, although he was interesting enough and athletic enough not to have been an outsider in the world of boys and men. Nonetheless, I sense a subtle bond between Portnoy and father beyond the negative identification. I believe that Portnoy feels his father's depression and fadedness and appreciates his pluck in not bailing out all together. Father is a survivor and he moves along with minimal nutrition. He feeds himself and is steady and reliable. His stubborn strength, in this regard, is admired by Portnoy and bodes well for his own survival in the face of narcissistic loss. Portnoy also knows that he is loved by his father and has never doubted this. There is something very gentle in the man for he never has retaliated for his son's early winning away of the love of his wife. Father is not a jealous father or a vindictive father. He genuinely wants the best for his son. Though there is not much open affection, I sense that Portnoy knows that he is not only admired by mother but loved and admired by father as well.

The negative side of all of this enmeshment, once again, is guilt. Portnoy is in conflict about separating from father as well as from mother. Father is a simple man and cannot comprehend Portnoy's complicated, contemporary ways. As long as Portnoy remains unfulfilled as a person, he maintains a strong relational tie to father. Portnoy is successful and much admired but he is never free or happy. Rumination is his form of constipation. Portnoy cannot live relaxedly or find his own idiom. However much he achieves in contrast with father, he is tied to father on the toilet bowl of rumination and dysphoria. Thus, Portnoy's psychopathology is not only related to his incestuous ties to his mother but to his adhesion to father's dysphoria. In this most unfortunate way, Portnoy is profoundly identified with father. The two of them are always worried about something and never experience contentment for longer than a bowel movement or an orgasm.

It is interesting that Portnoy's metaphor for true fulfillment in life is playing out in center field, with wide open space between himself and everyone else. His affinity for center field, embodied by the heroic Brooklyn Dodger, Duke Snider, reflects Portnoy's potential resolution. For one, Portnoy's father did play softball with the men in the community and sports was one form of connection with father and freedom from mother. Sports was an area of achievement that mother had no part of or interest in. In playing baseball or softball, he was more like father than mother. He found an ideal father in the handsome Dodger center fielder, and for those moments he did not find it necessary to ruminate, achieve, or masturbate. He could relax in the privacy of center field with green grass all around and no human intrusion in proximity. This was his space; dad was idealized and mother could not get near him. If Portnoy could have this space as something integral and enduring in his life, frantic masturbation and compensatory sexual exhibitionism would be unnecessary.

It is likely that Portnoy will always be a man that needs some reasonable distance from people. Intimacy will probably always be difficult. On the other hand, he has incorporated enough love from both parents so it is possible he can be capable of nonguilty love and be a man of great achievement in the work or creative realm. If Portnoy is able to control the distance and tempo of his relationships, as he is able to do out in center field, he may be in a position to let go of his penis and become a reciprocating or generous person, to some degree. This proximity issue will be a central one in the transference with any analyst, as will the question of the admiring versus the depriving stance of the analyst.

From my description of Portnoy as a person, it is probably

clear that I do not see drives as central in human development. With all of his sexual obsession and activity and all of the eroticism between Portnoy and his mother, it is easy to formulate a drive-based description of his development. This is most likely Spielvogel's point of view, judging from the blank screen analytic stance that goes hand in hand with a one-person drive psychology. It is evident from my reading of the data that I do not view the protagonist's drives as initiating the family configuration. I am more inclined to see the significant others, mother and father, as the precipitating force in Portnoy's intensely sexualized relationships. Portnoy does not have excessive drives, but an excessive mother who both overstimulates him and controls him. Mother was the cause, if you will, of her son's incestuous feelings, sexual preoccupation, and defensive need for control and domination over women. His perversions were not part of his biology but a reaction to real, external experience with the primary woman in his life.

Similarly, I view Portnoy's narcissism as a function of his overblown centrality in the family, more so than libido turned inward or deficient loving. Portnoy was too loved or too special, albeit mother's love was selfish as much as it was generous. He was no more preoccupied with himself than was his mother with him. Thus, his narcissism, also, was based on real, external interpersonal experience that gradually became internalized.

I have made an effort to describe Portnoy and his development from an interpersonal perspective. However, other nondrive or relational theorists may indeed understand Portnoy in a very similar way. That is, all relational points of view see human development as primarily a function of consistent, interpersonal experience. There is less likelihood than with Freudian theory to see individuals developing along clearly outlined lines or stages. Theory per se plays far less of a role in understanding the person and the descriptions may sound more like that of a lay person than someone using a technical or scientific language. Many interpersonal analysts downplay developmental theory as part of

an effort to avoid stereotyped, theory-based views of people and
this is true for some other relational perspectives as well. The
interpersonal psychoanalytic theory of therapeutic action, however, is somewhat distinct from the other relational positions and
quite different from Spielvogel's traditional blank screen.

PORTNOY IN ANALYSIS

Spielvogel, the Freudian blank screen, observed Portnoy for a
long period of time before telling him that he had not yet begun.
Why was he silent for so long and why did he finally and pithily
tell Portnoy that all his output was essentially meaningless
bullshit? Classical technique justified Spielvogel's silence. The
patient is supposed to reveal himself, the transference to unwind.
When the transference is solidly and clearly developed and the
patient has been free from analytic intrusion, it may then be time
to interpret. Spielvogel no doubt perceived Portnoy's exhibitionist
narcissism from the initial session. He watched it repeat and
repeat in the same form, while presuming to stay outside of the
picture, as the blank screen dictates. I contend that Spielvogel
was not outside of the picture at all and that his silence helped
him delude himself that he was. Spielvogel was watching a
brilliant, manic, exhibitionistic display from a most witty and
entertaining patient. I imagine that, indeed, the analyst enjoyed
Portnoy sometimes, or maybe frequently. Spielvogel also observed someone who he felt was narcissistically talking to himself
and not to the analyst. In other words, he felt that Portnoy was
consistently masturbating in front of him and asking him to
admire his beautiful strokes.

Based on Spielvogel's one comment, I believe that he eventually grew to hate Portnoy. His comment was like a retaliation:
"You think you are so special but you have been saying nothing
all of this time—wasting your own precious sperm." Spielvogel
probably felt that Portnoy just wanted his awe and admiration.

Self psychological technique would lead to a recognition of this and a likely decision to provide it for the patient. Spielvogel probably did provide it, unwittingly, but at some point felt unreciprocated and himself deprived. He watched his own countertransference but did not monitor it carefully. If he did, he would probably not have so devastatingly retaliated when he finally said something to his patient. From my perspective, he had to be destructively furious at this selfish, grandiose patient of his. Why else would he so thoroughly have wiped out everything that Portnoy had conveyed? I think he was telling Portnoy that this bland old man will not be treated like his father or his sister and will not admire him like his mother. Spielvogel was making the statement that he was more potent than his patient; he can castrate with one brief stroke. It was father's and sister's revenge for a life history of blandness and second-class existence. Spielvogel was not passive or sweet like father. He did not love his patient and he was not going down in defeat to this fascinating younger man. Spielvogel was the fierce rival Portnoy never experienced at home; he was the Germanic punitive agent in contrast with Portnoy's passive, *shtetl* Jew, inadequate father.

This blank-screen analyst is far from outside of the transference–countertransference matrix. He superficially acts like a neutral and objective observer but enacts his countertransference feelings with a fury. If Spielvogel did not conceive of himself as a blank screen, he would have recognized that his feelings were not being subsumed for the treatment but enacted or acted out within the analysis. This is inevitable and not problematic if recognized. Spielvogel's theory impedes his recognition of countertransference enactment and so it occurs anyway, under the guise of bona fide Freudian analysis, and reflects the absolute worst abuse of classical technique. Not all Freudian analysts are as smug as Spielvogel. Only an enraged analyst would be as severe as this one. Spielvogel had infinite opportunities to convey to Portnoy that the latter was exhibiting, competing, talking at and not to him, profoundly self-absorbed, using his intelligence to obscure his feelings, viewing the analyst as a bland nonentity father or an admiring mother or a cock-sucking girlfriend. If he had done any of this at any point, he might not have so stubbornly sat on his anger until it tersely exploded. Spielvogel was constipated on the toilet, like father. He was so angry at this special younger man's ability to defecate that he finally let go and drowned his patient in an exploding interpretation. He rubbed Portnoy's face in it.

The outdated traditional concept of resistance also lends credibility to Spielvogel's technique. He conceptualizes Portnoy as being in resistance by virtue of his narcissistic, exhibitionist display. Since resistance has dominated, the analysis has not yet begun. What, however, is nonresistance, or the correct material? Should Portnoy have been more out of control, nonsensical, freely associative? Maybe so, in some ideal world, but this is not who this patient is as a person. Portnoy was being himself and showing himself in the playground of the analytic relationship. What more or better can a patient do but be himself? This manic, self-absorbed, overideational man was indeed being those ways in the here and now of the transference. The concept of resistance implies that the patient is doing something wrong. It is an evaluative notion that is implicitly, if not explicitly, critical and judgmental.

Should Portnoy be somebody other than who he is? Would this make him a good patient instead of such a hostile, self-aggrandizing one? Invoking the notion of resistance is tantamount to telling someone to stop being who he is and to be more like what the analyst wants. It is one thing if the patient excessively misses sessions, comes late, does not pay bills, and so forth. These enactments threaten the basic structure of the relationship and physically impede analytic engagement. Portnoy is talking and pointedly conveying to his analyst one of the essences of who he is. Of course, he is not showing all of himself. Were he to do that he would probably be finished with his analysis. He is vividly displaying his defensive character structure and therefore doing all that an analyst could ever want his patient to do. Unfortunately, Spielvogel sits on his feelings and develops a hatred for Portnoy via a prolonged, judgmental silence, followed by a devastating talionic blow.

Interpersonal analysts are not more prone to love their patients or less prone to feel destructively hateful than are Freudian analysts. They are not nicer, kinder, gentler, or more decent human beings. The advantage of the participant-observation model over the blank screen model lies in analysts' greater likelihood of awareness of both countertransference feelings and enactments, particularly the latter. Were I in Spielvogel's place, I never would have waited so long to speak. Quite in contrast, I probably would have verbally intervened very early, perhaps even in the initial session. As exemplified by Gill, I would have likely addressed the transference themes as they emerged. I hope that I would have pointed out to Portnoy that he was talking at me and not to me, that he was being exhibitionistic and looking for my admiration. I would have told him that his words and ideas and his brilliant mind often obscured his genuine feelings. When I was feeling admiring or awestruck by his brilliance or his incredible wit, I would have conveyed that he was trying to impress me or perhaps have me adore him as do his mother and his girlfriends. At times when I felt overwhelmed, competitively infuriated, bland in comparison to his sexual exploits, and so forth, I may have pointed out that he probably views me as similar to father or sister. I would likely address his disrespect for me and his powerful desire to be different than my depressed, constipated self. In short, my comments would be guided by my reflected upon, countertransference feelings. They would not normally be disclosures of my feelings but a transposition of my feelings and enactments into a description of what I believed was transpiring in the here and now. In addition, to the extent that the here and now countertransference field resembled historical patterns of interaction, the links of similarity in pattern would be made. My comments would be more descriptive than interpretive. They would likely address the "what" rather than the "why." The analysis would consist of moving back and forth from the field of the here and now playground to history and to current life, lining up the consistent patterns of interaction.

From my perspective, there is no value in waiting as long as Spielvogel did to intervene. The transference themes emerge immediately and if analysis of transference is the sine qua non of the process, the best road to it is to address transference themes from the beginning. In addition to this being more economical in time, it is less mystifying. The silent analyst makes himself into someone more profound than he actually is. It gives too much power to the analyst, who, after such verbal deprivation, sounds like a genius when he says anything. Spielvogel is Germanic, authoritarian, and judgmental, and his technique easily fits these personal characteristics. The interpersonal analytic philosophy is more democratic. It is a two-person psychology and not a relationship between a sick, distorting patient and a well, neutral, and objective analyst. Analytic commentary, from the beginning, more visibly portrays the analyst as visible and fallible. Comments are not for this purpose or to have this effect but it is an artifact of the method of working. It lends itself to a view of analyst as co-participant in contrast to expert or authority. The patient is more encouraged to comment on the nature of the content and form of the analysts' participation.

In the blank-screen method, the patient's commentaries tend to be more toward the analyst's depriving silence while the participant-observation method stimulates a wider range of observation on the patient's part. The freedom for the analyst to address the here and now themes from the beginning serves as a control for the buildup of feelings within the analyst. If Portnoy's anger, selfishness, disrespect, and so forth are pointed out early, it is less likely that these feelings will fester within the analyst, as they did with Spielvogel. Even within classical analytic circles, there has been a shift away from the concept of transference neurosis. This is the concept that most validated long periods of silence in order to facilitate an ultimate transference crescendo. Most Freudian analysts currently believe that intense transference experience exists on and off throughout the entire analysis, in contrast with the one period of transference neurosis. From a more current perspective, the active pointing out of the transference themes from the early stages of analysis onward has many advantages over Spielvogel's archaic technique. This approach has always been characteristic of most contemporary interpersonal analysts.

Despite every effort at neutrality and objectivity as well as the intention to constructively use countertransference feelings, analytic enactment is inevitable. The analyst unwittingly plays out with the patient the fundamental patterns in the patient's interactional life and becomes enmeshed in the system. Analysis thus occurs from within the system.

Were I Portnoy's analyst, I would have viewed him as special from the beginning. His brilliance, wit, and professional accomplishments would likely have dazzled me. I am especially excited by humor and I know that I would have laughed with Portnoy on many occasions. Portnoy led a life of being special—in his family, in academic and professional circles, and with women. He did everything he could to invoke this feeling in his analyst and although I can only assume Spielvogel felt it at some time, I am certain I would have. I very possibly would have become lost in this specialness, looking forward to vastly entertaining as well as poignant session after session. Were I aware of Portnoy being so special to me, I would have commented on the issue of specialness. More than likely, however, I would have not articulated it to myself and simply enacted with him, some facsimile of all those who have been so admiring. He most likely would have loved my response (which would be in tone or form, not in content) and escalated his performance, as he actually did with Spielvogel.

As Portnoy became more grossly manic and exhibitionistic and his repertoire became more obviously a comic shtick, I might have woken up to having been part of a narcissistic experience. I would have felt deceived and tricked. What I thought was a genuine connection to me was really an unrelated show. I was nothing but an adoring mother, having fun during my workday, admiring my favorite patient. I did not exist as an entity except to service this dynamo patient with blow jobs. Or I may have recognized that I was a bland father or sister in comparison to this star. From this role, I could have felt like a competitive fool, a loser, sitting on the toilet while the hero is holding court on center stage or in center field. He was Duke Snider and I was a substitute player in the minor leagues. Degradation breeds the fury of the underclass. From both positions — the deceived mother or lover, and the loser father or sister — my awestruck admiration would likely have congealed to rage. I believe this was the revenge and hatred of Spielvogel.

I hope that I would have addressed the above themes as I was aware of experiencing them, and thus avoided massive talionic retaliation. Addressing these themes means using the feelings about which I am aware to point out what I see transpiring in the analytic field or playground; for example, "It seems to me that the only thing you value about me is admiring you as did your mother and your girlfriends" or "It appears that in your eyes, I am a dull, bland, and ineffective man, as was your father and your sister in contrast with you," or "If I am not excited to see you or don't find you very special, you feel as devastated as you did with your Israeli woman."

My efforts to directly address these themes from within the analytic dyad have two major purposes. The first reflects the emotional impact of the patient's awareness of transference issues in the immediate, and the second, the effort to form a new relational configuration. For all nonclassical analysts, insight is only part of what is mutative. The analytic relationship certainly does provide increased awareness; the more it takes place in the here and now, the better. This, however, is never enough. The analyst must also develop with the patient a relationship different in quality from what has been historically internalized. This new relationship is not prescribed in advance or consciously pursued as such. If so, it would be too artificial and inauthentic. To be valuable, the new relationship must occur naturally; an artifact almost of analytic inquiry, observation, interpretation, and so forth. In the process of trying to clarify experience, the analyst works out of the repetitions that are so compelling. When I became aware of how I was caught up in Portnoy's world, my use of countertransference would aid me in trying to emerge from my enmeshment. It is the analyst's effort to try to climb out of his embeddedness in the patient's world that ultimately leads to new and mutative experience.

What may have eventually emerged from my consistent monitoring of transference themes, as I saw them develop from the very beginning? I believe that Portnoy's "cure" would lie in my ability to work out of my awestruck, admiring response, my depressed and deflated response, and my angry and retaliatory response. Were I able to do all of this in the context of my analytic inquiry and observation, Portnoy's characteristic way of being in the world may have shifted and this movement internalized. The cured Portnoy ideally would be less self-involved and more related, less guilty about his achievements or assets, and more able to tolerate his depressed or inadequate aspects. Portnoy, I suspect, will always be somewhat narcissistic, overly ideational, and emotionally distant. He and I may have become teammates, as long as I respected his position in center field where he could be a bit of a hero and maintain a comfortable distance from me. With all of my interest in the here and now transference, I would have to be cautious not to smother the man, and to leave him enough grass to roam alone.

There are no brilliant analysts and no interpretation is a breakthrough. The process is long and difficult and it is quite clear that no particular analytic technique has proven to be superior over any other. Every analyst must do what personally makes most sense and this of course has much to do with every analyst's transference identification with his or her own analyst.

Spielvogel may recover from his destructive hatred; one awful comment does not spoil an analysis. I would have loved Portnoy as I loved Roth's book and I would have hated Portnoy as did the first analyst I consulted hate me. I would have loved to work with Portnoy, since in love or hate he is so talented and in so many ways quite special. I undoubtedly would be intimidated by his being so special and so much more brilliant and witty than myself. The key for his successful analysis with me would be to learn to live with my experience of inferiority to him and to not be either a simple admiring fool or a vengeful tyrant.

REFERENCES

Epstein, L., and Feiner, A. (1979). *Countertransference*. New York: Jason Aronson.

Gill, M. (1982). *The Analysis of Transference*. Vol. 1. New York: International Universities Press.

Greenberg, J. (1991). *Oedipus and Beyond*. Cambridge, MA: Harvard University Press.

Hirsch, I. (1985). The rediscovery of the advantages of the participant-observation model. *Psychoanalysis and Contemporary Thought* 8:441–459.

Hoffman, I. (1983). The patient as interpreter of the analyst experience. *Contemporary Psychoanalysis* 19:389–422.

Levenson, E. (1991). *The Purloined Self*. New York: Contemporary Psychoanalytic Books.

Mitchell, S. (1988). *Relational Concepts in Psychoanalysis*. Cambridge, MA: Harvard University Press.

Racker, H. (1968). *Transference and Countertransference*. New York: International Universities Press.

Searles, H. (1979). *Countertransference and Related Subjects*. New York: International Universities Press.

Singer, E. (1970). *Key Concepts in Psychotherapy*. New York: Basic Books.

Wolstein, B. (1975). Countertransference: the psychoanalyst's shared experience and inquiry with his patient. *Journal of the American Academy of Psychoanalysis* 3:77–89.

8

Self Psychology Perspective: Portnoy's Shame and Self-Vulnerability: Illuminating the Porte-Noir

Andrew P. Morrison, M.D.

Through Philip Roth's biting, penetrating prose we learn of Alexander Portnoy's pain—his anxieties, his compulsive sexuality, his castration fears, and his ambivalent oedipal strivings. We also learn of his deeply embedded shame and humiliation and of the precarious state of his sense of self, ever teetering on the verge of disintegration and doom. Portnoy is driven by shame—over his Jewishness, over weakness and impotence, over concerns about being dirty—into desperate attempts to shore up his ambivalent, tormented self and to attain the longed-for self-image of grandiosity, strength, and perfection that so dominated his youth. Through Portnoy's meanderings we can discern the essential outline of anxious, narcissistically vulnerable contemporary man, the alienated self pathology that has attracted the attention and concern of current, post-Kohutian psychoanalysis. We can anticipate the challenges to Spielvogel as he listens and associates to his patient. Were he informed by the perspectives of psychoanalytic self psychology in addition to the dominant listening mode of 1967 when his patient's "kvetchings" took place,

139

he might have been sensitive to the issues of vulnerability that I shall emphasize in this chapter.

There can be no doubt about the importance of oedipal conflict, guilt, and superego-dominated ambivalence in this scion of the Promised Land. However, it is the language of shame that cries out so stridently at the analytic surface, and that must be addressed and accepted before attempting to penetrate to the conflictual depths of Oedipus. Quoting his own paper on "The Puzzled Penis," even that expert Spielvogel himself (in the introductory definition of "Portnoy's Complaint"), speaking of Portnoy's lack of sexual gratification, notes that fantasy and act lead to "overriding feelings of shame and the dread of retribution, particularly in the form of castration" (p. i/i). Further, the workings of Portnoy's shame carry with them their own depth, their own conflicts, their own inferiority, which must themselves be analyzed. His are the intrasystemic conflicts and tensions of aspirations and ideals that I have termed the *dialectic of narcissism* (Morrison 1989)—Portnoy's conflict over whether he should be totally self-sufficient and independent, without need, or loving, dependently merged with an idealized other. Before delving into the complexities of Portnoy's material, however, I will give a brief overview of my perspective on narcissism and shame, which will provide a framework for this case discussion.

Central to all narcissistic manifestations and phenomena is a longing for a sense of absolute specialness and uniqueness, a wish to be the "only" to an important, idealized other (Morrison 1986, 1989). This is the self's wish to matter, to be significant, which Heinz Kohut (1966, 1971) has demonstrated to have a legitimacy in treatment as in life, and which becomes expressed during analysis in the emergence of the selfobject transferences (for mirroring, idealization, and twinship needs). To the degree that these age-appropriate needs are adequately responded to and provided for during early development, the individual attains (or inhabits) a cohesive, reasonably stable, accepting and respecting self. Without such attunement and responsiveness—growing up in an atmosphere of inadequate or failed empathy—the self feels shaky, fragile, and depleted. It is not fruitful to debate the idea of the self as an *actual* entity in a process of disintegration or the existence of ego or id as tangible structure. Rather, it is the fact of the patient's *experience* that draws our attention and commands our interest. Analytic concern is necessary about our patients' pain and self-doubt, and their attempted regulation through grandiose self-aggrandizement, which, perforce, brings attention to matters of narcissism.

Shame is the central dysphoric affect of narcissistic conditions, much as guilt and anxiety serve for neuroses (Broucek 1991, Lewis 1971, Morrison 1983, 1989, Wurmser 1981). It is no coincidence that shame became a focus of psychoanalytic or development interest only in recent years as narcissism also attracted attention for study and treatment. I have found it particularly useful to conceptualize the experience of shame in terms of *failure in the attempted satisfaction or attainment of a goal or ideal*. My approach to shame involves the clarification of which ideal put forward by an individual is *not* being achieved, and then working with the patient to experience, better understand, and sometimes to modify ideals, either unattainable or unrealized. The dialectic of narcissism involves, as I conceive of it, a tension between the ideals of autonomy and worthiness for merger, with emphasis on one inevitably involving a feeling of failure vis-à-vis the other. Shame obtains, then, from a conviction of unworthiness arising from failure regarding the conflicting narcissistic models of perfection inhering in this dialectic.

More explicitly, shame is experienced about the state of the whole self, in contrast with feelings of guilt over particular pain-inflicting actions or thoughts. As guilt generates confession in an attempt to gain forgiveness for the "superego transgressions" (Piers 1953), shame tends toward hiding and concealment of the meager, lowly state of the self. The antidote to concealment in the treatment of shame involves the process of recognition, acknowledgment, and, ultimately, acceptance of the flawed, imperfect, weak, dirty self. Shame tends to generate its own language, and it becomes important to recognize the shame and humiliation that lie behind such phenomena as rage and contempt, and such self-descriptions as "insignificant," "pathetic," "ridiculous," "invisible," "a loser," "not good enough," "a freak." This language of shame, no doubt familiar to the readers of Roth's novel and certainly observed in our clinical practices, may be used clinically as an opening to work with the affect of shame and related narcissistic vulnerability.

With this brief overview of narcissism and shame from my perspective as a self psychology–influenced psychoanalyst, I turn to the case of Alexander Portnoy. Some of the foregoing discussion must have pointed to where I plan to go in considering Portnoy's complaints, for it is his *shame proclivity based on a vulnerability of self experience* that I consider central to understanding his difficulties.

Throughout the book, Portnoy quests for a clearer understanding of who he really is, of what constitutes his true identity. Is he the brilliant, good, obedient little Jewish boy of his parents' imaginings, or is he an evil, dirty, lustful man preoccupied with degrading women? Is he strong, forceful, and independent, or is he a weak, sniveling, and dependent baby? Is he capable of loving another, or is he totally preoccupied with pleasing himself alone? These are the questions that perpetually plague him. As Portnoy himself says about his Jewish parents,

> they were able to make us little Jewish boys believe ourselves to be princes on the one hand, unique as unicorns on the one hand, geniuses and brilliant like nobody has ever been brilliant and beautiful before in the history of childhood—saviors and sheer perfection on the one hand, and such bumbling, incompetent, thoughtless, helpless, selfish, evil little shits, little *ingrates*, on the other! [p. 118/129]

This statement, from Portnoy's own lips, succinctly expresses his narcissistic dilemma, the dramatic conflict of the dialectic, between his perfect uniqueness or his devastating shame. I refer to this conflict in terms of the expansive and contracted poles of the narcissistic dialectic (Morrison, unpublished).

He yearns to be the good, loving boy of his youthful memories — "A nice little Jewish boy? Please, I am the nicest little Jewish boy who ever lived! Only look at the fantasies, how sweet and savior-like they are!" (p. 247/260); the bar mitzvah *kvelling* expansively at the rabbi's praise: " 'devoted son, loving brother, fantastic honor student, avid newspaper reader . . . entered Weequahic High School this boy at the age of *twelve*, an I.Q. on him of 158' " (pp. 201–202/214). His grandiose fantasies move on to chief justice, ambassador, but rapidly he reverts to the image of pimp, self-reviling, chained for eternity to a toilet bowl. Arguing meekly that he felt the stirrings of love toward his object of lust, his imaginings retort that all he knows is self-love, preoccupation with self. These meanderings of a man with a shaky sense of self, moving abruptly between expansive grandiosity and contracted self-loathing, the oscillations in self-esteem regulation described by Reich (1960), I have referred to in terms of the dialectic of narcissism.

Aware of the fragility of his self-esteem and his longing for a firmer, cohesive sense of self, Portnoy yearns for his doctor to help him attain this greater strength. He calls out, "Bless me with manhood! Make me brave! Make me strong! Make me *whole*!" (p. 36/46). Along with fragility, Portnoy feels about himself that he is truly isolated, unconnected with others, alone. "*Oh*, so alone! Nothing but *self*! Locked up in *me*!" (p. 248/261). A dilemma that runs throughout Portnoy's exegesis is his doubting about his capacity to love. We have noted the "stirrings" of love that he felt momentarily toward The Monkey. "*A human being! Who can be loved*! But," he questions, "by *me*?" (p. 194/207). Later, equating himself with a "freak," he laments, "Lover of no one and nothing! Unloved and unloving!" (p. 251/264).

These qualities delineate, I suggest, the character structure and symptoms of a narcissistic character disorder. Alexander Portnoy describes for us, readers of his "text," the widest possible swings of self-assessment—from the grandiose, expansive extremes of great self-congratulation to self-debasing, contrite, and contracted feelings of smallness and worthlessness. He continually expresses the narcissistically vulnerable person's concern about the state of his self—its cohesion and firmness, feelings of self-regard, emptiness, capacities for attachment and love. Informed in our assessment by the writings of Kohut and self psychology, Portnoy represents a narcissistic personality disorder reflecting the *mirror-hungry personality* (Kohut and Wolf 1978): "Mirror-hungry personalities are impelled to display themselves to evoke the attention of others, who through their admiring responses will perhaps counteract the experience of worthlessness [and low self-esteem]" (Wolf 1988, p. 73).

How did Portnoy become so vulnerable, so exploitative, so needy? We must look to his own *experience* of his childhood, of his parental/caretaker environment, for answers about Portnoy's development. This position invokes the nature–nurture polemic that has so engaged psychoanalytic thinking since its beginnings; psychoanalytic self psychology directs our attention specifically to the quality and nature of Portnoy's selfobject experiences, which are so graphically detailed in his rantings. By selfobject, Kohut and his followers refer to *dimensions* of the intimate relationship in which the *function* and *responsiveness* of the object, rather than its *configurational* qualities, are in the foreground. Kohut (1971, 1972) emphasized that the selfobject is experienced as part of (an extension of) the self, under the self's control. Recent writers have emphasized that selfobject is best understood as experience rather than actual relationship (Lichtenberg 1991), and may be created totally from illusion as a "phantasy selfobject" (Bacal and Newman 1990, p. 196).

From Portnoy's many colorful descriptions, we learn that he viewed his mother as overwhelming, undifferentiatingly worshipful, yet simultaneously unattuned to her son's needs and unaware of her own destructive intrusiveness. He feels that she set him up to expect total approval and admiration from an attentive public, and in no way prepared him to *work* for his aspirations, to love another, in order to attain substance or self-worth. Certainly, his desire was stimulated by her seductiveness, her sexualization of their interactions, and clearly the oedipal origins of his sexual appetites is apparent to him, as to the reader. However, those elements assuredly will be discussed and elaborated by others in this volume. It is the elements of selfobject failure, and their impact on the evolving self-experience of Portnoy, that I wish to emphasize.

His mother's transgressions, her failure to adequately mirror and appreciate her son's needs for individuality and boundaries, are recounted in great number. Wielding a knife at him for refusing to eat what she placed before him, sending him for a box of Kotex when he was struggling with his own masculinity, laughing at his wish for a bathing suit with a jockstrap, the guilt that she invoked for his not telephoning regularly enough. "Why was this woman so grossly insensitive to the vulnerability of her own little boy" (p. 42/53). Why indeed! Yet, clearly Portnoy's experience and memories of his mother were of a woman unable to attune to her son's needs, intruding instead on his developing self, unresponsive to his desires for autonomy and privacy. His solace came from those rare times when he was able to participate in sanctioned times away from her invasiveness. As in baseball: "Thank God for center field! Doctor, you can't imagine how truly glorious it is out there, so alone in all that space. . . . Oh, how unlike my home it is to be in center field, where no one will appropriate unto himself anything that I say is *mine!*" (p. 68/78–79).

Faulty mirroring, repeated empathic failures on the part of his mother-as-selfobject, is delineated by Portnoy in his incantations against Sophie. But there is another pole in the "bipolar self" (Kohut 1977) — that of the idealized selfobject, whose function is to provide strength and calming, to allow for participation in the grand, admired stature of the powerful other. This function is usually provided by the father (Morrison 1984), and certainly there are moments when Portnoy captures that yearned-for sense of his own father. "Thank God! at least *he* had the cock and balls! . . . he was constructed like a man of consequence, two big healthy balls such as a king would be proud to put on display, and a *shlong* of magisterial length and girth. And they were *his*" (pp. 40–41/51). Differing from oedipal competition or castration fears, in this context at least we find Portnoy relieved and proud to have something — his physical/genital attributes — to admire in his father. This is especially striking in the context of his own experience of testicular retraction as a child.

But his genitals and physical strength alone seem all that Portnoy can find to admire in his father. Rather, the rest of his descriptions are of disappointment, disillusionment, and contempt. The failures of his father to satisfy Portnoy's needs for an idealizable selfobject are frequent, and are as important to his narcissistic vulnerability as are his mother's failures in mirroring. Kohut (1977) suggested that the idealized parental imago (as he called the idealizable selfobject) offers a "second chance" for the attainment of self-cohesion and esteem, and can to a degree repair the damage inflicted from inadequacies of the mirroring selfobject. One potential function of the idealized selfobject is to atone for, or protect against, the failures in mirroring.

Instead, Portnoy finds his father completely unable to counter or to protect him against his mother's intrusiveness; after describing the knife episode, for instance, he asks, "And why doesn't my father stop her?" (p. 16/26). Instead of the assertive, protective father who might invite idealization, Portnoy's early recollections of him are of a weak, constipated man "with a suppository up his ass," already the loser in competition with his precocious son. While playing baseball with his father, his disillusionment is profound as he realizes that his father can't hold the bat right; "I am suddenly overcome with such sadness: I want to tell him, *Hey, your hands are wrong*, but am unable to, for fear I might begin to cry — or he might!" (p. 9/19). His longing for a strong father is so great that he fantasizes giving his father strength through his own successes: "In my liberation would be his—from ignorance, from exploitation, from anonymity. To this day our destinies remain scrambled together in my imagination. . . . Still hoping, you see, still if-onlying, at the age of thirty-three" (p. 7/17). As selfobject, Portnoy's father disappoints, fails. Toward him Portnoy feels contempt and pity, and even fantasizes not only that he could succeed in murdering his father but *"Chances were he would help me along!"* (p. 40/50). To provide for himself, to enhance his father, Portnoy has to act as idealizable selfobject to the older man.

We find, then, that Portnoy's father has failed to provide strength, protection, admirable qualities in all but the genitals department, and thus had not been available to offer idealizable selfobject functions for his confused son. If anything, Portnoy felt that his own destiny would elevate his father, and his family's stature, out of the abyss in which they found themselves. "To make life harder, he loved me himself. He too saw in me the family's opportunity to be 'as good as anybody,' our chance to win honor and respect" (p. 3/13). Thus, not only were Portnoy's needs for responsive mirroring and idealization not fulfilled, but he was called upon to provide selfobject functions for each of his parents. We hear him yearning wistfully for a strong father whom he can idealize and with whom he can identify, a firm, assertive man who would help him set boundaries against the insensitivities and intrusions of his mother.

How does Portnoy attempt to establish self-integrity, cohesiveness, and meaning? Clearly, the realm in which he lashes out, gropes for sensation and aliveness, is through sexuality and sexualization. His forays into sexual stimulation are legion, including his early, compulsive experiments with masturbation, and his perpetual combat between love and utilization of the pornographic object for gratification of his lust. Throughout, Portnoy upbraids himself for his desire, equates himself with an animal, and recognizes the dangers and limitations on his sense of self imposed by his compulsive sexualization. "Question: Am I to consider myself one of the *fragmented* multitude? . . . Is it true that only if the sexual object fulfills for me the condition of being degraded, that sensual feeling can have free play?" (p. 185/198, emphasis added). Certainly, the incestuous and oedipal elements of this dilemma abound, and will be discussed elsewhere in this volume. But I suggest that Portnoy suffers fundamentally from a self disorder, with principal narcissistic concerns about disintegration, fragmentation, and depletion, for which his compulsive sexualization served primarily as an attempt at restitution and stabilization.

This point of view represents self psychology's perspective on compulsory sexual activity, whether masturbatory, perverse, or with a partner, by which sexualization represents a "disintegration product" from the self unresponded-to by inadequate or nonattuned (mirroring or idealizable) selfobjects. Such unempathic selfobject responses, including those from the selfobjects of the oedipal period, result in developmental arrests and those self-impairments leading to the kinds of difficulties that Portnoy describes. In a chapter on the therapeutic process in his book on self psychology, Wolf (1988) writes, "Pathological and neurotic sexuality are conceptualized as deriving from faulty selfobject experiences which have fragmented the self and yielded disintegration products that have been organized into neurotic symptoms or sexualized behavior" (p. 121n). Similarly Meyers (1991) states, "Sexualization . . . is the psychological use of sexual activity to avoid painful affects of fragmentation anxiety, emptiness, and depression, due to a loss of selfobject function." For Portnoy, compulsive sexualization is an attempt to regain a sense of aliveness and agency hindered by his usual tenuous involvement with others, and his overall feeling of deadness and lethargy.

For example, about masturbation Portnoy told his analyst, "Doctor, do you understand what I was up against? My wang was all I really had that I could call my own" (p. 32/42) (this from an era when "wang" meant other than computer hardware!). He questioned, ". . . alone on my bed in New York, why am I still hopelessly beating my meat? Doctor, what do you call this sickness I have?" (p. 35/46). Were I Spielvogel, I believe that I would be thinking about sickness of self, narcissistic vulnerability, with its one potential avenue of assertion and self-reassurance—genital stimulation and desire. Related to this conundrum, the disappearance of Portnoy's testicle into his abdominal cavity caused him to fear for his very masculinity, among other things another challenge to the integrity and consistency of his sense of himself, engendering the sexualizing solution to his self-doubts. "What if my penis went dry and brittle, and one day, while I was urinating, snapped off in my hand? Was I being transformed into a girl?" (pp. 37–38/48). In a later fantasy of catching syphilis from a girl whom he encountered along with his high school friends, he imagines his penis as a "black, plastic thing" having fallen off onto the kitchen floor, causing frenzy in and evoking humiliating descriptions by his hysterical parents.

Portnoy's sexual descriptions turn, now, from masturbation to copulation, and The Monkey enters his interpersonal world. "Already two months had passed since the pickup on Lexington Avenue, and still, you see, the same currents of feeling carrying me along: desire, on the one hand, *delirious* desire (I'd never known such abandon in a woman in my life!), and something close to contempt on the other" (p. 184/196). In The Monkey, in *shikses*, Portnoy finds a vehicle for his contempt, a container for his own self-loathing (which I will discuss shortly), and an object who affirms his sexual activities as he strives toward the longed-for self-reparation. She knows that he spews degradation upon her—" 'It's just practically humanly im*possible* for anybody to be as stupid as you think I am!' " (p. 196/209); " 'There are those fucking orbs already picking out every single thing that's *wrong* with me! . . . I mean I can't even give you the time of day without *the look*: oh shit, here comes another dumb and stupid remark out of that brainless twat.' " (p. 211/224). Words like "leper," images of groaning with "disgust," delineate Portnoy's feelings toward the woman he easily picked up on the street.

This disdain and loathing toward the woman who elicits Portnoy's greatest sexual excitement and provides for previously unimagined gratification is consistent with the view of his sexualizations as attempts at repair of a shaky, potentially disintegrating self. His sexual excitement, coupled with contempt for the object of his lustful desires, reflects disintegration products of his fixated and damaged self. The contempt that he feels toward The Monkey and others are externalizations, projective identifications, of his own self-contempt and self-loathing, attempts to relocate his own self-hatred and shame into a receptive "other" (Morrison 1989). No wonder that he fails in his attempts to feel some tenderness and love toward her, when it is so important for her to serve as container for his own self-degradation and fragmentation. No wonder, also, that Portnoy fails in his quest to feel sexual desire and satisfaction, or to attain closeness with those "uncontaminated" Ivy-Leaguers, "healthy . . . as milkmaids," who could *not* provide the appropriate vessel into which to evacuate his self-loathing.

In Israel, as in other encounters with ambivalently held women, Portnoy is rendered impotent when he cannot readily discharge his contempt. Familiar as the madonna–prostitute dichotomy of classical oedipal dynamics, it is the case that certain women fail as sexual objects for Portnoy because they do not allow for him to dispose of his own self-hatred and products of his self-disintegration, paradoxically adding to his humiliation through the body failure and fragmentation of impotence. Those who do serve that function—the receptive selfobject—cannot possibly be loved because of the smearing contempt engendered from Portnoy's own self-fragmentation.

Whether through his masturbatory activities and fantasies, or through comingled sexualization with The Monkey or her "sisters," Portnoy's sexuality and his perverse fantasies and inclinations are fundamental expressions of the deep despair and arrested self-development that have become his lot. We have considered his self-difficulties from the perspective of narcissistic vulnerability, and have examined the developmental sources of his fragile self as failure in appropriate responsiveness of his parental selfobjects. Portnoy presents with the panache of apparent oedipal conflicts, but he himself constantly calls our attention to his tortured, inchoate self. Thus, the oedipal caste of his difficulties represents a pseudoneurotic patina to a fundamentally narcissistic character disorder — the type of confusing picture that so frequently emerges currently in our consulting rooms, and that Kohut has helped us to sort out through our understanding of the emerging selfobject transferences.

With this background on Portnoy's narcissistic imbalance and issues, I turn to the matter of shame as revealed in *Portnoy's Complaint*. As I said at the beginning of this chapter, shame lies at the heart of narcissistic phenomena, whether in response to overwhelming grandiosity or to the defeat and constriction about self-failure and despair. Portnoy reveals his shame and humiliation at practically every turn in the book — consciously, directly, and not hidden from his own awareness, as may alternatively be the case in other shame-immersed patients. What I have called the "language of shame" permeates each aspect of his lamentation, and these feelings about himself are absolutely central to his problems. Without focusing attention on his shame, any attempt at successful treatment of Portnoy would be doomed to failure.

Let's look, then, at the manifestations of Portnoy's shame, and how they relate to his psychopathology. First, we have Spielvogel's defining statement about Portnoy's "overriding feelings of shame" (p. i/i) — so prominent were they, that even this classical analyst of the 1960s (when shame was all but ignored by psychoanalysis) was impelled to comment on them. Further, in our previous discussion of narcissism, vulnerability, and self, shame has been purposely circumvented but palpably implied; now we can fill in the spaces.

For instance, as Portnoy speaks of his longings to find
something admirable in his father's qualities (e.g., his coarse-
ness), he laments, "If only I could have nourished myself upon
the depths of his vulgarity, instead of that too becoming a source
of shame. Shame and shame and shame and shame—every place
I turn something else to be ashamed of" (p. 49/50). Competing in
fantasy with other Jewish sons about the noxiousness of their
respective parents, Portnoy jousts, "I can match you, you bastard, humiliation for humiliation, shame for shame" (p. 118/129).
In his final exegesis on shame, as he reflects on Diaspora Jews
and his encounter with Naomi, Portnoy recalls her as saying that
the Diaspora "had produced just such disagreeable men as
myself—frightened, defensive, self-deprecating, unmanned and
corrupted by life in the gentile world" (p. 265/278); and "Temptation and disgrace! Corruption and self-mockery! Self-
deprecation—and self-defecation too! Whining, hysteria, compromise, confusion, disease! Yes, Naomi, I am soiled, oh, I am
impure—and also pretty fucking tired, my dear, of never being
quite good enough for The Chosen People!" (p. 266/279).

We thus learn of the ubiquity of Portnoy's shame feelings; their
relationship to his longing to find something admirable and
idealizable in his father; and the self-definitions of "unmanned,"
"disgrace," "soiled," which give shape to his shame experience.
Everywhere he looks, Portnoy finds shame—not surprisingly
since the shame he feels defines each aspect of himself. He
describes qualities about his own shame that are characteristic of
men's shame in general, such as weakness and lack of masculinity. (Shame in men tends to be characterized by feelings of genital
inferiority and impotence, as well as concerns about competence
and efficacy. These represent failures, falling short of ideals,
which men tend to set forth for themselves within our cultural
context. Failure in achievement does not seem to be one of
Portnoy's major problems.) Manifestations of Portnoy's feelings
of shame include the episode of his mother's taunting him about
his "little thing," his concern about his "disappeared" testicle and

feared transformation into a girl, and of his varied experiences with impotence. Another characteristic of shame that Portnoy reveals is the sense of being dirty, "soiled," the childhood remembrance of never being able to rid his anus of the "zitz" that marred his underpants, leaving the telltale mark for his mother to see.

Portnoy fears that he will never be quite good enough for the "Chosen" — his mother, his rabbi. We recall the little Alex striving to do and think everything just as his mother would have him do. He sets for himself impossible ideals to attain — nothing short of perfection. "I drop to the doormat to beg forgiveness for my sin (which is what again?) and promise her nothing but perfection for the rest of our lives" (p. 14/24). He cites his sin for which he seeks forgiveness, but characteristically he cannot figure out what it is. This is one instance, I believe, where Portnoy confuses shame with guilt — sins are specific actions that one confesses and for which one seeks forgiveness. Shame, on the other hand, is unnamed, amorphous, and all-encompassing. The only antidote to shame is, as Portnoy promises, perfection; reparation from shame comes not from forgiveness but from self-acceptance — the very opposite of the scorn and self-deprecation that he heaps on himself.

He finds himself "never quite good enough," but not good enough for what? It seems to me that his quest is to attain those ideals, well-symbolized by the "Chosen People," that he sets forth for himself, or that he felt mandated by his society or his insatiable maternal selfobject. These ideals (or goals or tasks) include cleanliness, strength, potency, cleverness, morality, and the capacity to love. His shame represents the conviction of failure, inferiority, defect, and unworthiness that leave him ever feeling that he falls short of attaining his cherished aspirations. [For a similar perspective, described for depression but equally relevant for shame, see Bibring (1953).] Whether as a morally worthy Assistant Commissioner of Human Opportunity, a diligent and devoted son, a phallically assertive and gratifying lover, or a human being capable of compassion and love, Portnoy always experiences himself, in failure, left alone with the pangs of isolating shame.

In the shame exegesis just quoted, Portnoy used the constructs of disgrace; elsewhere, he talks incessantly about humiliation. These are the public, interpersonal arms of shame — where there is humiliation, there is a humiliator (usually a highly significant other). Similarly, where disgrace occurs, a valued audience is present or anticipated to witness the weakness, soiling, passivity, or indiscretion. About his relationship to The Monkey, for instance, Portnoy fantasizes, "the whole neighborhood will know at last the truth about my dirty little mind. The so-called genius will be revealed in all his piggish proclivities and feelthy desires" (p. 200/213). Similarly, his fantasied retribution for mentioning his masturbation to his old high school friend Arnold Mandel was, "Mistake! What if he blabs to the *Daily News?* ASST HUMAN OPP'Y COMMISH FLOGS DUMMY, *Also Lives in Sin, Reports Old School Chum.* The headlines. Always the headlines revealing my filthy secrets to a shocked and disapproving world" (p. 174/186). These concerns about revelation underscore the element of secrecy, hiding, and privacy that form an important part of Portnoy's (and everyone else's) shame. Of course, an additional element about these concerns is their grandiosity, underscoring the relationship of Portnoy's shame to his narcissism. His fantasied exposure presumes that everyone in the neighborhood has no greater preoccupation than Portnoy's indiscretions, or that the *Daily News* would certainly feature them as their primary new item.

This public augmented quality of Portnoy's shame must be contrasted with the very private, personal, internal experience that he feels in isolation, alone, and that he associates with his sense of utter aloneness, unlovability, and personal doubts about his capacity to love. These qualities he identifies with one of the paramount signifiers in the language of shame — "The *freak* I am! Lover of no one and nothing! Unloved and unloving!" (p.

251/264). Here Portnoy feels his own isolation, condemns himself with self-deprecation; no one need be present to observe or scorn his freakishness. Portnoy condemns himself for his lack of loving attachment in this passage, as throughout the book, because of his own failure, his own ideal of libidinal intimacy. Certainly there are others who excoriate him for these same failures—The Monkey, Naomi—but their criticisms fall on his own self-loathing about his lack of loving attachment. This is a major example of Portnoy's private shame, felt about himself even when concealed from others. Other examples include his doubts about his values and worthiness compared with his childhood ideals, and his integrity in serving in his present job. These illustrations of what might be called "moral shame" belie the earlier (psycho-analytic/anthropological) view of shame, which claimed that it was always social, external, and superficial, compared with weightier guilt.

It is worth noting that Portnoy feels shame not only about the state and qualities of his self—his thoughts, his sexual behavior, his unworthiness for the job he has been awarded—but also for his feelings, his sense of passivity, his shame itself. He feels ashamed of the contempt and degradation that he recognizes and expresses toward The Monkey. Similarly, he experiences shame at the fear and passivity with which he approaches life. "Oh my secrets, my shame, my palpitations, my flushes, my sweats! The way I respond to the simple viscissitudes of human life! Doctor, I can't stand any more being frightened like this over nothing!" (p. 36/46). This shame over feelings (especially about shame itself) is *secondary* shame, in contrast with the shame that Portnoy feels about attributes of his self (*primary* shame). Another relevant distinction to be made—although not one of great prominence to Portnoy—is that between the affect of shame itself and the more cognitive awareness of potential shame, which serves as a *signal* of behaviors or attributes that might engender future shame. This has been called *shame anxiety* (Levin 1971), and serves a signal function similar to signal anxiety itself. Portnoy, however, seems quite at home with his shame, familiar (perhaps even wallowing) in it, and not particularly given to changing his character or behavior to avoid it. This is not to suggest, though, that Portnoy's shame is not a source of great pain and disturbance to him; later in the chapter I will discuss the relevance of shame to Portnoy's analytic treatment and the potential technical approaches in that treatment.

No discussion of Portnoy's shame would be complete without a consideration of his complex relationship to his Jewish heritage. Certainly, one potential source of shame relates to one's membership in a cultural or social group, either by exclusion or by forced inclusion. "What is wrong with me that I cannot gain acceptance by (Group X)?" or, alternatively, "How can I ever achieve goals or ideals as a (Y)?" Much has been written in the social psychological literature about shame and self-hatred among lower castes, blacks (e.g., Tocqueville 1838), and Jews (e.g., Allport 1954, Lewin 1941). Indeed, Portnoy's florid self-castigations might serve as a text about ambivalence. The sabra Naomi berates him with, "'Mr. Portnoy,' she said, raising her knapsack from the floor, 'you are nothing but a self-hating Jew'" (p. 265/278). Certainly, we might argue that Portnoy is much, much more, while agreeing that his Jewish self-hatred is an important piece of his self-image.

Consider his fantasied attempts to hide his Jewishness while ice-skating with "*shikses*," while dining with The Pumpkin's family, and the retribution he delights in as he imagines passing venereal disease on to the sabra community through intercourse with Naomi: "Screw off, Jewboy! Get off the ice and leave these girls alone!" (p. 149/161); "Oh, what's the difference anyway, I can lie about my name, I can lie about my school, but how am I going to lie about this fucking nose?" (p. 148/160). Portnoy's goal is to hide his Jewishness, but he realizes that he cannot carry his pretense beyond what he feels to be his telltale nose: "You have got J-E-W written right across the middle of that face—look at the schnoz on him, for God's sakes! That ain't a nose, it's a hose!"

(p. 149/160–161). From this, Portnoy fantasizes sacrificing his authenticity by concealing his origin, pretending to another. His delicious image of his name being a "corruption" (another shame-related word) from the French " 'porte noir, meaning black door or gate. Apparently in the Middle Ages in France the door to our family manor house was painted . . .'. . . 'You seem like a very nice person, Mr. Porte-Noir, but why do you go around covering the middle of your face like that?' " (pp. 148–149/160). Along with his self-hatred, deception, and anger goes envy of the Christian world, from which he has felt permanently excluded: "So don't tell me we're just as good as anybody else, don't tell me we're Americans just like they are. No, no, these blond-haired Christians are the legitimate residents and owners of this place. . . . America is a shikse nestling under your arm whispering love love love love love!" (pp. 145–146/157).

Portnoy's shame over his Jewish identity, his embarrassment about his Jewish physiognomy, and envy of and longing for the shikses, alternates at other times with disdain for the same Christians after whom he lusts: "'What kind of a dream am I living in? Being with such a person is for me all wrong! Meaning-less! A waste of everybody's energy and character and time!'" (p. 209/222).

Self-hatred, concealment, dissembling, envy, and contempt of self and other — ingredients all of the psychology and language of shame. Each of these elements reflects the inevitable manifestations of narcissistic disequilibrium. We have examined Portnoy's self-condemnations and shame, and here we see his attempts at self-explanation about his shame in regard to the external world. His own self-loathing is externalized, projected onto an all-too-willing or appropriate "other." He tries to rid himself of his shame through this externalization, and yet he remains caught in the dilemma of envy/contempt toward that "other," as well as a similar dilemma in the conflict between disdain and (self-protective) grandiosity in his view of himself. These are the conflicting issues that I have discussed previously as the expansive and contracted poles in the dialectic of narcissism (Morrison 1989), particularly in a man with similar dynamics in the case of Cristophe; even the fictional name I gave this patient reflects similar pretense as "Porte-Noir" does for our protagonist.

We are left, then, with the challenges to Spielvogel. How does a self psychology approach to the treatment of narcissistic vulnerability and shame inform the analysis of Alexander Portnoy? First, self psychology, like all good analysis, requires the existence of a trusting and accepting ambience, and it seems, through the intimacy and lack of self-conscious reserve in Portnoy's expressions, that such an ambience is present. We note relatively little attention to any of Spielvogel's *configurational* qualities, but rather that Portnoy relates to him, believes in him, as an interested, potentially helpful listener. We hear none of the specific assumptions or attributions toward him that would reflect transferential displacement from either father or mother. Rather, we note Portnoy's wish to be heard, understood, and to have his dazzling rhetoric admired. Kohut's teachings about the inevitable emergence of selfobject transferences in the treatment of the narcissistically vulnerable patient seem relevant here. In his use of Spielvogel, Portnoy has created/experienced a good *mirroring selfobject*, serving as an empathic listener to the emergence of his self-needs, and providing the (presumed) function of attentive responsiveness. The challenge to Spielvogel will be to *allow* himself to remain in that (faceless) role, without the need to prematurely interpret, to otherwise impose his own self-structure into Portnoy's universe, and to contain his own inevitable countertransference reactions at being placed in an undifferentiated role without retaliating with boredom, withdrawal, or anger.

While the analytic ambience seems affirming and able to generate adequate trust to call forth Portnoy's complaints, more feedback and clarification of the analyst's presence, understanding, and acceptance of the analysand's feelings would have been helpful. For example, when Portnoy recalled his father's pathetic harangue about taking piano lessons, he laments "But what he had to offer I didn't want—and what I wanted he didn't have to offer. . . .Why must it continue to cause such pain? At this late date! Doctor, what should I rid myself of, tell me, the hatred . . . or the love?" (pp. 25–26/36). The analyst might have replied something like "A real dilemma, this, about love and hate. You wanted so much from him, and it felt like you got so little. Yes, the pain, the longing, the disappointment."

In a related segment, when Portnoy brings together images of Jewish suffering, his compulsive masturbation, shame ("secrets," "flushes," and "sweats"), and fright, he pleads with his analyst to make him brave, strong, and *whole*. Here would have been a good moment, it seems to me, for Spielvogel to have brought together his understanding of Portnoy's father-longing for a strong man to help him out of his self-debasement, and his yearnings for an idealizable selfobject within the analytic experience to provide him with the power to heal his (fragmenting) self and to attain cohesion. Spielvogel might have said, noncritically, "So you would like for me to be the one to make up for your father's failures, to stand up to your mother, to show you how to become whole." This, without the traditional tendency to confront him about unreality or entitlement, might have represented a self psychology intervention and transference interpretation. It also would have shifted the sense of agency from the analyst "making" him whole, to that of helper and guide in that project.

Again, when Portnoy recalls his mother's humiliating response to his wish to be given a bathing suit with a jockstrap, Spielvogel might have acknowledged the humiliation and pain, and then have affirmed Alex's experience that "Your memories of your mother were of a woman who didn't leave you with much room or freedom to develop, to grow independently. As though your testicle were still in hiding in your abdomen, the way you recall her assaulting and ridiculing you." He might even at this point have inquired about Portnoy's potential pain or anger, trying to help him to identify and gain access to his childhood affective experience. In addition, he might have acknowledged the self-conscious origins of his patient's feelings of shame, indicating that these feelings could have been the poison from which derived so much of his behavior, compulsive sexualization, and feelings of fragmentation. Such a comment would have indicated his acceptance and understanding of much of Portnoy's distress, and have pointed to connections between these feelings that might ultimately provide a unifying developmental integration.

Essentially, then, I am referring to an analytic approach that allows for the flourishing and embellishments of the patient's longings, self-deprecation, and despair, coupled with the unfolding of selfobject transferences that address his needs for attunement and acceptance (i.e., mirroring), and for participation in strength and wholeness (i.e., idealizing). This ambience, and these feelings themselves, become, then, the focus of analytic exploration, including particularly those ruptures in the analytic bond that usually relate to earlier problematic caregiver experiences (i.e., empathic selfobject failures). In suggesting some possible interventions available to Spielvogel, I have tried to indicate ways that he might have forwarded this process. On the other hand, the patient's uncritical openness and willingness to reveal his feelings suggest that he felt comfortable enough in the analytic ambience.

I will end, as does Portnoy, with Spielvogel's first (and only) words, since these are the best indication we can get about his technical stance, and because I find inferences made from his comment to be particularly troubling from a self psychology point of view. "So [said the doctor]. Now vee may perhaps to begin. Yes?" (p. 274/287). While it is certainly possible that Spielvogel was referring to the end of evaluation and the beginning of treatment proper, I hear it differently. This comment suggests that Spielvogel considered everything that had preceded in the analysis — Portnoy's whole narrative — to be mush, avoidance, digression, irrelevancies, that the *real* work of analysis would be something else. It implies that Portnoy's stance toward himself must somehow change, that he must be a different patient from the one he is or has been, that he must become more self-analytical and curious, less kvetchy and demanding.

I fear that the doctor's real message is that Portnoy has, up until now, been inadequate as a patient, and that what has gone on so far has not mattered much. Among other things, I think it is apparent how actively humiliating and shame-provoking such an assertion would be to an analysand. But beyond this, it implies that the analyst sits in judgment, discerns what is relevant and what is not, and determines authoritatively what the content and process of analysis should be. It also trivializes the whole matter of analytic ambience that I have just discussed. It seems to me that Spielvogel is suggesting that the analytic context has been, so far, either irrelevant or incorrect. A more charitable (and probably more prevalent) view would be that establishment of an ambience or environment of safety (i.e., therapeutic alliance) is a necessary context in order to hold, or allow for, the unfolding of the *real* analytic work (which is pure interpretation and reconstruction of the genetic past as experienced in the transferential present).

I believe that in the unfolding of the self-deprecating and shame-infused feelings of Portnoy's diatribes, and in the beginning evolution of the selfobject transferences that I have described, the analytic work is already well under way. Portnoy is able to share his pain—his fears, his shame, his feelings of insubstantiality. These feelings are *not* to be treated simply as defenses or digressions from something else, from some more fundamental feelings. Rather, the observations and feelings themselves are true, relevant, and will be the coinage of the shared universe that will continue to evolve between analysand and analyst. The analyst will have countertransference feelings stirred up by Portnoy—points of identification, resonance with his own shame experiences, revulsion—and these will or will not be shared or utilized with his patient. By staying with his patient's subjective experience, the analyst will discover and make known connections between shame over weakness and father-hunger, between oedipal lust and guilt, and feelings of smallness. Portnoy's fright and shame will, at times, be seen to defend with passivity against feared retaliation for positive oedipal longings and competitive feelings within and outside the transference. But the self-psychologically informed analytic attitude would never include pushing aside our patient's efforts with the implication that somehow they had not been adequate. With what I hear Spielvogel revealing of his attitude toward Portnoy, I fear for the future of their joint venture.

REFERENCES

Allport, G. (1954). *The Nature of Prejudice*. Cambridge, MA: Addison-Wesley.

Bacal, H. A., and Newman, K. M. (1990). *Theories of Object Relations: Bridges to Self Psychology*. New York: Columbia University Press.

Bibring, E. (1953). The mechanism of depression. In *Affective Disorders*, ed. P. Greenacre, pp. 13–48. New York: International Universities Press.

Broucek, F. J. (1991). *Shame and the Self*. New York: Guilford.

Kohut, H. (1966). Forms and transformations of narcissism. *Journal of the American Psychoanalytic Association* 14:243–272. [Also in *Essential Papers on Narcissism*, ed. A. P. Morrison, pp. 61–87. New York: New York University Press, 1986].

———— (1971). *The Analysis of the Self*. New York: International Universities Press.

———— (1972). Thoughts on narcissism and narcissistic rage. *Psychoanalytic Study of the Child* 27:360–399. New Haven, CT: Yale University Press.

———— (1977). *The Restoration of the Self*. New York: International Universities Press.

Kohut, H., and Wolf, E. S. (1978). The disorders of the self and their treatment—an outline. *International Journal of Psycho-Analysis* 59:413–425. [Also in *Essential Papers on Narcissism*, ed. A. P. Morrison, pp. 61–87. New York: New York University Press, 1986.]

Levin, S. (1971). The psychoanalysis of shame. *International Journal of Psycho-Analysis* 52:355–362.

Lewin, K. (1941). Self-hatred among Jews. *Contemporary Jewish Record* 4:219–232.

Lewis, H. B. (1971). *Shame and Guilt in Neurosis*. New York: International Universities Press.

Lichtenberg, J. D. (1991). What is a selfobject? *Psychoanalytic Dialogues* 1:455–479.

Meyers, S. J. (1991). Panel on sex, sexuality, and sexualization. 14th Annual Psychology of the Self Conference, Chicago, IL, October.

Morrison, A. P. (1983). Shame, the ideal self, and narcissism. *Contemporary Psychoanalysis* 19:295–318. [Also in *Essential Papers on Narcissism*, ed. A. P. Morrison, pp. 348–371. New York: New York University Press, 1986.]

———— (1984). Working with shame in psychoanalytic treatment. *Journal of the American Psychoanalytic Association* 32:479–505.

———— (1986). Introduction. In *Essential Papers on Narcissism*. New York: New York University Press.

———— (1989). *Shame: The Underside of Narcissism.* Hillsdale, N.J.: The Analytic Press.

Piers, G. (1953). Shame and guilt: a psychoanalytic study. In *Shame and Guilt,* ed. G. Piers and M. Singer, pp. 15–55. New York: W. W. Norton.

Reich, A. (1960). Pathologic forms of self-esteem regulation. *Psychoanalytic Study of the Child* 15:215–232. New York: International Universities Press. [Also in *Essential Papers on Narcissism,* ed. A. P. Morrison, pp. 44–60. New York: New York University Press, 1986.]

Tocqueville, A. de (1838). *Democracy in America.* vol. 1. New York: George Dearborn.

Wolf, E. (1988). *Treating the Self.* New York: Guilford.

Wurmser, L. (1981). *The Mask of Shame.* Baltimore, MD: Johns Hopkins University Press.

9

Intersubjectivity Perspective: An Intersubjective Discussion of *Portnoy's Complaint*

Shelley Doctors, Ph.D.

INTRODUCTION

Woody Allen might have been speaking for Alexander Portnoy when he called masturbation sex with someone you love. How Portnoy, the compulsive masturbator, becomes a man unable to love and, eventually, unable to have sex, is the subject of this chapter. Can we understand the subjective meaning he has made of his life experiences? Further, will this understanding illuminate his eventual misery and dysfunction in a coherent, comprehensive, plausible, and appealing manner? My goal is to do just that by applying intersubjective theory to Portnoy's Complaint.

ON APPLYING INTERSUBJECTIVE PSYCHOANALYTIC THEORY TO A STUDY OF PORTNOY

Psychoanalytic interpretations of literature impose the conventions of one discipline on the product of another. Such hybrid activity ought to make us wary of what is claimed for the fruits of the process. It is important not to confuse an idea of our own (which the literary author's material may graciously illustrate) with a grander idea of what the literary material "really" shows.

Paul Ornstein (1990) has eloquently argued that when analysts offer their "own supposedly more accurate . . . responses [to an analysis presented by another, they are] already dealing with another analysis, the one . . . just conjured up [in the mind of the observer]" (p. 480). I respect the integrity of Roth's novel and recognize that its success derives, in part, from his having created a work that has an inherent coherence; we accept that the childhood described, the adult character, the symptomatology, and the analytic process portrayed are *intrinsically* related. Thus my comments are intended to elucidate my own psychoanalytic views. While I hope they may inspire others to consider the worthiness of such views, they should not be taken as an attempt to improve upon Roth's work.

It should be easy for analysts to grasp this nonrevisionist view quite personally if they consider how they might react if one of their interpretations were subjected to a variety of criticisms, literary or otherwise. I have always thought that the tenacity with which analysts defended their particular views of someone else's psychological reality (and the related ferocity with which differing psychoanalytic views are often attacked) might be related to the enormous difficulty attendant on the nature of psychoanalytic work itself—the attempt to gain access to someone else's subjective reality. One aspect of that essential difficulty is the fact that in psychoanalysis the observer is also the observed (Stolorow and Atwood 1979). The psychoanalyst, even when striving for so-called objectivity, is part of the field of observation. Thus the psychoanalytic situation has been defined by the intersubjectivists as the interplay between the differently organized subjective worlds of observer and the observed (Atwood and Stolorow 1984, Stolorow et al. 1987). Gaining access to the subjective organization of another is always attained through one's own already patterned personality. The analyst, attempting to enter another's world empathically, must also strive to be aware of the influence of her own organizing activity on her "understanding" of her patient and be alert to how her very activity is being organized by her patient.

Intersubjectivists are interested in how people structure their experience: What patterns and themes characterize the way they tend to experience the world? People tend to organize experience in such a way that certain motifs emerge as characterizing disparate domains in their lives. Through these unconscious organizing principles, a person's experiences of self and other begin to assume typical forms. These invariants, or personal patterns, are neither replicas of interpersonal events nor simple internalizations. A focus on the distinctive structure of meanings, which form the inner pattern of a life, provides a conceptual bridge for understanding the close functional relationship between character and personal conduct. The basic focus of analysis is the illumination of the structure of the patient's subjective experience. The goal of psychoanalysis is its transformation.[1]

The term *intersubjective* extends the idea of the structure of one person's subjective experience to the notion of the field created by the intersection of two subjectivities. Normal development and pathogenesis are both conceptualized as occurring in specific intersubjective contexts. In the psychoanalytic situation, the patient and analyst form the indissoluble psychological system through which the patient's psychological structure is to be elucidated and changed (Stolorow et al. 1987). With this as background, it is apparent that many intersubjective systems could be the focus of an analysis of *Portnoy's Complaint*:

1. The intersubjective matrix formed by the author and his work. This usually takes the form of speculations about

---

1. This discussion draws on the ideas expressed in Atwood and Stolorow (1984).

conjunctions between the psychology of the author and that of a character or circumstance. Such a project might be appealing, particularly because *Patrimony* (Roth 1991) provides an intriguing hint of a transformation in Roth's experience of his own father. For present purposes, this will not be undertaken.

2. The intersubjective field formed by my own psychological organization and those of the personalities of the novel. This aspect is acknowledged to be inevitably present, though no attempt will be made to analyze it explicitly.

3. The intersubjective systems within which Portnoy's psychological organization took form (the developmental relationships with mother, father, etc.).

4. The intersubjective field reflected in the evolving relationship between the Jews and the larger society, both as this interaction contributed to the personalities of Sophie and Jack Portnoy and as it affected the development of Alexander Portnoy's sense of himself.

5. The intersubjective systems implicated in the development and maintenance of psychological symptoms.

6. The intersubjective field formed by Portnoy and his analyst, Dr. Spielvogel, which defines the psychoanalytic situation.

I will analyze the last four intersubjective systems, believing that taken together, these four topics offer an intersubjective view of the nature of Portnoy's "complaint." The intersubjective approach is firmly rooted in self psychology. Unfortunately, at present, self psychology is often misunderstood as pertaining only to psychological disturbances that reflect inadequate structuralization. While an important achievement of self psychology is the extension of psychoanalytic treatment to people who, because of structural deficits, were previously believed to be untreatable (Kohut 1971, 1977), self psychology is highly relevant to people who have consolidated psychological structures that are too inflexible. Considering various intersubjective systems that pertain to Portnoy's pathology may shed light on the leitmotifs that rigidly characterize his experience. Portnoy exemplifies the severely constricted personality hobbled by defensive structures that operate inflexibly to prevent the emergence of emotional conflict and subjective danger — the quintessential neurotic character.

AN INTERSUBJECTIVE VIEW OF ALEXANDER PORTNOY'S DEVELOPMENT

Alexander Portnoy's "complaint" is an anguished plea for understanding from the beloved parents he can neither understand nor forgive. He pleads to be left alone, though he takes them with him psychologically wherever he goes. Implicitly, he seems to know that something about his importance to them and their obsessive devotion to him is contributing to the torment of his life. In psychoanalysis perhaps he can understand how this could be, and thus free himself. Functionally, he can work but can love neither himself, his parents, nor the women he beds. How did this happen?

Sophie and Jack Portnoy, first-generation American Jews, seem not to have expectations of actualizing their own potential greatness. Their frustrations and their dreams of fulfillment have all become focused on dreams of the glory that may be reflected from the accomplishments of their marvelous, brilliant son, Alex. In this way, their self-esteem is tied to his achievements and Alex's activities, unfortunately, become tied in his mind to his parents' well-being.

Three interrelated, problematic aspects of Alex's parents' powerful investment in their son's perfection and his experience of their investment can be delineated: (1) the oppressive attention paid to every facet of Alex's being, (2) the ever-present issue of whose needs determine the fate of an interaction, and (3) his experience of their need for him to fulfill them.

Alex grows up a pampered, overindulged child, whose every wish is attended to unless it threatens his parents' overarching plans for him. Often, he has only to murmur a preference, such as the wish to go over the George Washington Bridge rather than take the shorter route home to New Jersey through the tunnel, for his mother unhesitatingly to make his wish come true. His mother devotes herself to him. Alex has middle-class memories of milk and cookies after school, smooth, freshly laundered sheets, and his mother's ardent attention to his intellectual prowess. Though we may judge her obsessive cleaning of his ear wax and demands to inspect his adolescent feces as intrusive, Alex learns from this more than a mere obsession with his own body and hygiene. From the repeated association of intense interest and immediate, gratifying responses to incidental whims of his, he develops the expectation that the world at large watches his every action closely. He becomes self-centered and self-conscious.

Each time we see Alex expressing feelings and inclinations disjunctive with theirs, we witness negative responses from the parents. Their harsh responses range from belittling and teasing, to an escalating bullying of him. The coercive responses invariably end with the prediction by his parents that his abandonment of their wishes as the center of his self will result in his "killing" them. Alex's mother pressures him in his boyhood to submit to her will by repetitively invoking the groundless fear that his father may have a tumor. The coercion continues in the same form into his adulthood.

The question of whose needs are more important, mother's or Alex's, is played out in Sophie's memorable, denigrating reaction to Alex's shy, early adolescent assertion of his need for a bathing suit with a built-in jockstrap ("What, for your 'little thing'?"). Is she castrating? The anecdote may lend itself to that interpretation, but I believe it is more broadly indicative of her uninterested response to those aspects of Alex's interest that lie outside of *her* interests. As we shall see, the fact that his genitals and the pleasure they give are indeed his and his alone is one of the key elements of his compulsive masturbation.

Strong, condemnatory reactions occur in response to anything experienced by the parents as threatening to Alex's future, as they conceive it. Narcissistically vulnerable people, they have little tolerance for things they experience as threatening to their self-esteem. Thus he must promise and swear never to "eat hamburger out" and, by implication, not to allow his interests to become more important to him than their wishes. When his adolescent sexual interests lead him to a burlesque show, he has expectations of public broadcasts of his actions and vilifying deprecation of his shameful character. His expectations stem not only from his experience of being closely observed by his mother, but also reflect the unwavering expectation on his part of harsh, punishing reactions to desires of his that are particular to him and not shared by her (or them). The patterns of interaction become remembered and then expected (Beebe and Lachmann 1988). The parental response to spontaneously arising affect in the child becomes amalgamated with the affect. The child later experiences the parent's reaction as his own reaction to a particular affect (Socarides and Stolorow 1984/1985).

Other examples may further illuminate the intersubjective field. When 6-year-old Alex didn't eat because he wasn't hungry, his mother terrorized him with a knife because *she* needed him to eat. Similarly, he remembers being turned out of the house as a little boy as a means of punishing another of his infractions. Thus, while his fears of discovery and punishment at the burlesque show may be popularly understood as evidence of a "harsh superego," the sequence of the assertion of self-interest followed by expectations of annihilating response reflects the structuralization of a pattern that has actual origins in lived experience.

Alex is especially vulnerable to his parents' negative judgments of him, in part, because he has been seduced by their excessive idealizations of him. His natural desire to discover himself through them has been betrayed by their need to have produced a "little Einstein." While his positive sense of himself has become enslaved to their hyperbolic praise (and we laugh as Sophie's "little gentleman" compulsively says "excuse me" and "thank you" to the furniture as he ventures into the Gentile world), it is their criticism that carries special weight. However, the parents who affirm only those aspects in the child that conform to their needs are not likely to respond sympathetically to unhappy reactive feeling in the child. We hear less in the novel of the ways in which Alex expressed hurt and indignation to his parents than we do of their trivializing responses— "Mr. Hot-Under-The-Collar," "Mr. Hit-The-Ceiling." His parents cannot see, nor can they respond to, the ways that Alex has been compromised by *how* they have loved him. The anger and indignation Alex feels are associated with guilt and confusion because the things his parents do that frustrate him are always done "for his own good."

The parents' self-sacrifice and their need to gain fulfillment through Alex are two sides of the same problematic coin. Alex's struggles to escape his mother's imperious will and his father's impassioned pleas are short-circuited by his guilty awareness of their devotion to him. Would that they were more clearly devoted to themselves! He might then feel less guilty and more entitled to pursue his own desires. Their self-sacrifice creates a debt he can never repay. "Do me a favor *and don't do it for me*" (p. 116/127), cries Alex, bemoaning his terrible importance to them. He can never be successful in articulating how *their* interests swamp *his* interests because they claim their interests are his interests. Paradoxically, although his parents tout his perfection to him and to everyone he is "still somehow not entirely perfect" (p. 107/118), because, of course, he can never make up to them what they have missed in their lives. Despite the parents' unwavering devotion in pursuit of their goal, we know they must be let down, disappointed by Alex. He can never repay the debt unless he is willing to sacrifice himself for them, as they have sacrificed their own existence for him. (The suicide of Ronald Nimkin illustrates the death of the spirit that is inevitable when one person "lives" for another.)

As time goes on, Mr. and Mrs. Portnoy become more vociferous in laying claim to their prize and Alex becomes more frustrated and angry at the impossibility of his circumstances. By filtering their responses to him through the prism of their need to feel good about themselves, they have hampered his ordinary progress toward self-delineation. He barely knows who he is outside of their ideas about him. Further, because his nascent inclinations are so relentlessly associated in his mind with his parents' scrutiny and judgment, his own desires are the focus of unremitting guilt, conflict, and confusion.

Even when the parents' wounded narcissism is not directly engaged with Alex, the ambient home atmosphere provides countless opportunities to learn the ways of self-inflation and, crucially, the ways of contempt. Even though Sophie never tires of telling people her main fault is being "too good," she regularly denigrates those she believes are less worthy than she. The contempt expressed by both parents toward the world, which does not grant them sufficient appreciation, becomes central to their son's character.

ALEX AND HIS FATHER

Although Sophie Portnoy has become enshrined in the world of literature as the quintessential, pathogenic Jewish mother, Alex's frustrated wishes to idealize his father are an underappreciated source of his difficulties. On close examination, we see that Jack Portnoy engaged in dialogues with his son that were similar in structure to those between his wife and son. In those dialogues Jack seemed more easily defeated by Alex than was Sophie, an unfortunate and significant part of the picture. Both parents engaged in harangues intended to get Alex to accept their views of life, particularly as regards the rules that govern success. However, while the adolescent Alex consciously took pleasure in distinguishing himself from his mother's "pearls of wisdom," the feeling tone that surrounds Alex's recollections of his father's admonitions to study shorthand is one of sadness at rejecting what his father had to offer.

In *Portnoy's Complaint*, the only love untainted by doubt or contempt is reserved for the neighborhood men who played softball on Sunday mornings, when Alex was a boy. The manly camaraderie and competition he witnesses provides for him his warmest notions of growing up to be a Jewish man. Baseball serves as an organizer for Alex's attempts to identify with an idealized father, although the attempt is only partially successful. As a boy, playing center field affords him his truest moments of feeling at ease and competent. He has a model in mind of how to conduct himself; the almost seamless affiliation he feels with his own activity gives him a sense of the self-assurance he more generally lacks but knows exists.

Alex longed to feel about his father as he did toward his mother. She was established in his mind in early childhood as an awe-inspiring possessor of amazing powers. How he yearned to similarly admire his father's prowess! How disappointed he was to discover that his father's grip on the baseball bat was incorrect! He wants to believe his father has a great deal to teach him about being a man and follows his father's advice when it is not too obviously flawed. It is touching to imagine Alex imitating his father's way of entering the water to swim.

In his fantasy life, his father is a strong figure who stands up to his mother, asserting his right even to screw the *shikse* bookkeeper, if he so wishes. Alex yearned to find in his father a capacity to stand up to his mother, which might serve as a model for his own attempts to do the same. If he could experience his father's self-assertion and his mother's capacity to survive it, it might modify his sense of the danger to them all embodied in his desire for self-delineation. Indeed, in a neat reversal, if the father will not stand up to Sophie to protect the boy, the boy will kick Sophie in the shins for him!

Alex's father attempts to bring him with him into the world of men, taking him to the Turkish baths. But while Alex is in awe of his father's substantial *"shlong,"* he is not able to find in his father the masculine qualities of gusto, courage, and boldness he wants to discover as his birthright. It is likely that these qualities that Alex longs to idealize in his father and to develop in himself become concretely associated in his mind with the phallus he admires. This will contribute to the unconscious meaning he attributes to the growth of his own genitals in adolescence. He yearns to experience his father as resolute and strong. Alex develops the compensatory belief that it is his mother who is responsible for suppressing boldness and courage in his father and, further, that it is exclusively his mother who thwarts his development. His father is thus protected, in part, from Alex's disappointment and anger.

The episode in which Uncle Hymie breaks up the romance between cousin Heshie and his *shikse* girlfriend Alice reiterates the theme of a parent's felt entitlement to absolutely control the life of a child according to the parent's own vision. Heshie, on discovering his father's treachery, goes to the basement where he proceeds to break, one by one, his father's considerable inventory of bottled soda pop, screaming obscenities with each crash. His father, it is said, wrestled him to the floor where he held him for 15 minutes before Heshie "gave in." Alex ponders the story and wonders how his uncle succeeded in overpowering Heshie, the athletically built high school track star, who was likely to have been physically stronger than his father. Why, Alex wonders, did Heshie "give in?" We may never know the answer about Heshie, but I submit that the anecdote interested Alex because the motif of restraining frustration and anger toward the father to preserve the father's authority and power was a salient feature of Alex's psychology. The function of self-restraint was to keep alive and potentially available for his own (fantasied) participation the father's power and authority.

THE CONTRIBUTION OF JEWISH THEMES TO INTERSUBJECTIVE MATRICES

The structured belief systems that characterize the environment play a role in the development of social groups and individuals. Alex develops his particular sense of himself partially in relation to the meanings he ascribes to Jewishness; those meanings are inevitably related to his experience of his parents, their experience of being Jewish, and to his experience of the larger culture. Thus there is an infinitely receding background that each new participant endows with personal meaning.

The Jewish religion is organized around the belief that it is the destiny of Jewish people individually and together to aid in the betterment of the world. This belief has been sustaining during hard times and contributes to (but is not solely accountable for) the crucial value Jewish people place on the education and nurturing of their children. Sophie and Jack Portnoy are themselves first-generation American Jews, one generation removed from the ghettos of Eastern Europe and the long history of oppression. They are as much imbued with the positivism of America as they are with the Jewish "everything-for-the-kinder [children]" spirit. Their first-born son Alex carries the hopes and dreams of all his parents and their forebears might have been, had they been blessed with freedom and an education. He is also the product of the boosterish American mentality into which he was born. The confluence of the two streams produced a moment in time in which perfection seemed attainable.

Jack takes seriously his mandate to support his family. As an insurance agent for a WASP firm that will never promote him because he is Jewish, he steadfastly works the least desirable territory. Sophie is a veritable whirling dervish in her own, traditional domain — the house and children. Her energy can be contained neither by the narcissistic pursuit of a perfectly clean house nor by her use of her son. Wild exaggerations belie her frustration. Sophie's daughter becomes a teacher but another generation must pass before the women who spring from Sophie's loins are lawyers (like Alex), and judges as Sophie might have been in different times.

As an adolescent Alex refuses to participate in his father's Judaism. He rejects the sufferer (his father) along with the "suffering and heartache" of the people with whom Jack identifies. It is, I believe, Jack's weakness that Alex rejects, or more precisely, refuses to deify; that weakness is associated with the Jewish people through a history of persecution. What is experienced as noble by Jack is a shameful reminder of weakness to Alex. And, as we are beginning to see, questions of weakness and strength are central to the ways in which Alex organizes his experience.

For Alex, the atmosphere of his home becomes associated with Jewishness. He contrasts the home atmosphere with the normative surrounding culture, as it is transmitted by movies and radio. From this vantage point, Alex comes to experience Jewishness in terms of intensity, misery, and weakness, while, in his mind, Gentiles enjoyed niceness, an enviable blandness, and pure happiness. That Alex grew up believing "aggravation" was a Yiddish word is a testimony to his power to distill and abstract the essence of his environment, as he experienced it. His fantasies about genteel life among the Gentiles began early and will be explored further in the next section on symptom formation.

The Portnoy household maintained an intensely ambivalent relation to the larger society. As newcomers, they enthusiastically embraced many of its traditions (having "real" apple cider for Thanksgiving, for example). They were certainly eager for all of the opportunities the society offers. Yet their unfamiliarity with the culture and their precarious position within it led to a defensive devaluing of the "strange" ways of the dominant Christian group. The story Alex's mother tells him about how sick she was when Mr. Doyle tricked her into eating lobster is a story about her fear of non-Jewish people and their ways. It is also a parable about the danger that ensues when one is carried away by pleasure, a message assimilated by Alex into the litany of parental prohibitions against the exercise of self-interested pleasure. Alex was repeatedly exposed to the disparagement of non-Jews; this provided him with an important mode of psychologically asserting his superiority when it was required in relation to a love object.

THE INTERSUBJECTIVE SYSTEMS IMPLICATED IN THE DEVELOPMENT AND MAINTENANCE OF PSYCHOLOGICAL SYMPTOMS

Alex's compulsive masturbation in adolescence, his inability to fall in love, and his difficulty integrating sex and love (including his eventual impotence) are his "presenting complaints" in psychoanalysis.

In a paper known mainly for its elaboration of the well-known theme of the conflict between sexual needs and the demands of civilized society, Freud (1908) stated, "The sexual behavior of a human being often *lays down the pattern* for all his other modes of reacting to life" (p. 198). He appears to have referred to the same idea more obscurely in a later paper on masturbation (1912b): "The injury may occur through the laying down of a *psychical pattern*" (pp. 251–252). Freud did not elaborate on the processes by which the establishment of a pattern occurred. Later psychoanalytic writers (Eissler 1958, Nydes 1950) spoke specifically of the power of orgasm to reinforce the conscious thoughts and the unconscious masturbatory fantasies that accompanied sexual activity. Repeated experiences of masturbation, therefore, tend to provide the individual with an unconscious conviction about the truth of his unconscious fantasy (Eissler 1958). Sexual fantasies and enactments have increasingly become viewed "as psychic organizers which contribute vitally to the structuralization of the representational world" (Stolorow and Lachmann, 1980, p. 169) and "the sense of self in particular" (Atwood and Stolorow 1984).

With the onset of adolescence, Alex discovered imperative sexual desires and developed the capacity to think about who his parents were and who he was in regard to them. The developmental reorganization of self occurring in adolescence centered, for Alex, on the wish to liberate himself from the constrictions of a "good-little-boy" image that had been formed in compliance with his mother's close supervision of him and his parents' expectations of him. This yearning was unconsciously associated with a psychological threat to his parents, who "require" Alex to live for them. Masturbation became the locus of his struggle in an overdetermined manner. Sexual feeling became the center of Alex's existence because it offered a private domain where he could consciously experience himself apart from his parents and their agenda. His maturing penis was associated in his mind with masculine strength, courage, and greatness and its use affirmed those qualities as his. The orgasms he discovered introduced him to longed-for experiences of self-articulation. However, the unconscious meanings associated with his longings for self-delineation caused genital functioning to be overburdened for Alex, as it was associated with conflict, guilt, and confusion from the beginning. The freckle he discovered on his penis, and his related hypochondriacal fear that it signaled his demise, concretized the link in his mind between pleasure and self-destruction. For Alex, if it feels good to him, it must be bad for him.

The conscious thoughts that accompany his masturbation— "Big Boy, Big Boy, oh give me all you've got" (p. 17/27)—may represent his desire to be valued for the qualities *he* wishes to define as his own—masculine strength, independence, sexuality. The same words come perilously close to representing the parental demands that he live only for *them*. Alex's unconscious masturbatory fantasy involves the wish to affirm his own self-delineation coupled with the fear that the fulfillment of his wish might destroy his parents. Whether he fears his mother will open the bathroom door, or fears the sleeping girl on the bus will awaken and discover him masturbating, the "close calls" concretize the close association structuralized between wish and fear. If orgasm is understood as strengthening Alex's unconscious conviction in both his wish and its associated fear, we can understand some of the recursive aspects of his compulsivity — the repeated strengthening of his fears requires the reassurance of his fantasied liberation, which then brings with it a resurgence of his unconscious fear.

The adolescent experience of near-impotence with Bubbles Girardi is a demonstration of the psychic balance for Alex. He is more afraid of the fulfillment of his desires than he knows. The pattern of excited experiences of arousal followed by self-loathing is also reminiscent of the association established between his self-assertion and his parents' critical, guilt-inducing, disappointed responses. Now, however, self-criticism and guilt are associated with the affects associated with self-assertion and automatically follow them.

With his first girlfriend, Kay, he almost escapes a neurotic fate. It seems as if a comfortable sexual adjustment is achieved with her that is untroubled by the postcoital depression and contempt for the partner that accompanies later sexual activity. Perhaps for a while, the differentness provided by her Midwest Christian background is sufficient to lull Alex into believing he has left his problems behind in the Jewish neighborhoods of Newark. Interestingly, the relationship falters on the revelation of Kay's psychological maturity. When they are planning to marry, Alex half-jokingly asks Kay if she will convert. Her calm, "why would I want to do a thing like that?" (p. 230/243) tyrannizes Alex with its intimation of solidity and contentedness. It marks the disintegration of Alex's interest in the relationship because, I believe, it crystallizes for Alex a sense of Kay's psychological superiority in relation to him. While (later on the couch) his conscious experience is awe and respect for Kay's equanimity, the unconscious experience is an equation of Kay with his mother, whose power is associated with overpowering his father and his little-boy self. The pattern evoked is superiority/inferiority. Alex experiences the situation subjectively as one that will require his submission to a powerful other (although until that moment he and Kay had actually been egalitarian partners). The opportunity to change his subjective organization through the course of ordinary life experience passes.

This is a pivotal moment for Alex. Turning away from Kay with a notable, cool indifference, he turns his romantic interests toward women he is certain are not superior to him. Devaluation and contempt will henceforth operate rigidly to protect him from being in a situation that might again engage his central concerns about being overpowered by an other. These defenses determine his personal conduct and protect him from the subjective danger of a true and possibly transforming confrontation with his subjective organization. (Although he acts as if he is indifferent to his parents' emotional demands, he is still powerfully tied to them and unconsciously fears changing the nature of his relation to them.) Now his dilemma will emerge more clearly and more painfully. If he is successful in choosing a girlfriend he securely can look down on, she will, of course, never be up to his personal standards for a wife.

With Sarah, his debutante WASP girlfriend, it becomes clear that Alex is unable to be in relation to a woman who possess qualities he idealizes. Such experiences, which he consciously desires, are unconsciously assimilated into his subjective organization; the subjective danger of feeling inferior and powerless in relation to such a woman triggers defensive contempt and devaluation. As Alex says, he was "intolerant of her [Sarah's] frailties. Jealous of her accomplishments" (p. 240/253). His defensive structures are becoming even more inflexible.

The stage is set for Alex's relationship with The Monkey, the beautiful, sexy model whose total lack of education seems to promise that Alex will never feel threatened by her. Sex with The Monkey is phenomenal, protected as it is by Alex's certainty that he can never take seriously someone who can barely spell. They are together for almost a year. When Alex begins to recognize her natural, untutored intelligence he struggles, briefly, with the question of why he cannot accept her as she is. The problem is not in her, but in him. While Alex consciously aspires to a relationship between equals (he is, after all, Assistant Commissioner of Human Opportunity for the City of New York), there is no such possibility open to him in his subjective universe. Alex finally leaves her. The conscious explanation is that she is pressuring him for a commitment he cannot make; unconsciously it is because her pleading, hysterical ways of trying to influence him are associated with his parents, particularly his mother, who dominated him with those very tactics. Further, Alex cannot free himself from his rigid superiority/inferiority schema and thus has no way of assimilating his increasingly tender feelings for The Monkey into his psychological organization. Defenses of distancing and contempt protect him from the emergence of emotional conflict and subjective danger but progressively constrict his behavioral repertoire.

The Monkey had the capacity to view him alternately as marvelous and, when he demonstrated qualities that ran counter to her interests, to view him as a lowlife. This pattern, of course, recalls Alex's relation to his parents. Further, she blames her actions on him saying, "I did it for you," reviving the parental, self-sacrificial theme song that activates Alex's defenses against the loss of his psychological autonomy — distance, contempt, and devaluation. The pièce de résistance of the repetitive theme comes when The Monkey threatens to broadcast his sins to the world at large — to call Mayor Lindsay and Jimmy Breslin! This, of course, is the actualization of his own worst fantasies.

The Monkey complains about feeling degraded by having sex

with Alex and Lina, the Italian prostitute. It is my view that Alex's experience of that incident contributes to his leaving The Monkey. After sex with Lina, Alex throws up, as his mother did after unwittingly eating lobster. In his mind, he is going too far in the exploration of the possibilities of pleasure. His fear and certainty that he has contracted VD (despite his conscious awareness of a total absence of suggestive evidence) represents the engagement of a central organizing principle — if it feels good to him (but does not serve his parents) it must be dangerous to him.

Demoralized and confused, Alex flees to Israel to try to make sense of his predicament. There he confronts his inability to function in love relations with women and is, finally, impotent. He is unable to maintain an erection with a Jewish girl. Naomi is redheaded, six feet tall, and the woman with whom his neurotic compromise finally comes undone. Alex calls Naomi "the Jewish Pumpkin," The Pumpkin being his nickname for Kay, who he associates with Naomi because both were women of equanimity and strength.

In an attempt to understand his problem, Alex has read Freud (the title of the fifth section of *Portnoy's Complaint*, "The Most Prevalent Form of Degradation in Erotic Life" (p. 183/196) refers to "On the Universal Tendency to Debasement in the Sphere of Love" written by Freud in 1912) and is taken with the Freudian proposition, "where such men love they have no desire, and where they desire they cannot love" (p. 185/197). He is quick to adopt its thesis and believes that he cannot enjoy sexual pleasure with a Jewish, redheaded woman because he cannot fuse his tender, affectionate childhood feelings with his manly sensual ones. I think Alex has much more to learn in psychoanalysis. While choosing non-Jewish women has been important in assuring himself he was free from the misery of his childhood home, I believe that themes of dominance and submission are more salient for Alex than issues of finding nonincestuous love objects. His mother was much too dangerous to his sense of self to be

mainly remembered as a model for his desires. I think it is more
germane to focus on the patterning of relational experience, its
subjective meaning and functions, than to invoke a theory of
early fixation of a sexual drive.

Another important aspect of attraction to non-Jewish women
has been his sense of being superior to them, religiously. Sophie
and Jack's defensive contempt for Christianity has been adopted
by Alex. Early in adolescence, Alex rejects Judaism in an attempt
to distinguish himself from his parents' definition of him. His
reversion to their denigration of Christians is a further indication
of his failure to effect a genuine transformation of self in
adolescence. (In demeaning his Christian girlfriends he is also
fighting his father's battles with his WASP oppressors.) With
Naomi, his illusion of superiority is undone both because she is
Jewish and because she is psychologically solid like Kay. Further,
his inferiority feelings are activated by her self-righteous, ha-
ranguing criticism of him. These feelings are intensified by her
resemblance to his mother, who engaged in the same behavior,
and by her physical domination of him. When he is on the floor
looking up at her towering over him he bites Naomi's leg, as he
kicked his mother's shin so many years before, in helpless,
impotent fury!

Portnoy's impotence is a psychological symptom. Themes of
strength and weakness, dominance and submission, have become
salient in his (defensive) choice of partners. Such themes have
been strengthened by cultural concerns about oppression. Fears
of being subjugated to the will of another have interfered with
choosing partners he could take seriously. Yet the origin of this
theme lies in his experience of being dominated by his parents'
narcissistic need for him to serve them. Specifically, he has felt
overwhelmed by his mother and unsupported by his father, in
whom he could not find a model for standing up to his mother
without destroying her.

Sexual feeling emerged as the private arena in which Alex
could attempt to experience himself apart from his parents'

needs. Masturbation became the symptomatic locus of the trans-formation of self that he was attempting to effect in adolescence; he tried via his masturbatory activity to rid himself of the strictures placed on his self-delineation. His compulsive mastur-bation was an attempt to consolidate and solidify newly develop-ing, still wavering aspects of self experience (Doctors 1990). However, he was not able to free himself from the unconscious fear that the assertion of self-defined interests would lead to the destruction of his parents or himself. Rather, Alex responded to the engagement of his central organizing principles with increas-ingly rigid defenses; distance and contempt served to protect him from a confrontation with his psychological problems. In the end, he is impotent, a sign of his inability to experience his sensations and inclinations, which lie outside his parents' orbit, without succumbing (unconsciously) to fears of relational tragedy. The defenses that constricted his experience have now failed him. He is now helplessly in the grip of his unconscious belief that if it feels good to him, it must be bad for him. The pain of his inability to live for himself can no longer be avoided.

THE PSYCHOANALYTIC SITUATION

The novel presents itself as the beginning of a psychoanalysis, the text being the free associations and memories of Alexander Portnoy. In this section I will discuss what we may learn from the psychoanalytic material about the psychoanalytic situation and the probable transference themes occurring in this analysis. I will also discuss Portnoy's diagnosis and prognosis.

What are we to make of the fact that we read a monologue, not a dialogue? Not only is Dr. Spielvogel silent (until the last line), but The Monkey's analyst, too, is portrayed as conspicuously withholding of verbalized responses. Roth's 1969 novel draws on the notions about analysis that were popular in the 1960s.

Modern perspectives emphasize the field created by the interplay between two personalities.

We can also view Portnoy's monologue as an intrinsic part of his personality. A self-centered harangue might well characterize Alex's analytic behavior. Narcissistic preoccupation is a likely outcome of his mother's alternation between pampering and ignoring responses to Alex's inclinations. We might surmise that Alex does not notice his analyst's personhood any more than his mother noticed his.

As soon as we begin to speak of Alex's behavior in the analytic situation, we are speaking broadly of transference — how Alex organizes his experience of this interaction (Stolorow et al. 1987, Stolorow and Lachmann 1984/1985). I think of transference as consisting of two dimensions — the selfobject dimension, which consists of the patient's wishes for psychological experiences missed in the course of development, and the repetitive dimension, which consists of the patient's fearful expectations of being retraumatized. Defenses abound against the development of both wished for and dreaded transference experiences.

On the basis of what is known about Alex's development, we would expect the selfobject dimension of the transference to focus on his needs for self-delineation. He will want to experience the other as someone who can understand and affirm the particularities of his experience. The repetitive pole of the transference will be organized around themes of domination and submission: Alex's fears of subjugating his desires to the wishes of an other. It is my view that what we observe in the initial analytic work is evidence for defenses employed by Alex against the development of the transference.

Alex refers to his analyst as "Your Holiness," and says he has "already confessed" (p. 133/144). I suggest that Alex is manifesting a compliant stance toward his analyst, which is his defense against the emergence of his own needs for recognition, and that he is cynically contemptuous of his analyst, a defense against feeling overpowered by the person from whom he needs so much. (Given Alex's opinions about the inferiority of Christianity, we must take a jaundiced view of his borrowing their metaphors to describe his experience in analysis.)

Alex turns to a reading of Freud to try to understand himself as his doctor might and then tries to produce material that is in harmony with the theories he believes his doctor holds. More than a generalized resistance, this is an active repetition of the way in which his own self-delineation was originally subverted. In place of the hope to be understood by his analyst on his own terms, he attempts to discover what his analyst may need to believe about him and then attempts to conform to that. This is Alex's defensive posture in the selfobject dimension of the transference. In regard to the repetitive dimension, one wonders whether his contempt in the analytic situation is only an inevitable component of the analysis. Additionally, it may be iatrogenically stimulated by his analyst's silence. Alex needs help so badly, and yet his analyst says nothing. Alex, vulnerable as he is to humiliation, may need to distance himself and subtly denigrate the analyst to counter the mortification triggered by his analyst's silence. The rigidity of Alex's defensive structure is such that Alex has little choice. If he does not wish to feel criticized, he must be the critical one. Working over these themes in the transference should be critical to Alex's developing a more flexible, tolerant capacity to relate to others.

One further point about Dr. Spielvogel. (I will forego the pleasure of analyzing his name, for Alex does not name him, Roth does, and, therefore, that line of analysis is outside our purview.) Dr. Spielvogel is a man. This is never directly stated, and yet we believe it to be true. As we read, we implicitly think that the way Alex speaks to Spielvogel conveys his expectation that Spielvogel is enough like him to understand him. We assume Alex has chosen a man for an analyst, perhaps because he is seeking in analysis to affirm in himself "manly" qualities he believes have been compromised in relation to his mother. It is not that Alex could not be analyzed by a woman, only that the course of the experience would be significantly different.

All of what we think we know about Alex's experience in the psychoanalytic situation is delimited by our not knowing anything about Dr. Spielvogel. It is no longer tenable to think about the transference as determined exclusively by the patient's personality. The principles that pattern the analyst's subjective experience will be a factor in "the analytic arena which involves the mutually influential interaction of two subjectivities" (Fosshage 1992).

I believe that describing people by listing the pathological features they share with others is not as clinically useful as understanding the themes that pattern a person's subjective organization. Nonetheless, to interact with the points of view of others, I will briefly consider Alex from the point of view of current diagnostic standards.

Alex is suffering from a narcissistic personality disorder. However, his personality is structured at a neurotic level, not a borderline level. His self-centeredness and self-absorption are aspects of the characteristic self-importance often found in such people. The search for "ideal" love, pursued with a driven, pleasureless quality, is also a diagnostic sign, as is his concern about how he is seen by others (his greater concern about appearances than with substance). His affective experiences, ranging from cool indifference to marked experiences of rage and humiliation, are also typical. Exploitiveness and disregard for the integrity and rights of others are denied by him, but present. In his relationships, others complain of this and demonstrate its effect on them, but a lack of empathy, an inability to really recognize how someone else feels, makes it hard for him to see it. The characteristic alternation in relationships between extremes of overidealization and devaluation is markedly present. Other features of Alex's presentation are consistent with the diagnosis—

the eventual reactive depression and his preoccupation with physical symptoms.

Despite the formidable listing of pathological signs and symptoms, and despite the conventional wisdom that holds that such people are extremely resistant to treatment, I believe that Alex has a reasonably good prognosis in analysis. He is intelligent and highly motivated by his psychic pain. The fact that he has a well-developed capacity to work hard and to achieve long-term results indicates a good capacity for sublimation and the tolerance of frustration, both of which are positive prognosticators in psychoanalysis. Lastly, we must consider the substantial positive contribution of his real love for his parents. These features all are characteristic of Alex's neurotic level organization. While many consider narcissistic personalities to be fundamentally cold and uncaring, Alex is not. His problem stems from conflicts surrounding a deep love for both his parents. His self-delineation has become unconsciously associated with endangering his beloved parents and has been thwarted on that account. There is, therefore, a capacity in Alex to commit himself intensely to love relationships, which can serve as a foundation on which to build more mature love relationships. The little boy who became enchanted with language through his enchantment with his parents — Alex is transfixed by his mother's poetic, "a real fall sky" (p. 26/36) and by his father's enthusiastic, "good winter piney air" (p. 27/37) — now must discover in analysis the themes that patterned that love and transform his self-constricting ways so that he can love again.

CONCLUSION

Roth has provided us with a text in which the childhood, the adulthood, the symptomatology, and the analytic process appear to be intrinsically related. Intersubjectivity offers an experience-near mode of gaining access to the themes that give meaning to Portnoy's life. It is left to the reader to determine whether the meanings offered here are sufficiently coherent, comprehensive, plausible, and appealing to be acceptable. Tight, formulaic explanations do not, however, characterize real psychoanalytic experience. Actual analytic encounters are co-creations of the patient's subjective world in interaction with the analyst's subjective world. The way the themes that characterize the patient's life are lived out between patient and analyst (and therein modified and transformed) will vary with each unique analytic couple. All that can be said with certainty is that Portnoy's patterns would come into his analysis. The rest could never be known at the outset by an outsider.

REFERENCES

Allen, W. (1977). *Annie Hall*, screenplay. United Artists.

Atwood, G., and Stolorow, R. (1984). *Structures of Subjectivity: Explorations in Psychoanalytic Phenomenology*. Hillsdale, NJ: Analytic Press.

Beebe, B., and Lachmann, F. (1988). The contribution of mother–infant mutual influence to the origins of self- and object representations. *Psychoanalytic Psychology* 5(4):305–337.

Doctors, S. (1990). *The developmental splint: meanings and functions of symptoms occurring in adolescence*. Paper presented at Division of Psychoanalysis (39), American Psychological Association, Tenth Annual Spring Meeting, New York, NY, April.

Eissler, K. (1958). Notes on problems of technique in the psychoanalytic treatment of adolescents: with some remarks on perversions. *Psychoanalytic Study of the Child* 13:223–254. New York: International Universities Press.

Fosshage, J. (1992). *Toward reconceptualizing countertransference: theoretical and clinical considerations*. Paper presented at Division of Psychoanalysis (39), American Psychological Association, Spring Meeting, Philadelphia, PA.

Freud, S. (1908). "Civilized" sexual morality and modern nervous illness. *Standard Edition* 9:179–204.

———— (1912a). On the universal tendency to debasement in the sphere of love. *Standard Edition* 11:179–190.

———— (1912b). Contributions to a discussion on masturbation. *Standard Edition* 12:241–254.

Kohut, H. (1971). *The Analysis of the Self*. New York: International Universities Press.

———— (1977). *The Restoration of the Self*. New York: International Universities Press.

Nydes, J. (1950). The magical experience of the masturbation fantasy. *American Journal of Psychotherapy* 4:303–310.

Ornstein, P. (1990). How to "enter" a psychoanalytic process conducted by another analyst: a self psychology view. *Psychoanalytic Inquiry* 10:478–497.

Roth, P. (1991). *Patrimony*. New York: Simon and Schuster.

Socarides, D., and Stolorow, R. (1984/1985). Affects and selfobjects. *Annual of Psychoanalysis* 12/13:105–119.

Stolorow, R., and Atwood, G. (1979). *Faces in a Cloud: Subjectivity in Personality Theory*. New York: Jason Aronson.

Stolorow, R., Brandchaft, B., and Atwood, G. (1987). *Psychoanalytic Treatment: An Intersubjective Approach*. Hillsdale, NJ: Analytic Press.

Stolorow, R., and Lachmann, F. (1980). *Psychoanalysis of Developmental Arrests: Theory and Treatment*. New York: International Universities Press.

———— (1984/1985). Transference — the organization of experience. *Annual of Psychoanalysis* 12/13:19–37.

10

A Woman's Perspective: Psychoanalytic Musings on *Portnoy's Complaint*

Helene Kafka, Ph.D.

INTRODUCTION

My invitation to contribute a chapter as Alexander Portnoy's analyst was to write from a woman's point of view. When *Portnoy's Complaint* was first published in 1969, it created a sensation more for its explicit language, raunchy humor, and sexual content than for its abusive and dismissive treatment of women. Today, feminists may read more darkly the protagonist's derisive, depersonalizing behaviors with women. They might consider these indicative of patriarchal oppression. In my opinion, although the book is replete with male/female issues, this is not its essence. To consider *Portnoy's Complaint* a sexist novel misconstrues Philip Roth's intent. On the contrary, Roth draws Portnoy's portrait as a manifest of macho culture, not an exponent. With verbal and imaginal rawness, he portrays the psyche of an injured man compelled to seek women for solace, vengeance, and self-aggrandizement.

Nevertheless, the psychoanalyst, as with any ego syntonic

defense, needs to bring Portnoy's misogyny into his awareness. Perhaps a woman therapist might be more alert than a man to evidence of sexual harassment and abuse. I hope not. When I become Portnoy's analyst, however, I am not the arbiter of his morality. My endeavor is to help him gain sensitivity to the anxieties his machismo masks, to comprehend its historical origins, its cultural roots, and the ways the male stereotype both organizes and stunts his sense of self. Reeducation in psycho- analysis is subtle; it is neither by prescription nor by proscription.

There are many issues of gender in *Portnoy's Complaint*. I address the dilemmas they create for Alex Portnoy within the context of his personal narrative. During an analysis, gender issues become demonstrable in the transferences and counter- transferences they foment. Such is the case for Alexander Portnoy and me when he becomes my fictional analysand. I conjecture exchanges with him that the reader will discern reflect a woman's point of view, evocative of female upbringing and sensibility.

Portnoy is a creation born of Philip Roth's experience, but grown from his imagination. Similarly, part of my pleasure in writing this chapter was to play with the character of Portnoy's analyst, creating her from my experience, imagining interactions that potentially could happen. Although inwardly active, I follow the author's psychoanalyst, Dr. Spielvogel, in remaining silent. I read each chapter in the book as though I were listening to my analysand in session, accompanying his associations with my own thoughts and images, fastening on my countertransferences, those both particular to male/female issues and otherwise. I wrote down these musings after each fictional encounter. This ap- proach parallels the intertwining of psychoanalytic theories, professional experience, personal history, gender identifications, and personality that are at play in the analyst at work. Of course, the process of writing down my analytic associations changes them. When recorded, the simultaneous polyphony of thought, image, and feeling becomes linear, more static, and drawn out. I offer the result of this process.

MUSINGS OF A WOMAN PSYCHOANALYST

Session 1: "The Most Unforgettable Character I've Met" (Portnoy's title, p. 1/11)

This is a most unusual first session. No sooner are the preliminaries over than Alexander Portnoy lies back on the couch and begins to associate. Both in words and manner, he projects himself as beguiling, imaginative, playful, and literary, but also sardonic and stubborn. He appears well read in Freud and wants to do what he thinks I expect of an analysand. Yet he takes immediate control, recalls his childhood stories unbidden and ends the session with impeccable timing. Clearly he is telling me he needs to do this his way, to stay out. I will. I'll just listen, holding off any interventions.

Mr. P. is a carefully groomed, somewhat handsome man of 33, of medium height and build, with dark curly hair. His black-framed glasses, set high on his prominent nose, give him both an intellectual and predatory look. He seems quite proud of his work as Assistant Commissioner of the City of New York Commission on Human Opportunity, equally emphasizing to me his altruism and status. Interspersing Yiddishisms as he talks, he loses no time in letting me know he is Jewish. He seems oblivious to me, shutting me out, yet assumes we have this common bond. I wonder why his Jewishness enters so soon.

Portnoy tells me a fantasy he had when he finally decided to call me for an appointment. He offers it much the same way another analysand, at his first session, might present a dream of the previous night.

The fantasy is that as a result of our work together, I not only write a paper called, "The Puzzled Penis", but name a new diagnostic category after him: *Portnoy's Complaint*. How quickly he reveals his expectancy (wish?) that his penis will fascinate me and that its workings and malfunctions will provide me opportunity to advance both my career and his notoriety. Negative advertising of himself! Will he entwine self-aggrandizement and self-deprecation with projections of my ambition and exploitiveness? Is he pulling our respective legs, alerting me to Siamese needs to exalt and mock me? (His fantasy name for me is Dr. "Spielvogel." I'll have to find out what spielvogel means.)

Mr. P. carefully wrote down his preanalysis fantasy to give to me. It takes the form of an encyclopedic entry:

PORTNOY'S COMPLAINT . . . A disorder in which strongly-felt ethical and altruistic impulses are perpetually warring with extreme sexual longings often of a perverse nature. Spielvogel says: "Acts of exhibitionism, voyeurism, fetishism, auto-eroticism and oral coitus are plentiful; as a consequence of the patient's 'morality,' however, neither fantasy nor act issues in genuine sexual gratification, but rather in overriding feelings of shame and the dread of retribution, particularly in the form of castration." . . . It is believed by Spielvogel that many of the symptoms can be traced to the bonds obtaining in the mother-child relationship. [p. i/i]

So this is the way he sees his troubles. How come mother is the villain? What about "bonds obtaining" in the father–child relationship? Why has virtuoso sex versus shame and retribution become the language in which he casts his conflicts? What are the meanings of castration to him? Does he allow himself *any* gratifications, sexual or not? What are the anxieties and beliefs underlying this sexualization? I wonder how fervently he has embraced Freudian psychology to intellectualize and flee from feelings.

I am amused that Mr. P.'s fantasy analyst is a German or

Austrian like Papa Freud, and in reality he comes to me, an American woman named Kafka. Surely, for a man who seems scrupulously well-read, this is not accidental. Did he unconsciously choose a woman analyst to work out those "bonds obtaining" with mother? If he thinks it all started with Mom, will he expect this woman named Kafka to be The Judge, to put him on trial so that he may be punished further, and/or redeemed? Is "The Puzzled Penis" his own Kafkaesque metaphor?

Alex Portnoy seems to take nothing for granted. Before starting his free associations, he gives a title to what turns out to be a session-long monologue, "The Most Unforgettable Character I've Met." Although ignoring me as he sets forth on scenes from childhood, he seems to want to direct my associations. Or does he think I am too dull to catch the themes of his streams of thought (to appreciate the workings of his puzzled penis), or has he little trust that his thrust will be understood without his asserting control? (One session, and I am already beginning to think in his sexual language.)

He begins his story to me, a woman analyst, with his first separation from his mother. Alex describes the fantasies of the 5-year-old kindergartner; "She was so deeply imbedded in my consciousness that for the first year of school I seem to have believed that each of my teachers was my mother in disguise. As soon as the last bell sounded, I would rush off for home, wondering as I ran if I could possibly make it to our apartment before she succeeded in transforming herself" (p. 1/11).

He is telling me that he accomplished his first separation from mother by denying it was happening. With magical thinking, he succeeds in taking her to school with him, projecting superhuman powers on her to ease the unfamiliarity of teachers, children, and school. He does not tell me he was lonesome or scared, perhaps overwhelmed by the other children, and therefore had to pretend his mother was everywhere. Instead, he paints a picture of an imaginative child, awed by, but not unchallenging of mother's ubiquity and omniscience. (He lets me know at once how important *woman* is to him and perhaps to expect a volatile relationship.)

Nor does he admire his childhood capacity to help himself over a rough time. If he, the adult, does not recognize that at least from age 5 he was able to soothe separation anxieties himself, how does this affect his need for attachment? Will he contort himself to stay connected? Watch for inner emptiness, feelings of aloneness.

Mother, he claims (almost bragging), totally adores him. I wonder, was he named for Alexander the Great? Her adulation seems his elixir of life. She calls him Albert Einstein the Second. He calls himself "heir to her long Egyptian nose and clever babbling mouth" (p. 2/12). This is a troubled version of Lloyd Silverman's "Mommy and I are one." This child seeks the source of Mommy's power, on risk of punishment were his quest discovered. (Another transference possibility: He might project his strength onto me, only to challenge me for what is his own, expecting retribution for his assertiveness.)

No sooner does he establish that he is his mother's favorite than he introduces me to his father, a man who worships him just as much as does Mom. Alex alleges that Dad blockaded feelings of jealousy with constipated bowels, drowned frustrations, and outrages with mineral oil and milk of magnesia, while lamenting (boasting?) that maybe it would take an atomic bomb to do the job. The man coats the bitterness of his life's realities with idealism, as he does his intestines with cathartics. Mother's power is magical; father's is unfused dynamite, wrath turned inward, power held imprisoned in the bowels.

I wonder about Portnoy's preoccupation with female and male strength and control. He only talks of an older sister in passing with commingled contempt and sympathy, as toward a physically and mentally inferior but good-natured creature, echoing mother's attitude toward her. So far, I don't have a clue to father's attitude toward his daughter. Will she be more important in the family and for Alex than he now lets on?

Did these parents require that a man-child be born for their emotional sustenance, to fulfill their dreams? Is this part of his Jewish cultural heritage, exaltation of the boy, devaluation of the girl? Could this be one of the reasons he sexualizes his struggles, that through gender superiority he gains narcissistic grandeur, feels masterful? In my Jewish family, boys were cherished; girls were tolerated. Watch out for countertransference reactions based on this.

And yet, the penis is puzzled: strong Mom, invisible sister, inert father. Portnoy alerts me to what possibly may be basic elements in his relationships with women (and with me to come); he seems to seesaw between gloried submission to his mother's adoration and a fight for superiority and control. His associations suggest Portnoy senior behaves quite differently; Alex paints a portrait of a father who is proud but easily intimidated, doomed to a thwarted existence. His Dad is a committed life insurance salesman, slaving in a Gentile firm with little chance of promotion. "Nobody ever really gave him satisfaction" (p. 4/14). Considering father's inhibitions, Alex's conflict may be enormous over asserting mastery through male power.

I sense Portnoy's poignancy and anger when he says of his father, "Where he had been imprisoned, I would fly: that was his dream. Mine was its corollary: in my liberation would be his—from ignorance, from exploitation, from anonymity. To this day our destinies remain scrambled together in my imagination" (p. 7/17). He tells how, as a college freshman, he tried to educate his father, trying not to outdistance him. He curses him "this schmuck, this moron, this Philistine father of mine" (p. 7/17), recalling how he believed his father threw out and never read the *Partisan Reviews* he sent him. He reins in his rage with self-scorn, "Still hoping, you see, still if-onlying, at the age of thirty-three" (p. 7/17).

I listen, and identifying with Alex, I hope he will tell me in later sessions that he had been wrong, that his father had read the journals and understood what his son needed him to know. Why am I feeling so compassionate toward his father, yet think of his mother as a caricature? After all, Mr. P. caricatures them both. I think for a moment of myself and my father, aware now of the root of my associations: my wish for my father to come through for me. Then back to Alex, wondering how come, at age 33, he still must have his father be the man he himself is, or wants to be? He cites other instances of longing for Dad to be the hero, especially on the baseball field. With bitterness, he tells of the boy's sadness and disappointment when the child discovers that he is more facile and adventurous than the man.

Has Mr. P. made what Levenson calls a compassionate sacrifice (Levenson and Feiner 1968) for his father? Will he not go further in his life than he thinks his humiliated, shamed father can bear? And/or is he also blockaded with spite and defiance, enraged at being the designated savior of both parents? I really don't know yet how he sees himself, other than his initial sexualized presentation (Puzzled Penis, et al.). With that metaphor, his symptoms scream out that in *his* life as well as his father's, "Nobody ever really gave him satisfaction" (p. 4/14).

His most traumatic memory has the flavor of a screen memory: mother would brandish a knife near his heart when he refused to eat, exhorting him: which does he want to be when he grows up, weak or strong, a success or a failure, a man or a mouse? For the first time, Mr. P. turns to me, asking with bitterness in his voice, why the threat of murder, of annihilation, how could she expect him, a 6- or 7-year-old to bluff her out, why couldn't his mother let him win? (Is he appealing to me to be a different kind of mother?)

I think of another analysand whose mother would shout, "I gave you life and I can take it away!" And then of the patient whose father would chase her with a strap, threatening to beat her, although he never did. Why do I regard these as screen memories? I catch a sense that the analysands know that the abuse they report did not really menace their lives. I think their outrage, albeit unconscious, is that their parents assaulted their fundamental sense of self. They cannot forget nor forgive the attack on their singularity, their will, their right to develop their own way of Be-ing — self-dominion. At ages too young to sustain themselves, with need of nurture, support, and mirroring to empower their developing identities, such parental onslaughts impeded courage to be a self, alone. *The ultimate castration!* Alex, the smart boy he was, had to know his adoring mother would not kill him. After all, his lament was, "Why couldn't she let me win?"

Control vis-à-vis mother appears a paramount issue. Note: He introduced himself to me as a sexual dynamo, power without pleasure. Has he, through identification with his mother's knife-wielding, come to brandish his penis with women, trying to turn the tables in his struggle for supremacy? Does he compete at all with men? Will I become a transference object for domination or for his capitulation?

With exquisite timing, the session at its end, bemoaning his mother's knife-wielding, he asks me, "And why doesn't my father stop her?" (p. 16/26). Perhaps at this point he really does not want to know the answer. I speculate on P.'s question after he leaves (my homework assignment?). Did father at that moment desperately want his messiah–man-child (a) to defy his wife since he himself could not or (b) to be humbled, to cave in to omnipotent mom? Does his jealousy of his son hold back action against his wife's excesses? Or perhaps senior Mr. P. dismissed his wife's histrionics because he was insensitive to the distress of both wife and son.

Interesting — at the moment Alex tells of mother's misuse of power, he appeals to me to use mine to help him. I think that some of the work with P. (now he becomes for me like Kafka's "K."), will be to refocus the way he perceives the little boy who battled with his mother. He fixates on his mother's maddening inconsistency (she adores him one moment, belittles him another), as if he were but a passive reactor to her moods. It might be helpful for him to get in touch with his own strength, the instinctive struggle he was (is?) waging for self-determination, a combat in which he was both resourceful and provocative. Perhaps, as he comes to realize his inherent power, this embroilment with mother will abate.

I wonder whether Portnoy's inability to gain satisfaction with his life is encoded or symbolized by the dynamics of this mother/son/father trio in this knife-wielding screen memory. His experience of self may be integrally tied to his role in the family. Is Alex still in this power struggle, refusing to move on, to be the man his mother desired, the success his father wanted and feared him to be, the strong one both parents needed to compensate for their thwarted hopes and inner cowardice. Suppositions: Mother finds in him a twin self (à la Heinz Kohut); but in addition, each parent unconsciously wants to mold him into an omnipotent hero self (à la Ernest Becker). He, their American man-child, must be their immortal star, but his energy seems quashed. How *is* he shaping his manhood; does he see himself separate from them at all?

The more I listen to Portnoy, the more the family sounds like those I described in "Three Mothers of Narcissus" (1990):

> My thesis is that the narcissistic character disorder is a product of family disruption. It is a relational malfunction in which each of the personalities in the family system plays a significant part. The deeply troubled and troubling narcissistic person is not just a victim of primary narcissism gone awry or in developmental arrest, but of family transactions wherein s(he) becomes the spokesperson for the family's frustrated ideals, illusions, entitlement and grandeur. *It is also true that the child so "chosen" has a propensity for this adaptation.* In my opinion, a theory of the origins of narcissistic pathology needs to include parental and sibling relations as well as the particular interplay of mother's and father's needs with this "selected" and perhaps "self-selected" child.

I will be interested to learn more of the particular dynamics of P.'s family. In line with this, I think of the title he gave this initial session. Which member of his family will prove to be the most unforgettable character he's met? His mother, whom he caricatures? His sister, whom he writes off? His father, for whom he seems to have underlying compassion? Perhaps it is the little boy Alex, whom he idealizes as brilliant, imaginative, sensitive, amusing, *perfect*, the boy he continues to believe was victimized and exalted by an aggrandizing, hysterical mother and a vulnerable, frightened father. Perhaps the most unforgettable character in his personal narrative is this exploited, angry child with feelings already forgotten. It may be that this glorification of himself, the unforgettable wunderkind, prevents him from escaping his mental prison to face life alone. This defensive idealization of self enjoins his freedom as much as the parental imagoes he internalizes.

I have been writing these associations to this first session in more detail than I usually do. Am I in collusion with Portnoy over his specialness, and consequently my own? Is this intertwining similar, although more subtle, to his narcissistic imbroglios with his parents? (Resolve: from the next session onward, I will write my ruminations more briefly.)

Session 2: "Whacking Off" (p. 16/26)

Was I supposed to be taken aback at or feel violated by this title? As mother of three sons, I am not shocked at the street language in his exegesis. Rather, P.'s title vividly condenses much of what he goes on to tell me in the session. Boasting! Defiance! Self-will! Anger, hostility, and aggression! Illicit pleasure! Power in aloneness! Irony: joy in the power to whack off, to control his own body is linked with guilt for fooling everyone. Self-contempt seems always present. He feels himself the hypocrite, pretending to be the compliant model son when he knows he violates the family's beliefs and expectations. Says P.: "I am the Raskolnikoff of jerking off" (p. 18/29). He's constantly hiding signs of his perfidies, trying to outwit the authorities; yet "the sticky evidence

is everywhere" (p. 18/29). Q: What is the crime he commits that
he seems not to identify? A: He can and will do what he wants
with his body = Himself!

With P.'s initial fantasy of "The Puzzled Penis," he announced
to me that he is led by his cock. I think he can talk so freely to me
about masturbation because even though he might want to shock
or dazzle yet another woman, he, unconsciously, might also be
testing my reaction to his penis as symbol of autonomy. Like the
baby who sucks his thumb, the toddler who refuses to toilet-train,
or the child who bites his nails, P.'s masturbation proves he can
control his own body. He can use it for solace, to feel alive, for
spite or even self-punishment, certainly to flaunt independence
from parents (secretly). Does he want to know whether I will fight
his willfulness?

P.'s need for self-agency and sexual lust characterize the stories
of this epoch of his childhood. He regales us both with fantasies
of compulsive masturbation. At the same time he boasts of his
libido, however, he reveals a confused intermix of sexual desire
and derogation of females. Without a thought, he masturbates
into his sister's brassiere, regretting only that her cup size is so
small. In a subtle way, the young Alex accepts as a given — the
male is the doer, the female is the done-to, the object. He joins
friends in an abortive adolescent gang-bang that may foreshadow
the detached mistreatment of women he, the man, now labels his
pathological syndrome: *Portnoy's Complaint.*

On the other hand, he does relate now to a woman as a whole
person. He loves his mother's high school yearbook picture,
empathizes with her as a young girl. I am touched by his adult
compassion when he describes his mother's failed dreams, that of
the girl with the stringbean body and red hair whose yearbook
prophesied: " 'Red,' *She'll go far with her big brown eyes and her clever
head*" (p. 30/40). I think of my smart mother who fought my
grandmother to be allowed to finish high school, and her
subsequent surrender of ambition. She, too, was the family's
backbone, seemingly the source of life energy and demonic

power, a woman I appreciated far more when I was grown. Portnoy and I are of the same vintage and socioeconomic Jewish culture. Will this promote empathy or overidentification? Be aware!

I, like Portnoy, sought closeness from my more vulnerable, softer parent, my father. I am moved by Alex's story of going to the beach on hot summer evenings with his weary, bedraggled father after the man's workday. He recalls every detail of the little boy watching his father's rituals. "To this day I go into the water as he advised" (p. 28/38). Yet his derision is simultaneous with his compassion. "Oh he floats so still—he works, he works so hard, and for whom if not for me?—and then at last, . . . with a few choppy strokes that carry him nowhere, he comes back to shore" (p. 28/38–39). What does he want of his father: can he ever forgive him for not being the man he needed him to be and that he himself has had so much trouble in becoming?

I, like Portnoy, would go with my father for his swim. It was in the early morning at the beach before his long day at work. I loved this time alone with him when only birds and the occasional beachcomber were about. I was trying to "will" a closeness between us, an intimacy that never was achievable. How I wanted him to know I loved and needed him! Did the boy Alex feel these desires, too? Has the man Alex ever told his father these memories or that he loves him? Has P. been able to acknowledge his needs for closeness, for intimacy, be it with man or woman?

Tormented by fears, secrets, and shame, P. lets loose his anguish. For the second time, he appeals to me when our interaction must be aborted—at the end of the session. Is he fearful that letting me in might overwhelm him? In his distress, he both distances himself from rage at his parents and plunges into the victim position. "Who made us [Jews] so morbid and hysterical and weak? . . . Is this what has come down to me from the pogroms and the persecution? from the mockery and abuse . . . ?" (p. 35–36/46). He appeals to me to fix him. He seems to feel that the power to hurt or heal him lies outside himself. "Doctor . . . Make me brave! Make me strong! Make me *whole*! Enough being a nice Jewish boy" (p. 36/46). Narcissistic defenses collapsed, he reveals the trembling child for whom safety and strength depend on the omnipotence of the other. Right now, it does not seem to matter whether I be female or male. He deeply hungers for a protector. I would expect a period of rage toward me when I don't meet his needs directly and rage at himself for the humiliation of wanting me to take care of him. It might be some time before Alex trusts that a woman can be protective and not emasculating, that a man can be soft and still strong.

Again, what is the Jewish connection?

Sessions 3 to 5: "The Jewish Blues" (p. 36/46)

Session 3

I guess Portnoy and I are on the same wave length. His title for our next three sessions, "The Jewish Blues," focuses us both on what, for him, is the Jewish question. Going back to age 9, P. begins where he left off: with an intense sense of helplessness. Masking the child's horror with humor, he tells about how his left testicle went north, disappearing somewhere in the inguinal canal, "an archaic insurrection had been launched by one of my privates—which I was helpless to put down!" (p. 37/47).

His testicle's treachery epitomizes and magnifies his feelings of impotence. Immense body anxiety provokes the fantasy of the testicle's transformation into an egg inside his body—he becomes a boy-girl who can have babies. How gender and role confusions troubled this child! He is terrified of being transmuted into femaleness by his (identifications with?) knife-wielding mother, a fate spared him by successful hormone shots. No sooner does he mention mother's power or taunting sexuality, than he rails against father's weakness for being the woman in the family, "enfeebled by a tender heart." "But what a mix-up of the sexes in our house!" (p. 40/50). The murderous rage of his confused adolescent self is palpable.

Does P. believe that manliness eschews tenderness; does he embrace this stereotype of masculinity? I, too am a product of the patriarchal culture. Male dominance and female submission also were interchanged in my household, atypical of most Jewish families. I remember feeling shamed by my mother's aggressiveness and my father's sensitivity. I know how this confused my notion of what were acceptable feminine and masculine behaviors. Men were supposed to be strong, but could a woman be assertive and still be feminine? Contrast with today where studies like Aube and Koestner's (1992) suggest power is "in" for males and females. I recall reading that girls and boys who display typically feminine interests and traits have lower self-esteem and more adjustment problems than those who identify with so-called masculine traits. How might the interchanged roles of Portnoy's parents have contributed to his puzzled penis, his compulsive womanizing, and what he calls his "perverse" sexuality?

More particularly for Alex, what makes it so fearsome to be female? Multifarious associations: His father's "femaleness" epitomizes not only secession of power to woman, but the weakness of The Jew! Both are "oppressed," "powerless." They may despise and ridicule their victimizers, but dare not vanquish them and flout the triumph. If this hypothesis is true, young Portnoy needed to deny and undo his terror that father is prey. He tells me that senior Mr. P. has testicles "a king would be proud to put on display, and a *shlong* of magisterial length and girth" (p. 41/51). Ambivalence toward Pop? The boy may have been relieved to know his father was so well endowed but chagrined at the comparison of his own child-size penis. Poor Alex, how obsessed he became, so young, with his penis's size as symbol of strength, backbone, and power.

His penis has been puzzled, it seems, since age 4 or 5. In the rest of this session, P. swings from descriptions of mommy's love songs to his enraptured little boy self, through hatred of her sensuality that invites yet repels, to envy and relief at being with his father of the coveted apparatus in the *shvitz* bath, relishing their primitive male bonding away from the "double threats of Goyim and women." Misogyny seems growing within him, consequence of anxieties about commanding women, powerful Gentiles, and men with superior genitals. Whatever P.'s association, he is never free of guilt for forbidden wishes or fantasies, be they incestuous, parricidal, or desire to desecrate. I empathize with this little boy, who struggles to be perfect, but never feels good enough, an empathy that grown P. might not yet be able to feel for himself.

I speculate that Alex again is expressing an enormous, unsolvable conflict in terms of his body functions. Elevated by both parents to messianic heights, the child's fall is preordained. Humiliation and shame are inevitable, for failing to meet their and his expectations. Ignominious defeat! Rage for being lured and cast down might underlie his stories of mother's seductiveness. When he feels ready for a jockstrap, mother scoffs, "For *your* little thing?" (p. 50/60). Rage for being unchallenged might underlie his derision of father's passivity. Impassioned love/hate for them both! His own avenging fantasies might underlie his emphasis on mother's knife-wielding, menstrual blood, uterine surgery, and his allusion to the House of Atreus. Orestes fatally slashed his mother and her younger lover for their betrayal and murder of his father. Symbolically, Orestes murders the incestuous, parricidal side of himself, then survives. In this play, Sophocles killed off the whole family except for Orestes. In his fantasy identification with Orestes, Portnoy vents hostility toward men as well as women.

Session 4

Alex continues to explicate his Jewish question. To avoid anti-Semitism, the family moves to an all-Jewish neighborhood, close by his father's oldest brother, "the potent man in the family — successful in business, tyrannical at home" (p. 50/60) — the more typical Jewish patriarch. He remembers the rambunctious cheers of Jewish high school students, who assert the superiority of difference, claim preeminence by dint of their persecution by morally inferior Gentiles, on whom they lavish their own hate. His child-self seems sensitive to the stench of hypocrisy. No wonder he is so proud of his work with inner-city, deprived people; his adolescent idealism propelled him into meaningful sublimations of anger against all prejudice.

Then comes the unhappy saga of macho cousin Heshie's brief but defiant life. To the family's horror, Heshie loves a *shikse*, a Gentile girl. Alex says, "We are not a family that takes defection lightly" (p. 57/68). Uncle Harold callously ends the affair; father and son violently battle; muscular Heshie, the weight lifter, allows his father to overpower him body and soul; Heshie goes off to the war and dies.

So here was a horrendous primer for young Alex. Death results from surrendering your self to filial obedience, to tribal loyalty! Love for a *shikse* can be a defiant proclamation of emancipation. Failure to be true to that love can be life-threatening. This is the first time P. speaks of love. He neither derogates the girl nor isolates her as a sexual object. She symbolizes freedom from past confusions of the female with sadism, and with Jewish vulnerability. But which holds more terror for Alex, losing the *shikse's* love or separating from his parents? Would disavowing his family ties be even more calamitous than renouncing a love that holds hope of autonomy?

Session 5

Portnoy answers my unspoken question with an unspoken Yes! His stories reveal that defiance of the laws of the tribe results in EXCORIATION AND IMPRISONMENT OF SELF: GUILT . . . SELF-HATRED . . . SELF-ABUSE . . . LIFE-LONG PENANCE. He tells of Alex, the 14-year-old post–bar mitzvah adolescent, refusing to go to synagogue on Rosh Hashanah, bashing his outraged father's arguments, reducing the man to tears, sister Hannah trying to soothe them both, while mother recovers from uterine surgery in the hospital. His self-directed diatribe becomes bitter, intense, and severe for not giving his father affection and obedience in the man's extreme loneliness and vulnerability. "Because my need is not to give it to him! Oh yes, we'll turn the tables on him, all right, won't we, Alex, you little prick! . . . Alexander the Great!" (p. 62–63/73).

So here we have it again — the humiliating fall from his parents' exaltation, Alexander the Great plummets to Alex of the little prick (Mother's diminishing words internalized, "*your* little thing.") Self-hatred results when he acts out secessionary thoughts. I empathize with P.'s pained awareness of his dilemma. He avows "I sense some enigma at its center, a profound moral truth, which if only I could grasp, might save me and my own father from some ultimate, but unimaginable confrontation. *Why did Heshie capitulate? And should I?* But how can I, and still remain 'true to myself!'" (p. 63/74).

It is difficult for me to remain silent, but I know I must. I want to say to Alex Portnoy that the profound moral truth he senses, which will connect father and son, is *compassion*, each for himself and for the other. I suspect that P. knows this too, albeit unconsciously, for I feel it so much in his stories about both parents. What stops him from consciously experiencing compassion? Is it pent-up anguish and rage that demands continuing battle? Does fear of taking responsibility for his own life prevent forgiveness? Does he feel so unempowered that his blaming of parents helps ward off loneliness, feelings of inner emptiness, the castration of non-being? The more I listen to P. the more I think he will answer these questions soon enough.

Portnoy continues to tell tales of adolescence. In some ways this sophisticated man is so naive. He appears not to know how natural was his adolescent rebellion. He bounces from feelings of pride and pleasure in his idealism to self-contempt for fighting with his parents. I feel touched by his turning round to me to assure himself that I, a woman, could understand and accept his ode to baseball and his sense of power in the aloneness of Alex, the center fielder, chasing the ball shouting, "It's mine!" (p. 68/79). He exults at being in center field, "where no one will appropriate unto himself anything that I say is *mine!*" (p. 68/79).

With this last exclamation, Daniel Stern's (1985) description comes to mind of a particular kind of failed attunement. Mother, in her overeagerness to respond to her baby's play, aggrandizes and exaggerates the tempo, intensity, and feeling of what he is doing. The result: the child stops, is at a standstill—initiative aborted! Baseball is P.'s happiest metaphor so far, for the possibility of self-expression, self-control, exuberance, and self-transcendence! This game, that helps so many inarticulate men bond with each other, epitomizes genuine autonomy for Portnoy. His affect soars as he tells these tales. (I am reminded that I learned *spielvogel* is a Yiddish idiom for "like a lark.") I think baseball might prove a useful metaphor in our work together; it is his joyous symbol for self-determination, for the experience of freedom in life. Ambivalence disappears in center field. There, he is alone but connected, doing what is his to do, yet still an integral part of the team. In contrast, the metaphor of the puzzled penis is fraught with angst.

Then comes P. the apostate, declaring his atheism, his train of associations making its final stop of this week's sessions, the journey he titled, "The Jewish Blues." Renunciation of his faith seems crucial in his fight to separate himself from his parents and the kind of maleness they promulgate. Weak! Feminine! Power built on exclusion and flaunted superiority! What pain and conflict as he describes his hatred of Jewish xenophobia! He castigates his mother's deference to its rabbis of hypocrisy, a deference he believes is owed his father if anyone.

The next moment, he strangulates his empathy for father's despair, sneers at their joint vulnerability, as no more than the "saga of the suffering Jews! Do me a favor, my people," he shouts, "and stick your suffering heritage up your suffering ass— *I happen also to be a human being!*" (p. 75/85–86). P. appeals to his sister in the past and to me in the present to end his confusion and torment. His sister, with her husband, offers divergence from orthodox ritual while accepting Judaism, moderation that only aggravates P.'s conflict. He finds solace with neither her nor me as the session ends. He cannot cast off his Jewish (female) identification, however, realizing without self-acceptance, that when he cries for himself, he inescapably cries also for the Jews (perhaps for humanity?).

The Jewish Blues? *Ambivalence*! Ambivalence about attachment and aloneness, about male and femaleness, about difference and similarity, about being the outsider and insider, about dominance and submission, about abuse and victimization, about filial piety and hatred, about being for self and others, about finding safety in oneself and outside the self, finally about reifying persecuted Jews as "chosen people" who suffer their suffering. How black and white his world is! How impossible it seems to him to resolve the contradictions within! He has no notion that it is okay to feel all of the above, often at the same time. Poor Alex.

Why do I again think, poor Alex? Do I echo his self-pity and self-judgments? Do I need to distance myself from him as he pushes me away, as he stonewalls, disallowing any assistance? My constraint echoes his passivity. Ambivalence precludes activity. It becomes for him an unconscious massive restraint, a defensive strategy that prevents any attempt to emotionally connect. Yet his anguish draws me closer to him. I recognize that *ambivalence* is but one obsessional tool that helps him to maintain inner cohesion in his fight against dependence and fears of apartness. It diverts him from awareness of his aloneness.

Sessions 6 to 10: "Cunt Crazy" (p. 77/87)

I feel assaulted by P.'s title for our next week's sessions. Is this his way of reasserting control? Did he sense my "Poor Alex?" Until now I have not been offended by his street language or sexualization of his conflicts. Indeed, I have regarded it as self-saving.

I have been aware that he needs to talk to me, a woman, in a manner different from the nice Jewish boy talking to his mother. It also helps him avoid his penchant for intellectualization. If P., however, is responding to my condescension with his title, "Cunt Crazy," he might be diverting anxiety or anger into sexist harassment. This is the first time I feel feminist ire, because I sense this inbred male mode to regain dominance over a woman who may appear threatening. (The male/female dance for superiority exemplified in this interplay? Will this be one of our transference/countertransference dances?)

But I cannot help but feel empathy for Alex. He is tormented by his sexual compulsions. His anguish and flashes of self-awareness arouse my concern. When frightened and unable to cope, he seems trapped into gender-stereotypic behavior just as a woman might when she feels powerless and vulnerable. His emphasis on the size and workings of his penis and the many ways he denigrates women are typical machismo defenses men unconsciously deploy when they feel empty and deflated, unable to connect. The title, "Cunt Crazy," I think, denotes the forces that seize him and from which he is trying to escape.

Change of focus as I listen to Alex. With his need to let his penis do the talking in each epoch of his childhood and adolescence, I feel I am being led through a picaresque tale of the psychosexual stages of development. Fantasy, humor, ridicule, exaggeration, bitterness, sudden moments of helplessness with mocking or sardonic appeals to me — all characterize his associations. He presents conflicts of identity and individuation as if it were his penis, not himself, that compulsively rebels from Jewish proprieties and chases sexual satisfaction. I note, however, a change in him since we began. He seems to be seeking an ally. He directs more questions to me, albeit rhetorical, still wary of my possible intrusiveness.

Alex's stories tell me that while both mother and father are open to seduction, mother, the all-powerful, is the biggest seducer of them all, enjoining him to collude against father. I sense he worries that I, too, might seduce him into further separation from his manhood, with consequent alienation of self. Indeed, after an angry tirade against his parents, he both expresses this fear and undoes his hostility with: "Is it the process, Doctor, or is it what we call 'the material'? . . . I hear myself indulging in the kind of ritualized bellyaching that is just what gives psychoanalytic patients such a bad name with the general public" (p. 93/104). He worries lest I isolate him from parents and society even more than he himself has managed to do.

Ambivalence reigns supreme in these sessions. He shifts rapidly from hostility to self-ridicule, prompted it seems by anxieties of entrapment. P. tells of himself, the naive, clumsy, frightened adolescent unable to make it with the Gentile girls he desires except through defiant acts of self-jeopardy (masturbating on a bus into a *shikse's* skirt). When he boasts of his sexual pranks, he is totally unaware that the girl, herself, means nothing to him, or that she might even be considered. His pattern continues to develop: obsession with sex to prove manliness, to revenge feelings of victimization, to defy and separate from his family, to isolate himself from his feelings. (Anatomy of a date-rapist?)

Alex, the good Jewish boy, while boasting of his sexual mutiny from the family with *shikses*, does not stop flagellating himself for betraying his seductive mother. Guilt gives way to blame. His sexual obsessions, he wants me to know, arise from early incestuous experiences. He tells how intense was Mother's pre-school passion and adoration for him "during those five years when we had each other alone all day long" (p. 94/105), how, even when he was older, she sexualized their relationship, greeting him with, " 'Well, how's my lover?' " He feels lured into reversing roles with an unknowing-unknowable father. He gives me proof of mother and son's joint oedipal desires, of his temptations and revulsions (reporting that another thus-plagued Jewish son killed himself), invites me to join him in derision of Jewish mothers.

Portnoy certainly feels his mother sexually abused him. I

wonder, as we work together, whether he will report actually being physically molested by her? His rage, feelings of victimization, of enticement and conflict, his compulsive masturbation, adult promiscuity, denigration of women, inability to have a serious relationship can be, perhaps, symptoms of incestuous involvement far more serious than the Oedipus complex from which he claims he suffers. This is an hypothesis that awaits much more data.

Whether or not this proves true, I do not agree with Alex that his Oedipus complex is the crux of his torment. True, he feels caught in emotional quicksand. But it is not the family romance that pulls him under, that captures him. It is not the oedipal mother, but his preoedipal need of union to maintain a narcissistic fix, to feel power through merger with mother, thus to diminish threat of annihilation. In the twinning with his mother, in their affective symbiosis, he experiences himself as a wonderful potentate. Narcissistic grandiosity is the food that temporarily fills his emptiness. He knows few other ways to feel a strong sense of self and to connect. Without mother, he is nobody. This is his entrapment.

The castration he fears is not loss of penis, but loss of empowerment, of grandiose entitlement, and emotional intensity. Father inadvertently participated in Alex's preoedipal castration, sacrificing his baby son's individuality to a wife he could neither satisfy nor help realize her ambitions. Portnoy's danger from father was that the man was all too willing to capitulate to the boy. He deprived the child of the opportunity to test his mettle in challenges to a parent well-secured in his adult, protective, generative role.

Portnoy's parents, denying their vulnerabilities and failures, pinned their hopes on the little boy, spurring him to be their omnipotent hero. Therein they committed their worst abusive acts. They did not provide him the attunement, support, and modeling he required to develop inner solidity. Instead, his sense of self was inflated like the huge Thanksgiving Day balloons, tethered by adoring parents. Without this attachment, he is unmoored, loses stability and self-confidence; his sense of agency collapses. Portnoy remains stuck and tortured, because he needs to keep the grandiose myth going and not face his inner desolations.

P. sexualizes terror of aloneness, preferring to keep himself in the role of oedipal victim, whose overworked, puzzled penis has been enlisted in the struggle against incestuous wishes. Then he worries that his sexual perversities will be broadcast, destroying his prestige, status, and image as Portnoy, the humanistic commissioner, the idealistic helper of the downtrodden. I think the unmasking he fears is that he indeed feels impotent, more mouse than man (as mother threatened), always in need for an attachment fix. Sexual activity helps him gain whatever inner cohesion he can, lest . . . lest he experience the emptiness and depression of a deflated self. To avoid such a painful, anguished state, he might need to create some transference struggles with me as oppressive, tantalizing mother.

Portnoy lapses into a frenetic fantasy of himself urgently grilling a friend for every detail about the adolescent sex he missed. Although it sounds like a typical macho tirade about sex—disconnected, alienated—I hear his hysterical quizzing on what sex is all about as his desperate need to know what he lost, his frantic attempt to ease apartness in his search for connection. At the session's close, his pressured monologue reaches an emotional climax of yearning to have it all. He reminds me of Molly Bloom in Joyce's *Ulysses*. Alone, masturbating, prattling in a joyous stream of consciousness, she gives herself over, "Yes!" to sex, "Yes!" and life, "Yes!" Portnoy, the self-tortured, agonizing ambivalent Jew, is yet to joyously sing of sex like Molly, or fly like a *spielvogel*!

Session 10: "The Most Prevalent Form of Degradation in Erotic Life" (p. 183/196)

OK. Here it is. More homework. With this title for the present week's work, P. sends me back to Freud, just as his "Dr.

Spielvogel" sent me to a Yiddish scholar. But his associations refresh my memory. He struggles with his inability to love, recognizing the need to degrade the women with whom it might be possible. The story continues in Alex's self-minimizing, sexualizing fashion: of his failures to feel a cohesive sense of self and intimacy in adult life, as told by the puzzled penis in its ins and outs with *shikses*. I feel bored with his sexualizations and self-pity, that is, his sardonic "self-laceration is never more than a memory away, we know that by now" (p. 217/230). Why am I feeling so impatient and irritated with him?

His use of me is the same as with his *shikses*. He makes me his cohort in superego restraint one minute, his partner in sadism another, mocks or reveres me along with Freud (at least I am in good company), simultaneously asks for help to buttress crumbling defenses and shuts me out with self-analyses, forestalls my responsiveness, cuts off my initiative, deflects any possible contribution that might intrude on his no-win self-immolating/ aggrandizing/amusing/irritating/touching patter. If Alex is the imprisoned analysand, as Roy Schafer (1983) so brilliantly describes, I am feeling like the imprisoned analyst.

I sound angry! My irritation bespeaks our conjoint frustration and futility. I am identifying with the *shikses*, experiencing how compelling he is, whether he attracts or repels. I am identifying with him as he attempts escape from bondage (internal and external) to parents. I am identifying with his mother as he, Mr. Ambivalence Portnoy, both courts and rejects me.

Ready to listen again to Alex, several things strike me. Despite his condescension toward the woman he derisively calls "The Monkey," he realizes that there were moments with her when he could feel tenderness along with his lust. And to her crushed, shamed, abused child-self he brought possibility of connection and self-acceptance. She loved him for redeeming her, for feeding her soul, he says, filling her emptiness. The most poignant session this week was his tortured recognition that he could not surrender himself to loving her. Despite his flirtation with Freud's narrative line — oedipal incestuous wishes inhibit lust

with the beloved—he knows now it is possible for him to love more fully. This augurs well. Alex revels in his sexual abandon with Mary Jane (The Monkey). She comes close to refuting his dogma that nobody ever gave him (and father) satisfaction. But it is his own narrative of imprisoned Alex that interdicts deepening the relationship with Mary Jane. His conviction—that love threatens engulfment by the other's needs—sentences him to solitary guilts and penances.

Bitterness, born of annihilation anxiety, prompts his defensive bark, "Get it now? The perfect couple: she puts the id back in Yid, I put the *oy* back in *goy*" (p. 208/221). I want to say, "So what would be so bad?" but I think his guilt cannot tolerate even a temporary reprieve. I think terror of obliteration also underlies the narcissistic wound he feels when his midwest *shikse*, the woman he calls "The Pumpkin," secure in her own identity, says that were they to marry she would not convert to Judaism, *"Why would I want to do a thing like that?"* (p. 230/243). With this statement, she unwittingly wipes out his unconscious superiority as chosen child, his grandiose defense against nothingness. She unloosens the shaky ties that bind him to his family and Jewish suffering. He rages against such unshackling; it terrorizes, threatens separation from his parents. Erich Fromm (1976) so wisely described the unanchored person's impetus to escape from even the idea of freedom.

A peculiar phenomenon: with all of Alex's exploitations and derogations of women, with the sexual encounters that sometimes sound like date rape, I think he is as much a victim of the patriarchal culture as any of the women he assails. He has bought into the machismo myth: that men assert superiority through subjugation of women. He is tortured, inwardly shamed, always feeling inadequate, unsafe, and perilously alone; yet he knows no other ways to feel alive, powerful, and less lonely than to masturbate, have sex, or talk sex. The need begun in childhood, to exhibit self-dominion with his penis, has become a compulsive drive to find cohesion and connectedness. If I were to read about his sexploits in a newspaper, or to meet him at a party, I would

feel angry and repelled. But he is my patient, and I feel compassion for his being pulled into the fantasy that his penis can provide pride and pleasure that he cannot feel about himself otherwise.

A case in point: believing his and his father's destinies entwined, he maintains that his sometimes sadistic behavior with *shikses* (The Pilgrim especially) vindicates his father's humiliations as a Jew oppressed and defeated by wealthy Gentiles. The puzzled penis is used here to vanquish this crucible; only were he to cleanse his father's shame would he be able to accept him, be apt to love and identify with father as man and Jew. Only then would Portnoy be able to separate, individuate, and taste freedom. In telling me of his cruelty with women, P. already is on the way to linking these basic anxieties and conflicts with his exploitative behaviors.

It is still so painfully difficult for Alex to allow open despair, and it is even harder for him to express rage without undoing it or abusing himself. Yet in his histrionic mimicking of the admonishments of mother and father, he does acknowledge his fearfulness, blaming both parents for his insecurities. Also, through jokes again, he tells me his *shikses* are his instruments of revenge against his family. Once again, he demonstrates how the macho ethos leads him into sexual activity, preventing his addressing and resolving his conflicts. Sexual activity with Gentile women is multidetermined for Portnoy. He seeks them to escape the Jewish woman's engulfment, to retaliate for his father's castration in the world of non-Jews, to separate from and betray his parents. Both guilt for his hostility and fears of estrangement prevent his finding satisfaction with his *shikses*. Always ambivalent, he must undo his desires for vengeance to parents and tribe. But then, this frightened, fragile, "nice" Jewish man can neither shaft his parents nor separate from them.

Session 12: "IN EXILE" (p. 241/254)

Portnoy's title, "In Exile," aptly speaks for this man with little constancy of self, wherever he may be. His stories and uncon-

scious journey lead to an attempt to heal himself, as man and
Jew, by a pilgrimage to Israel for rebirth and redemption. He
professes, it is "*to watch the men* . . . to convert myself from this
bewildered runaway into a man once again—in control of my
will, conscious of my intentions" (pp. 245, 252/258, 265). On the
plane, he reminisces on boyhood pleasures when he and father
would watch the neighborhood men play softball, times that he
longed to be and felt sure that he would grow up to be a Jewish
man. At the same time he mocks their conformity, these nice
Jewish men grown from nice Jewish boys.

P.'s pilgrimage to Israel is also a quest to reunite with mother,
to recapture their joy in each other that had provided the little
boy with confidence, hope, and safety before he became so
alienated and alone—perhaps before the relationship was
sexualized. His search for rebirth begins when he flees from a
sexual Walpurgisnacht abed with two women in Rome
(sensational sex he assures me he did not enjoy). He tells of an
impotent encounter with a wholesome Israeli lieutenant he calls,
"The Jewish Pumpkin," and then reveals a story of total
self-abasement and humiliation with a redheaded sabra. She
reminds him of his mother in her yearbook, the clever girl with
so much spunk and promise. I am not surprised when he tells me
he could not maintain an erection in the Promised Land. To do
so would be to succumb to family and tribe. Ambivalence about
his identity, oddly enough, provides this fragmented man with
the little sense of self he has. He refuses commitment, therefore
he won't be devoured or misused.

And later, after detailing his desperate sexual escapades,
impotence, self-debasement, and the guilty panics over VD
injuring his penis, he avows with typical ironic self-awareness, "It
surely never crossed my mind that I would wind up trying to free
from bondage nothing more than my own prick. LET MY
PETER GO!" (p. 251/264). I recall something from the previous
session. It is P.'s insightful, "If I could be somehow sprung from
this obsession with fellatio and fornication, from romance and

fantasy and revenge — from the settling of scores! the pursuit of dreams! from this hopeless, senseless loyalty to the long ago!" (pp. 218–219/231–232).

Yes, I agree with P. that he must free his peter because it has become his split-off alter egos. It is at once Alex, passive prisoner of obsessions and compulsions, and Portnoy, active seeker of vengeance, retribution, and selfhood. This pseudo-autonomous male body-part symbolizes his imprisonment and emotional estrangement. He unconsciously uses it (and his Freudian oedipal interpretations of its meanderings) to repeatedly victimize himself or bring out the worst in others, especially women. He thereby convinces himself that this is what life is about: destiny is unalterable; intimacy need not be risked.

I find myself wondering whether P.'s stories about the Israeli women are fantasies. Of course, the events may be real. His internal and external worlds, however, are so similar. These women are uncanny representations of the splits within him; they condemn him with the fierce judgments he hurls at himself, as creature of "Temptation and disgrace! Corruption and self-mockery! Self-deprecation — and self-defecation too! Whining, hysteria, compromise, confusion, disease!" (p. 266/279). The women, self-righteous and idealistic, scorn him and his defunct penis, feel disgust for this cowardly, self-hating Jew with his ghetto humor. I think it is a positive sign when he finally ends his self-immolating diatribe to the sabra with "I am soiled, oh, I am impure — and also pretty fucking tired, my dear, of never being quite good enough for The Chosen People!" (p. 266/279).

Alex then comes closer than ever before to acknowledging his despair. He laments, "How have I come to be such an enemy and flayer of myself? And so alone! *Oh*, so alone! Nothing but *self*. Locked up in *me*!" (p. 248/261). Alexander Portnoy, whose " 'Acts of exhibitionism, voyeurism, fetishism, autoeroticism and oral coitus' " bring him " 'overriding feelings of shame and the dread of retribution, particularly in the form of castration' " (p. i/i) has become an egregious victim of machismo, disseminated by vulnerable parents seeking the American dream of power in a patriarchal culture.

At the point of emotional collapse, defenses weakened, P. puts himself on trial. This imprisoned Alex Portnoy gets more and more wound up as he prosecutes himself for his actual and fictitious crimes against humanity, simultaneously mocking and defying his inner prosecutor for the ridiculous disproportion of his guilt. And then the comedy is over for this exiled man. He emits that anguished howl, without words between it and him, between me and him, a howl that sounds primordial, a howl that is pain itself (I flash on giving birth), a wailing howl that begins with a dirgeful moan, goes on and on and on and ends in *release*!

Aaaaaaaaaaaaaaaaaaaaaaaaaaaaaaaaaaaaaaaaaaaaaaaaaaaaaaaaaa-
aaaaaaaaaaaaaaaaaaaaaaaaaaaaaaaaaaaaaaaaaaaaaaaaaaaaaaaaaa-
aaaaaaaaaaaaaaaaaaaaaaaaaaaaaaaaaaaaaaaaaaaaaaaaaaaaaaaaaa-
aaaaaaaaaaaaaaaaaaaaaaaaaaaaaaaaaaaaaaaaaaaaaaaaaaaaaaaaaa-
aaaaaaaaaaaaaaaaaaaaaaaaaaaaaaaaaahhhh!!!!! [p. 274/287]

In the quiet that follows I tell him there is a saying of Nietzsche that he might know, "You must have chaos within you to give birth to a dancing star." I then ask him to join with me in committing to our work together, "So, perhaps now we can begin. Yes?"

REFERENCES

Aube, J., and Koestner, R. (1992). Gender characteristics and development: a longitudinal study. *Journal of Personality and Social Psychology* 63: 485–493.

Fromm, E. (1976). *Escape From Freedom*. New York: Avon.

Joyce, J. (1922). *Ulysses*. New York: Random House.

Kafka, H. (1990). *Three mothers of narcissus: the mirror entrapped by its image*. Paper presented at Division of Psychoanalysis (39), American Psychological Association, New York.

Kohut, H. (1977). *The Restoration of the Self*. New York: International Universities Press.

Levenson, E., and Feiner, A. (1968). The compassionate sacrifice: exploration of a metaphor. *Psychoanalytic Review* 55:552–573.

Schafer, R. (1983). The imprisoned analysand. In *The Analytic Attitude,* pp. 257–280. New York: Basic Books.

Sophocles. *Elektra*. London: Penguin, 1953.

Stern, D. (1985). *The Interpersonal World of the Infant.* New York: Basic Books.

11

Comparing Schools of Psychoanalysis: "So, Alexander, How Are They Treating You?"

Stephen Appelbaum, Ph.D.

Psychoanalysts evaluating their work, students deciding what school of psychoanalysis in which to be trained, and patients deciding what psychoanalyst to entrust themselves to have more than a little interest in comparing schools of psychoanalysis. The task, however, is daunting—many are the claims, little is the evidence; often each claimant knows little about what the claimant considers inferior competing approaches; and what happens behind the consulting room door may or may not match what is described.

This book offers help with the task of comparing schools of psychoanalysis. It controls some of the major factors confounding many other kinds of comparisons by portraying, to a variety of psychoanalysts, the same patient, about whom they all have the same information gathered in the same way. Basking in the relative comfort of this research design one has the opportunity to learn about and assess the differences between a variety of psychoanalytic approaches.

As can be seen in this volume, there are a good many

similarities among the analysts, notably the general outlines of their diagnostic formulations. But the differences between them are substantial, in theory and in consequent technique. If anyone needs a graphic demonstration of how different people putatively practicing the same profession nonetheless greatly differ, this book provides such a demonstration.

From one point of view such a finding is gratifying. Even apart from the differences in orientation and beliefs each psychoanalysis is by its nature unique — each patient, each analyst, and each patient-analyst unit is one of a kind. So if all analysts saw and worked with the patient in the same way, their differences could only be obscured by the analysis being grotesquely general and superficial. From another point of view such diversity as demonstrated in this volume gives one pause. Patients will have much different experiences — and perhaps much different results — depending on which analyst espousing and acting upon which set of ideas the patient chooses.

Portnoy does not have unlimited choices; his possibilities have been selected by the editor. Portnoy might have been offered a different kind of relationship, different styles of analytic work, different emphases even within one analytic tradition. (One can get as many disputes between members of the putatively same approach as one gets between approaches.) Or Portnoy could have been offered a variety of nonpsychoanalytic therapeutic methods.

In addition to the selection of approaches that the editor has made he has also provided a subtext delineating the current tensions between what is polarizingly thought of as the orthodox, Freudian, classical, drive psychoanalysis; and one or another variety of object relations, intersubjective, interpersonal, self-psychological, relational psychoanalyses.

Attaching names to the groupings of these approaches immediately plunges one into controversy. Some interpersonal theorists object to including self psychology and object relations along with the interpersonal because of the former's persistent, if murky, connections with what seems suspiciously like Freudian drives. The development of self psychology and object relations (originally British style) was spearheaded by one-time committed Freudians, Kohut and Klein. The fear is that drive-thinking may interfere with theoretically central and clinically mutative inter-personal transactions. Such transactions, in their view, make the analytic world go round. Some Freudians object to being referred to as "classical" for fear that implies they have not made the shift from id to ego or are uninfluenced by modern psychoanalytic thinking.

It is difficult to cut the semantic Gordian knot without damaging the knotter. With due apologies for any conceptual butchery or injured sensibilities I shall use *classical* to refer to orthodox, traditional, drive, Freudian psychoanalysis, and *relational* to refer to one or another version of object relations, interpersonal, intersubjective, and self psychology approaches. (I can almost hear classical psychoanalysts complain that they, too, are relational; and relational analysts complain that they, too, deal with motive, needs, and insight. The life of a discussant, indeed any thoughtful student of psychoanalysis, is not easy.)

Would one predict that psychoanalytic theory and practice 100 years from now will be exactly the same as it is now? If so, then case closed; there is no reason for a book such as this, or for further experimentation with different means of selection and training, or for debates and competitions between people's ideas. However, it is unlikely that most workers in the field would be so sanguine as to assert that psychoanalysis is a finished, perfect, product. The present Babel-ing, competitive marketplace of ideas certainly portrays unsettledness and dissatisfaction, as well as busy ingenuity at work.

Thus, a book comparing approaches is welcome, if not neces-sary. As noted, the principle on which the organization of the book is founded is sound. Its implementation has afforded much potentially useful and certainly intriguing information. Yet problems inherent in such a method of comparing need to be considered.

One relatively minor problem is the difference between what one says as compared to what one does. It is difficult to know from written or oral reports what actually transpires beyond the closed doors of the consulting room. Those who supervise psychoanalysis know full well how much the reporting analysts vary in their ability to elucidate the stuff of the therapeutic experience (just as patients vary in how well they communicate their experience). That analysts are routinely shocked when they hear or view transcriptions of their analytic work suggests among other things the distance between what they think and intend from what they actually do. Case histories are infamous for slanting material for one or another conscious or unconscious purpose instead of offering an accurate rendition of what transpired.

Granting that the analyst's reports of what the analyst would or did do in the consulting room are congruent with the analytic reality, there is still the problem of generalizability. If what is offered is a case of one drawing upon some general ideas, then what you read is what you get, and we know how the analyst thinks and what the analyst would do. But if, as is done in this volume, the analyst is selected to represent a general point of view, a school, a tradition, then one has to deal with the many issues that often skew, limit, or distort generality. For example, how homogeneous is any particular approach — how expectable is it that a dutifully labeled member of its class would do and think the same as other members of the same class?

Take, for example, "classical psychoanalyst," so often used as a synonym for Freud. Well, which Freud? The Freud who believed in one or another of his four instinct theories developed over many decades? The Freud who emphasized oedipal matters, or the Freud who wrote so tellingly of the oral, anal, and phallic persons engendered by those preoedipal fixations? The Freud who wrote about technique, or the one who practiced so differently from his writings? The Freud who thought and wrote metapsychologically about drives, economics, and topography of the mind, or the Freud of the consulting room? The Freud who sounded at times authoritarian with colleagues and patients, or the tactful, gentle, caretaking Freud? Depending on which of these one chooses, and how selectively one reads in psychoanalysis, one comes up with quite different pictures of a classical psychoanalyst and how such a psychoanalyst works.

The contributions in this volume by the more or less Freudian psychoanalysts — Bettelheim, Adler, and Hanlon — illustrate the problem of generalizing. Bettelheim portrays at times some of the characteristics that others in the volume decry. He sometimes is didactic, considers being more authoritarian and insistent, and grandiosely believes he can know almost immediately (and certainly without the aid of psychological tests) whether the patient can or cannot be analyzed. He does so without apparently taking into consideration that properly *analyzing* characteristics likely to be inimical to success in psychoanalysis might drastically change the prognosis. He considers that another analyst might do better with Portnoy but only on the basis of that analyst being non-Jewish rather than being more talented, or a better match in various ways with the patient, and especially if the analyst was skilled in working with character and defense. Hanlon would have given Portnoy the chance to develop what, in Bettelheim's view, Portnoy lacks in analytic gravity and orientation to the work of analysis. Many classical analysts would analyze rather than indict, threaten, manipulate the environment, or blame the patient, as Bettelheim does. However, he does give the lie to the accusation that psychoanalysts deal only with oedipal matters, as he centers Portnoy's difficulties in pregenital areas.

Hanlon, too, views Portnoy in preoedipal terms, and in the light of the vicissitudes of early development more than in neurotic conflict. She bases her understanding in a theory as used and practiced by analysts (Mahler, Pine, Bergman, and others) who would, at least in comparison to others in this volume, be considered to be classical.

Elliot Adler, presenting himself as very different from Bettelheim and Hanlon, detoxifies the image created by Bettelheim by warning against irritation with the patient, and arguing for empathic, experience-near, understanding of the reasons why Portnoy behaves as he does. Adler takes seriously the one fleeting moment of love reported by Portnoy, seeing in it the possibilities for genuineness and the nurturing of workable motivation for change. If one surrounds Adler's comments about empathy, self-esteem, identification, the preoedipal, and drives as mediators of relationships, with other attributes of the relational points of view, one is hard put to know where classical psychoanalysis ends and the newer psychoanalyses begin.

I, myself, trained in psychoanalysis at the Topeka Institute, member of the American Psychoanalytic Association, certified for the practice of adult and child and adolescent psychoanalysis, could qualify as a classical psychoanalyst. More substantively, I believe in the unconscious, resistance, transference, use of dreams and the couch, judicious silence, and free association. Yet I see psychoanalysis as part of the ancient and grand tradition of healing, and thus as a participant in many other components of the healing process. By contrast with some other classical analysts I emphasize ego functions. I am radical in my belief that there is a purpose for all behavior. I believe there are subtle, sophisticated ways of incorporating will and action, even to a degree positive thinking, within the boundary of classical psychoanalysis. I believe strongly that the more one is able to experience life from the patient's point of view and cast one's language accordingly, the better. And I at least wonder at times about combining psychoanalysis and activities of the nonanalytic therapies (Gestalt, imagery, biofeedback, body therapies, etc.). Maybe I should be called a "psychoanalytically opinionated eclectic."

If people generalized less about the psychoanalytic other, there would be less of the tendentious polarizations so characteristic of the psychoanalytic landscape. People would realize that in addition to discordance on the basis of individual differences in practitioners, apparent differences often are semantic, the result of ignorance or misunderstanding of the other (genuine, prejudiced, or malicious), or come from mixing of levels of abstraction. They would recognize that practitioners may share more with each other, especially in what they do with patients, than the often stridently expressed differences suggest. The caricatures drawn in this volume from time to time were drawn so heavily in order to make a point. These caricatures falsely imply that all members of a named group behave similarly.

More likely one or another analyst's questionable behavior stems from poor selection, inadequate training, or basic lack of talent (there are lots of violinists, but only one Heifetz). Such reasons as these are at least as likely responsible for some psychoanalytic behavior as is one's analytic orientation. (Aerodynamics need not be questioned because some pilots are poorly selected, inadequately trained, and were drinking with the flight attendants at the time of the crash.)

Some of the authors of these chapters, especially some of the relational ones, espouse frankly revisionist positions. They often do so in the form of invidious comparisons with classical psychoanalysis. One can understand their occasional argumentative tone in sociopsychological terms. All varieties of psychoanalysis stem from Freud, the first assertion of the way psychoanalysis should be done (the "basic model") was set forth by Freud, the theory on which the practice was based was Freudian, the organizing and proselytizing functions were performed by Freudians, and official and quasi-official standing was first accorded to Freudians.

Classical psychoanalysis has itself changed through the years, on scientific bases as well as in response to the dynamics common to all groups. But despite their scientific disputes, psychoanalysts, especially in the United States, arrogated to themselves an elite status. By identifying themselves as members of a medical discipline, psychoanalysts traded on the prestige and the political and economic power of organized medicine; they felt free to take on the cloak of superiority engendered by exclusivity. Such a situation is an invitation for revisionists to try to bring down the aristocracy of the early settlers in order to make a central place for themselves. So responsible scientific explorers were joined by those motivated by political and economic considerations, the whole saturated by hurt feelings. (It is probably no accident that all but one of the contributors to this volume are Ph.D.'s, long barred from membership in the American Psychoanalytic Association.)

The revisionists put forward their antitheses to the classical psychoanalytic theses. Such antitheses include emphasizing the person versus mechanistic conceptions of people; subjectivity versus objectivity; hermeneutic versus physicalistic; egalitarian versus authoritarian. If this dialectical game is to be played successfully, there have to be clear theses against which to tilt the antitheses. Thus, there is the temptation to exaggerate if not misrepresent in order to make the case. Some of the contributors to this volume succumb to that temptation. They regale us with the image of a classical analyst as being cold, intrusive, mechanical-acting, self-absorbed, and dictatorial. Such classical analysts are alleged to be interested in perpetuating theories through persuasion while being heedless of the unique needful patient. Such analysts deal only with conflicts, especially oedipal ones, in apparent ignorance of or lack of interest in earlier developmental needs, and always cast thoughts, sometimes even verbal interventions, in terms of "drive theory." (The corresponding caricature of relational analysts, particularly self psychologists, is of an infantilizing, patronizing, aggression-blind do-gooder.)

While the representation of the classical psychoanalyst is overdrawn at best — indeed is contradicted by much of the classical literature and by some of the contributions in this volume — much can be learned from these criticisms. But it takes some work on the part of the reader to ferret out the useful from the misleading.

A good many of the criticisms boil down to, or are extensions of, the notion that classical analysts are, in one way or another, hard-hearted. The selection of one or another school of personality, as with all things, is in part motivated by the kind of person one is. The classical–romantic dichotomy runs through all human affairs (Appelbaum 1990). Classical psychoanalysis is, in this broader sense, classical — it adheres to form, is patient with time, requires evidence, and prizes thought before action. Some classical analysts *do* conceive and practice the calling in emotionally isolated and intellectualized ways, one reason being that psychoanalysis is heavy with theory — metapsychological, clinical, as well as first-order and experience-near. Some people find it difficult to keep these separate, and especially not to think and even speak in metapsychological terms instead of evocatively and in plain English.

Classical medical analysts may tend to esteem hard science and objectivity too much, to the detriment of emotional engagement. After all, it was the admission officers of medical schools who picked the pool of physicians from which psychoanalysts used to be drawn. Those officers did so according to criteria that might fit orthopods but are much less suitable for future psychoanalysts. Acceptance into and graduation from medical school requires facility with hard science, which is more correlated with a predilection for facts rather than for feelings. This may be one reason why some classical analysts deify the "facts" of insight and veridical reconstruction of the past while overlooking less factual, more emotional and interpersonal growth-producing factors that function in the therapy (Appelbaum 1975).

The elite status of physicians in the United States probably disposes practitioners toward authority–submission interactions rather than the egalitarian ones that are more conducive to the practice of psychoanalysis. Freud divined all this early on, and of

course favored "lay analysis" as befitting a man of broad humanistic interests. But he, too, was subject to his physicalistic and
biological training as well as to the need to meet the criteria of
prevalent hard science, so as to further the acceptance of psychoanalysis. We are only now emerging from the legacy of
physicalistic and biological models, as, increasingly, psychoanalysis recasts itself in hermeneutic, relative, and interpersonal
terms.

Note that psychoanalysis is easy to do, but hard to do well.
Instead of dealing with that, in many ways, unpalatable reality,
we have treated psychoanalysts as just another academic discipline, the completion of a course of study that is expected to turn
out competent practitioners. Psychoanalysis fitted itself into
existing educational procedures because these procedures were
there as a means of legal and, later, insurance acceptability, not
necessarily because they were optimally designed to turn out
psychoanalysts. The field has not yet delineated with subtlety and
depth those characteristics that make for good analysts. (I call
attention to one such systematically overlooked characteristic
below.) It is easy to spot flaws in individual practitioners, and
dangerous to do so when these flaws are taken as evidence of
theoretical and conceptual lacks. So here are a few additional
ripostes to some of this volume's criticisms of classical psychoanalysis.

While Freud emphasized the centrality of the Oedipus complex, he also wrote tellingly of pregenital issues and the charac-
terology derived from them. Indeed, as the inventor of the
psychosexual scheme of development, beginning with the trauma
of birth, he could hardly do otherwise.

Drive theory seems a particularly attractive target for criticism
in this volume and elsewhere. When drive theory is used in
metapsychological discussions, it is, by definition, of a different
order of abstraction — *meta*psychology — from experience-near
phenomena. Some of the argumentation on this subject could be
dispensed with on the basis of that recognition. Another argu-

ment reflects the prevalent confusion between Freud's instincts and the drive to repeat one or another interpersonal pattern. Consulting room behavior need not be as discordant as these theoretical arguments suggest. However, there is a substantive difference between those who conceive of the matrix of behavior as stemming *de novo* from interactions between persons as compared to innate, fantasy-driven, and, therefore in a sense, predetermined ways of behaving. To oversimplify, the latter leads to the treatment task of decoding fantasy and understanding motivation cognitively; the former leads to correctingly reexperiencing relationships.

The relational theorists have some conceptual work to do if they wish to rid psychoanalysis of drives. They need some way to account for the affects from which feelings are derived and the connection of affects with the viscera (one does not flood the body with multitudinous varieties and shades and nuances of feelings, often accompanied by bodily manifestations, as stemming from the big toe). Drive revisionists need a way to explain and replace the connections and correlations between Freud's psychosexual stages and a staggeringly wide variety of childhood behavior and eventual choices—of clothes, hobbies, occupations—and self-experience. They must also explain the *modes* of relationships—cuddling, exhibiting, intruding, and caretaking, for example. That all such behaviors are derived solely from interactions with others, interpersonally, is to imply that the infant is a blank slate, bringing nothing to the formative interactions with others except a need for people (could one not say a drive for people?).

Why should one care about a relationship if not "driven" toward it? If a relationship is to be anything more than trivial, it becomes a vehicle of passion, and passion must be accounted for as an expression of the body and as providing color for the wish-driven fantasies and symbols about people. Such conceptual work need not impinge on the essentials of the clinical interaction, the healing that takes place when people meet under unique clinical conditions. Emotionally sensitive and humanistically inclined analysts of all persuasions, indeed all healers through the ages, have known that, and, one would hope, have implemented it in their interactions and transactions.

As to the canard that Freud thought and practiced clinically solely guided by the idea that people only want to reduce tension through indiscriminate drive-reduction, note Freud's description of instinct—instinct has a source, an aim, *and an object* (italics added) (Freud 1915). True enough, however, the object is subject to displacement, and may or may not always include whole persons.

Of the writers in this volume Hirsch is probably the most critical of the critics of classical psychoanalysis. He sees it as an individualistic enterprise in which behavior emanates primarily from the patient to be observed by the analyst from an objective distance rather than as a construction of both analyst and patient. (Where in his formulation is transference and countertransference?) He regards this solipsistic state of affairs as stemming from Freud's turning from the interactional person in a turn-of-the-century environment conducive to theories of seduction and attack by males upon innocent females (the seduction theory) to explorations of intrapsychic fantasy.

Citing the metaphor of the analyst as a blank screen Hirsch envisions the analytic interaction as one in which the analyst claims to be the repository of objectivity and thus able to judge the patient's perceptions, usually as inaccurate. In this characterization countertransference is the analyst's mistake. This way of conceptualizing countertransference was doubtless true at one time, but thankfully is now superseded by the recognition that countertransference can be an aid to understanding the patient and a construction by both parties rather than simply evidence of an unresolved conflict of the analyst, which interferes with objectivity. Despite his sharp critique of classical analysis Hirsch offers a view of the therapeutic process with which most analysts would agree, and in fact is rooted in Freud's repetition compulsion and transference as well as the poorly named "corrective emotional experience": the analysis provides an opportunity to destroy problematic behavioral patterns through the patterns repeating themselves in the analytic situation, there to be dealt with differently from the way they were dealt with in the past. As an illustration Hirsch uses his own horrendous experience in applying for analysis in which the interviewing analyst turns him away as being narcissistic rather than neurotic. (That is a particularly dreadful example of what can give analysis a bad name.) The statement does, however, point to a theme that runs through most of the contributions in this volume — the recognition that Portnoy's character and defenses need to be dealt with before "content" interpretations can be of any use. If one cannot do that, as evidently Hirsch's interviewer thought he could not, successful analysis would be impossible.

Despite their stated differences, practically all of the contributors zeroed in on Portnoy's problematic character and flamboyant defensive maneuvers. Even Pape, who as a Lacanian has less in common with the others than they do with each other, recognizes the false self that Portnoy employs in part to screen off his real self. So impressed is Pape with the antitherapeutic implications of Portnoy's defensive style that he deals with it through the draconian measure of simply stopping the session as a means of stopping the character defense. Morrison, instead, sees the analyst's task as analysis of Portnoy's narcissistic character in order to delineate the vicissitudes of shame that drives and is embedded in the narcissism.

I found myself in greatest agreement with the interactional people when they expounded upon the need for empathy and the experience-near. As it happens I had read Heinz Kohut's paper, "Introspection, Empathy, and Psychoanalysis," when it appeared in the *Journal of the American Psychoanalytic Association* in 1959, before Kohut became *Kohut*. That paper still stands out in my mind as a brilliant contribution, and one that proved to be seminal. I resonated, also, in this volume to the emphasis on the analyst–patient interaction, and share the belief that the essence of healing can be found in that interaction. By the same token I believe that relations between people ("object relations") are crucial, especially as they are part of an interacting system, each component of which influences the behavior of the other parts. I appreciate the distinction between pathological idealization to be interpreted away, and people's need for a vision for which to strive and with which to identify one's self as embodied in another. I further appreciate the wise diagnostic discrimination between those patients whose difficulties are best thought of as stemming from conflict, requiring certain emphases in technique, and those best thought of as needing to complete and enrich development under more benevolent conditions than they originally had. Between the lines of many of this volume's chapters I happily felt the deemphasis on pathology as compared with the recognition that the patient is doing as well as the patient can at the moment, with sometimes more, sometimes less efficiency with regard to the patient's goals rather than the goals of others for the patient. Medical thinking in the parochial sense of naming and focusing upon pathology is one of the unfortunate legacies of the historical context of the development of psychoanalysis.

I fear that the many helpful contributions of the relationists may get lost in a shuffle of their own making. In addition to marring their contributions through creating and then destroying straw men, to some they arouse unnecessary ire in presenting their ideas as brand new rather than as emphases. For example, the self psychology position on aggression seems little different from the hoary academic frustration-aggression hypothesis. Worse, I fear that the way many of the relationists discuss aggression opens the door to collusion between analyst and patient not to deal with aggression as a fact of life. The species would not have survived without aggression and how one deals with that biological fact can be discussed, like anything else, in an ultimately salubrious and benevolent atmosphere. To believe otherwise is to share the patient's erroneous belief that the whole subject is too fraught with danger to be dealt with safely and helpfully. Rather than endangering the healing relationship, an honest, direct, brave discussion of all of aggression's facets ultimately enhances rather than endangers the healing relationship.

Relational analysts indulge their penchant for putting forth their ideas as if they were discoveries rather than elaborations, reminders, and emphases in various ways. They do it concretely by way of creating a new language ("selfobjects," "transmuting internalizations") through separate meetings and associations of the initiates, and other ways of suggesting that they are possessors of novel, even arcane knowledge. Finally, as I have suggested, before dismantling such matters as drives and structures, they need to have thought through replacements adequate to the task of explaining all empirical data.

Ad hominem as it is, one is entitled to consider the psychology of leaders, particularly their often prominent narcissism, as instrumental in the way they present their ideas. People who choose to become leaders prize specialness and exclusivity. They want to see their name above the title. They enjoy having followers. Modestly advanced contributions to someone else's work is not their style.

One should consider, also, practical calculations as to how best to win friends and influence people. Modest presentation of emphases might have gotten lost; a movement, by contrast, forces attention. Whatever the reasons, one can only hope the moves toward separatism and gratuitous stirring of ill-will among colleagues does not distract from the messages that require hearing for the good of psychoanalysis.

Two influences on the outcome of psychoanalysis are adumbrated in these pages though not dealt with directly. One is a radical application of Freud's discovery of unconscious motivation. This discovery is overlooked even by some Freudians who, as Roy Schafer (1976) has pointed out, deal in nouns rather than verbs, stasis more than dynamics, and by implication, therefore, unmotivated rather than motivated (at least to the degree of depth and complexity that full exploration of motives requires). Thus the patient is seen as *having* the symptom of intrusive ideas, or as *being* psychotic, rather than as a person who intrudes ideas *for a purpose*, or who behaves *for a purpose* in ways labeled as obsessional or psychotic.

At times relational analysts seem to imply that understanding, insight, and exploring motives may interfere with both analyst and patient contacting the patient's unique experiential world. The danger in concentrating too much on experience is that the analyst may stop short of trying fully to explain all the possible *reasons* why patients choose to experience or behave as they do.

It may seem like carrying coals to Newcastle to remind classical psychoanalysts about motivation, the exploration of which was central to Freud's discoveries. But I sometimes see in myself and others a softness in the execution of that belief, and in the pursuit of purpose in all behaviors, exempting an occasional reflex like the knee jerk. Exploration as to why the patient creates guilt, anxiety, depression, or one or another symptom or behavior encourages patient responsibility and sense of power, which are necessary for durable, useful change to occur. Why people behave as they do is at the heart of psychoanalysis. When explorations of motives are carried out carefully, tactfully, evocatively, and empathically they are complementary to the discovery of self-experience rather than opposed to it. Thus, the fears that Newirth, as representative of a good many others, expresses on this subject are needless.

Portnoy's Complaint offers a good illustration of another often overlooked variable that is crucial to the success of the analytic process. Upon finishing the book one *knows* Alexander Portnoy, as he exists in others, and as he exists in ourselves. Compare that experience of knowing with what one feels after reading the typical psychological case history. No fair, one might argue, Portnoy was portrayed by an artist, not just a clinician. Therein lies the truth in my conception of "evocativeness," a largely overlooked influence. It *is* the task of the clinician, as much as the artist, to evoke within himself and within the patient the essence of persons, vivid, lifelike representation, their depth and breadth, and above all their experience.

Evocativeness is the difference between Marlon Brando's reading aloud the phone book, making it interesting to listen to, and the dullness of most of the rest of us if we tried to do that. Evocativeness is the difference between leaving the theater and having forgotten the play by the time one hits the street, as against remembering the play for the rest of one's life. ("Attention, attention must be paid!" I remember from Arthur Miller's *Death of a Salesman* a long time ago. It comes to mind as I think about summoning rapt, emotionally meaningful "attention.") Such vividness enables not only memory, but instruction. One learns what one cares about, or can be made to care about by the artist or clinician. Not only do the artist and clinician share a common task (though with at least somewhat different goals) but they employ similar means — setting, tone of voice, choice of words, rhythm, timing of delivery, facial expression, whatever contributes to or detracts from compellingness.

How disproportionate is the time clinicians spend on learning the rightness of their understanding as compared with learning how to convey that understanding (including helping patients develop it on their own). If, as I suggest, evocativeness is a crucial, uncontrolled variable, the implications are profound. The capacity for evocativeness would be attended to in the selection and training of clinicians. It would add to the importance of the training analysis as a means of alleviating obstacles to evocativeness. It could make for significant differences in the effectiveness of treatment. Whatever the astuteness of the insight and technical actions of the clinicians writing in this volume, their usefulness to Portnoy would be enhanced or impeded by how they rate on the variable of evocativeness.

That not one of the writers alluded to this quality is unsurprising. I wrote about evocativeness more than 25 years ago, including comments about the personality characteristics that likely contribute to it and some ideas about how to measure them (Appelbaum 1966). In the subsequent more than two decades I have read practically nothing about it; it is not cited in works where its citation would be relevant. One reason might be that it was a poor piece of work, perhaps insufficiently evocative, even though it did have what I thought was a catchy title, "Speaking with the Second Voice." In my admittedly prejudiced view, however, it more likely fell under visionless eyes because of its unsettling implications. For those whose tolerance for being profoundly moved is sharply limited it could be seen as threatening, as beyond them. Worse, it could be thought of as, say, musical talent is. One is or is not tone deaf, substantially independent of dynamic reasons. (Some people cannot learn to play the violin, no matter what.) While training can make a musician, at least of a sort, in most of us, there are wide individual differences in how good we can be. Those who aspire to be Heifetz but are condemned to be only journeymen would not like to be reminded of their limitations. Some of them would not like to take the hint to practice their instruments more, either.

If I were to guess the evocative ranking of the clinician-authors in this volume I would put Dr. Kafka at the top of the list. Her sensitive revealing (of herself and Portnoy) illustrates the point I am trying to make about evocativeness. Others may have conceived of their task in this book differently, and perhaps in the consulting room are as evocative as I assume Dr. Kafka is. I am trying to be fair, but in truth I believe we tell of our capacity for evocativeness in almost everything we do, even when writing a "scientific" paper. For one thing language is a key element in evocativeness, and reveals its creator whenever the creator uses it. (Newirth especially emphasizes language in his chapter of this volume.) The wild card of evocativeness may be tilting the outcomes of treatment whose results we disproportionately ascribe to theory and consequent technique.

Silence, too, can be evocative. See Harold Pinter, see John

Wayne, see Dr. Spielvogel. As noted, some of the analysts in this volume took grave exception to Spielvogel's silence. They felt it to be punitive, withholding, reflecting dislike of Portnoy, and as a means of missing therapeutic opportunities. Note especially Morrison, Doctors, and Hirsch. I saw it quite differently. Through relative silence Spielvogel respected the patient's need and ability to speak of things important to him without interruption. After all, the technical rule is to do nothing without a therapeutically relevant purpose. Every intervention, no matter how accurate and ultimately helpful, is at the same time an interruption. Answering questions and offering interpretations stop inquiry; they make associations less free. Without, I hope, the unsavory connotations to many people, including some of the analysts in this volume, of a "blank screen," silence and the withholding of information about the analyst are, to put it mildly, useful. They make possible the transference neurosis. They are remarkably effective ways of reevoking the often warded-off dimensions of the personality. As with an inkblot, the more ambiguous the stimulus the more revealing the response. What the patient makes of the silence and limitation of offered information about the analyst in itself enables patient and therapist to learn a great deal. For example, does the patient feel cheated, deprived, disregarded, or lonely in response to the analyst's silence; or does the patient sense and enjoy the opportunity silence offers to learn from their conjectures and fantasies, or to feel held in silence's cradle?

The famous verbal intervention by the analyst, as far as we know the only one made by Spielvogel—". . . may perhaps to begin" (p. 274/287)—is subject to many interpretations, some of which we have read in this volume. I too would like to offer my take on it.

I appreciated its ambiguity, especially for this patient. Because it is connotative rather than denotative it will likely put the patient to work. He already knows a great deal, and in a first session (which I take this to be) one risks redundancy and superficiality at saying what, to this clever patient, is already known to him. The alternative of demonstrating that one is able to offer something not already known to him risks frightening him, and creating the impression that the analyst is showing off how much he can learn in just one interview. An ambiguous remark avoids such dangers, and more importantly invites the patient into a therapeutic alliance organized around the work of understanding, work that may often be ambiguous and challengingly difficult. This patient, in particular, so used to easy admiration and tending to disparagement of those less intelligent and informed than he is, requires a work orientation to the task ahead, as Bettelheim frustratedly reported in his chapter. Such an orientation informs that the analyst is not merely going to be an audience to whom Portnoy can display his penis-cleverness. Let the patient wonder what the heck the analyst means by that remark. Portnoy may even come up with the understanding that the analyst knows that beneath the patient's loveless, exploitative self is another self struggling to feel safe enough to get out, a person who just might be capable of love. So let us perhaps to begin — to find that self.

I liked (found evocative) Spielvogel's single words at the beginning and end of his oft-quoted, "So. . . . Now vee may perhaps to begin. Yes?" (p. 274/287). With the "Yes?" he asks Portnoy if Portnoy is ready to participate in a joint effort, a demonstration of respect for the patient's requirements, especially for his need for a feeling of autonomy, a reassurance that the patient may retain control as needed. The "So" with its Yiddish resonance introduces calmness into the patient's frantic experience. It says, "Alexander Portnoy, my son, it can't be all that bad; anyway there is something we can do about it, and the time is now." Across the ages and generations comes the chicken soup of hope and healing. Alexander the Great now has his chance really to become great.

REFERENCES

Appelbaum, S. A. (1966). Speaking with the second voice. *Journal of the American Psychoanalytic Association* 14:462–477.

———— (1975). The idealization of insight. *International Journal of Psychoanalytic Psychotherapy* 4:272–302.

———— (1990). Reflections on the role of theory in psychoanalysis. In *Tradition and Innovation in Psychoanalytic Education*, ed. M. Meisels and E. Shapiro. Hillsdale, NJ: Lawrence Erlbaum.

Freud, S. (1915). Instincts and their vicissitudes. *Standard Edition* 14:117–140.

Kohut, H. (1959). Introspection, empathy, and psychoanalysis. *Journal of the American Psychoanalytic Association* 7:459–483.

Schafer, R. (1976). *New Language for Psychoanalysis*. New Haven: Yale University Press.

Credits

Index